THE
DEPARTMENT

Kevin L. Ramos

ISBN: 0615846270
ISBN-13: 978-0615846279 (Kevin L. Ramos Publications)

For additional copies please visit: www.thedepartmentbook.com
Contact: kevin@thedepartmentbook.com

Dear Reader,

The tales you read in this book are inspired by actual
events. However, this book is a work of fiction. Any
resemblance of characters to actual persons, living or
dead is purely coincidental. The Author holds exclusive
rights to this work. Unauthorized duplication is
prohibited.

FOR

DAD

KEVIN L. RAMOS

CONTENTS

KEVIN L. RAMOS

ACKNOWLEDGMENTS

I think the Hip-Hop group **Dilated Peoples** said it best in their lyric, *"Worst comes to worst my peoples come first"*. This sentiment describes how I feel about the few individuals who made me feel whole and important enough to put my thoughts and soul on paper. If it wasn't for them, this book would surely never have been written. Firstly, I'd like to give a special thanks to my beautiful wife, Morneque who worked unmercifully to keep our family afloat financially and spiritually as I embarked on this project. Your love and support is why I smile today.

…David, Joshua, Paning, Paul, Glad, Renee, Warren, Bubba, Jaz, Joi, Zinga, Jay, Shad, Robin, Barbara, Bobby Jr., Bobby Sr., Jesus, Armenta, Marcus, Omar, Leman, Ralphie, Andrea, Yvon, Profess, Margie and friends — I thank you all.

…I also want to thank all the child welfare professionals, past and present, who've given their lives to keep children safe. Where would this world be if it wasn't for your daily efforts and sacrifice?

And lastly I'd like to thank the great State of Florida for allowing me to work in its child welfare system for over 10-years. The experience was definitely a journey that made me a better person.

I wrote this book because I wanted people to know how it really is working in one of the most difficult, selfless fields imaginable. There is no quick fix in repairing a complex system such as this one, but it does start with education and truly understanding why things are the way they are. I guess this is my meager offering at initiating change. Please enjoy THE DEPARTMENT.

-Kevin L. Ramos, June 18, 2013

i

1 FAMILY VALUES

August 31, 2000
(Liberty City)

I stared aimlessly at the Speed Queen commercial dryer. As the load of whites spun, the clanking of loose coins and other stray matter in the machine made for an unpredictable cadence. Coupled with the other ambient noises found at Bucky's Washhouse like the sound of running water and the banter of its patrons, no one in their right mind would ever think you could be at peace here. This wasn't the case for me… when I was plugged into my portable CD player nuthin' distracted me! Bucky's Washhouse was located on: Northwest 54th Street and 19th Avenue in the heart of Liberty City— just eight blocks away from the 2-bedroom/1-bathroom apartment I called home. I shared the apartment with my brother, Marcus aka Poo and my mama Denise Lisa Collins. Mama raised us the best way she could. A single mother of two, she worked as an usher at local Miami stadiums and venues like the American Airlines Arena, the Miami Arena, the Orange Bowl and Pro Player Stadium. This evening "Ms. Denise"— the name everyone addressed her by, was scheduled to work the University of Miami's opener against obscure, McNeese State. Although we missed her immensely, Poo and I loved when Mama went to work because she'd usually bring back platters of leftover concessions from the events— hotdogs mostly, but every now and then Ms. Denise would bring back somethin' special: cotton candy and candy apples courtesy of Ringling Bros Circus and one time Mama procured 215-medium-spiced Hooters Buffalo wings in 1995. Unfortunately, the Miami Hooters Arena Football team folded later that year, but our family had some of those left over wings in our deep freezer for months and months after.

"Poo help get this stuff into the buggy." I requested.

Annoyed, Poo reluctantly eased his Gameboy Advance into his pocket and then helped me lift two sacks of clothes into the old Winn

Dixie shoppin' cart. Then I took the bleach and washin' powder and placed it in the compartment where a baby or toddler would normally be seated. I found the buggy to be much more convenient then walkin' with these huge sacks for blocks. I thanked the unknown, resident of the Sycamore Rental community for commandeering such a fine piece of equipment. If it wasn't haulin' laundry or groceries, kids in the complex would take turns pushing each other in this squeaky cart on the uneven sidewalk in front of the Sycamore. The combination often yielded disastrous results.

"Queen, can we stop off at the A-rab store befo' we go home"? Poo begged

I took a quick audit of our finances, when I reached into my plastic Hello Kitty clutch and counted approximately $4.58 in US currency.

"Okay, but when we get home, you need to bathe and get ready fo' school tomorrow."

Before heading to the laundry mat, I made sure that our homework was complete since a stint at the washhouse could last hours. Fortunately for us, the school year just began on the August 28th so there was little to no homework assigned this first week. I was only 15-years old, but I was mature for my age. Truth is, Mama trusted me more than she did most adults. Aside for having the demeanor of an older lady, I physically looked the part; I could easily pass for 22. When I walked down the street it wasn't uncommon to be barraged with a flood of cat calls and car honks from horny old men that would pull up next to me tryin' to get my name and number. The cover of night didn't help; the only way you could tell I was a child is if you looked at my face. I was "thick", a brick house with a shape and curves most women would pay thousands of dollars for a plastic surgeon to replicate. The extra attention never bothered me one bit. I just hit play on my CD player and kept it movin'. Next track, Erykah Badu's 'Bag Lady'. I sang the lyrics to myself quietly as we walked down Northwest 54th Street.

Bag lady you gonna hurt your back. Draggin' all them bags like that.

Familiar noises echoed in the distance, car honks followed by a few hisses. Undaunted, I turned up the volume enough where I could hear the music and still listen to the noises of my surroundings including approaching footsteps. Poo, on the other hand, was constantly on guard, surveyin' the area for our own safety. Of the half dozen or so compliments/propositions I received this evenin', the most insulting an' least original was *"Hey Bitch, you wanna' ride!"* My "perceived" lack of concern for my safety always perturbed Ms. Denise. Mama told me—mostly during breakfast time, to always pay attention to my surroundings. Just this morning she provided a similar sermon, *"Girl, you just haven't run up on the right one… two licks to the head and you gonna find yo'self wakin' up in some perverts backseat!"* As a consolation, I always walked on the sidewalk against the grain of traffic so I could see what's comin' at me and I had my own system of dealin' with these horny automobilists. If approached by a *creepa*, a guy in a car who pulls up beside me tryin' to run his game, I'd smile at him and politely say, "No thank you, I have to get home to my kids." I could not fully ignore Mama's warnings, if a creepa was desperate and brazen enough to pull up to a complete stranger walkin' down the street, he'd be desperate and crazy enough to attack you and toss you into their backseat or trunk in a heartbeat. Being polite always has its benefits. A polite letdown might be the difference between you making it to your destination or you ending up a statistic. The "…get home to my kids" portion of my anti-creepa line was truly ingenious. "Kids" suggests responsibility: 6 out of 10 times the mere mention of kids had creepas pushin' forward—no questions asked. Havin' Poo draped over the side of the old Winn Dixie cart as I pushed it down the Ave served as a convincing prop. When the song's chorus kicked in, I sang louder and stronger:

So pack light
Pack light
Pack light
Ooh ooh

The last line was punctuated by three blasts of an unknown driver's car horn. Some say I am beautiful, while others say I am brainy, one thing I know I wasn't was vocally-blessed. I could only wish I had a fraction of the tonal gifts my daddy Songbird possessed. By the time the song finished, we arrived at our destination, Liberty Food Mart on Northwest 54th Street and 17th Avenue.

"Awright Poo, you get to choose three things and get me a blue Ritz and couple of pickled eggs from the bottom of the jar."

Poo smiled and grabbed the money outta my hand and ran into the store. I remained outside with our laundry— even sacks of used clothing were targets for potential theft in the City. I looked at the facade of the establishment, signage for Schlitz Malt Liquor and Newport Cigarettes adorned the front of the Liberty Food Mart and on the sidewall of the building was a hand-painted mural of Dr. Martin Luther King Jr. The spot was unusually empty for a Thursday night. I marveled at the A-rabs resolve. *It takes extreme courage to keep yo' doors open after 7pm in this neighborhood!* This particular establishment has been robbed four-times this past year. The owner's cousin, Abdul was shot dead in the third robbery. At the intersection of Northwest 54th Street and 17th Avenue, I smiled when I saw the newly-installed solar powered street name signs. Minutes later, Poo emerged from the A-rab store with a plastic bag filled with ghetto treats: two-12oz cans of Ritz Blueberry soda, an 8oz bag of Andy Capp's Hot Fries, a 1oz Chick-O-Stick, and two Red Smith pickled eggs (carefully fished from the bottom of the jar). After I approved the procurement, we headed home.

"Poo you need to hop in the bath, and I'll fix you a plate!"

As always my brother dutifully obeyed me. He bolted to the bathroom, strippin' off his clothes in route to the tub. He eased his body into warm bathwater. When we were out of Mr. Bubbles, I filled the bathtub half way, squirted some dishwashin' detergent in the water and then continued to let the water run to create makeshift bubbles. Poo enjoyed bathing especially when I placed one of his toys or any other random item that floated in the water (a plastic bowl, a foam flip flop slipper, a tennis ball). It was the Collins family mantra to "always make do." Before my daddy Daryl "Songbird" Collins passed away in

1997 due to complications attributed to lung cancer, he taught us the importance of leading the most normal life possible amidst the most adversarial situation or environment. "Just 'cause you live in the ghetto, doesn't mean you have to act ghetto…" he'd bellow in his captivating baritone voice, "…so if you have water, soap an' a wash rag, wash yo' ass!" This adage resonated especially with me. Each time I drew a bath, washed a dish, folded a shirt or assisted Poo with his homework, you knew where I picked up my fantastic work ethic and responsible nature from. Ms. Denise was the same way. Regardless of how chaotic things became or how depleted the family's finances were, she always strived to give us a semblance of normalcy. As a result of her hard work and dedication to her family, we never missed a school fieldtrip, lacked school supplies, left the house dirty or ever went to bed hungry.

After whippin' up some turkey Sloppy Joes with a side of original Lays potato chips (the yellow bag), I checked on Poo and made sure that he actually scrubbed and wiped before exiting the tub. Poo would play in the bath water for 10 to 15-minutes; he knew it was time to scrub down as the water's temperature cooled. Since I could remember, Poo had this affinity with water. After a quick toweling, I reached into our pile of freshly laundered clothes for a pair of boxers and an undershirt for my brother, no need for anything else since the tonight's forecast was slated for a balmy 78-degrees. We plopped on the sofa feastin' on Sloppy Joes on Dandee white bread topped with a slice of American cheese, my eyes were transfixed at a new show that was just released a couple of weeks ago, **Dora the Explorer** on Nickelodeon. It featured a little Hispanic girl and her escapades accompanied by her red boot-sporting monkey named Boots and her talking backpack and map.

"Yum, yum, yum, yum, yum. Delicioso!" The backpack exclaimed.

In the distance, a string of gunshots rang out. Seconds later, another six shots followed. *Return fire.* Like soldiers in wartime, we became immune to the sounds—and even the sights of our environment. As I watched the show I thought it had such a novel concept, teaching English speaking children basic Spanish phrases at an age when they are most susceptible to learning—*and what better place to be bilingual than in Miami, Florida!*

"Queen, what does *delicioso* mean"? Poo asked

"It means delicious."

"These Sloppy Joes are delicioso!!!" Poo said grinning. The Sloppy Joe juice smeared around his mouth looked like red clown paint. "What time is Mama coming home"?

"She'll be home around midnight. Thanks for helpin' with the laundry." I said smiling, while wiping the residue from Poo's face.

"You're welcome Queen."

"I remember when Daddy used to make us Sloppy Joes too. Boy, those things were good!" A Kool-Aid smile enveloped my face as I reminisced. "...he had the whole house smellin' and soundin' good."

I sank back into the Lazy boy and thought about Daryl "Songbird" Collins. I missed him so much and the role he played in caring for our family like the last Thanksgiving dinner we shared in '96 before he passed away. The dinner was awesome and the entire meal was prepared prior to him workin' a double at Miami International Airport as a skycap. He slaved 10-hours that day preparin': a 15lb-fried turkey, a sweet-ham, homemade giblet dressin', and fresh collard and turnip greens. For dessert, he prepared peach cobbler and a sweet potato pie. That day he must have sung the entire Al Green catalog—the Soul legend was my daddy's favorite artist. But Songbird's repertoire was not limited to Soul and R&B. He knew so many songs from so many different genres: Rock, Pop, Latin, Country, and one time he surprised us with a worthy rendition of Dancehall hit, 'No. No. No.' by Dawn Penn. It's not a surprise my love of music came from my daddy. As a skycap, he racked up on tips because of his impeccable customer service and his ability to belt out a tune, while heaving a 55lb-piece of luggage onto a conveyer belt or luggage cart. On flights from South America and the Caribbean, he'd croon Jon Secada 'Otro dia mas sin verte'– (Another Day without You) or Jerry Rivera's 'En Las

Nubes'. If they flew in from Cali, he serenaded them with The Eagles 'Hotel California' or Dionne Warwicks' 'Do you know the road to San Jose'. Songbird perfected his culinary skills working as an "L (Leading) Chef" in the Navy and on the cruise ship the Crown Victory which sailed out of the Port of Palm Beach. On some nights, he polished his vocal skills working as a quartet singer on the latter. After pleas from his family to find job on dry land, Daryl Collins gave in and applied for a job as a skycap for Tower Air.

Sunday, Monday, Happy Days!
Tuesday, Wednesday, Happy Days!

As we watched TV, I felt myself losing consciousness as Poo sank into my bosom sound asleep. The Itis was kickin' in. This lethargic feelin' attacked you after ingesting a satisfyingly heavy meal. The tryptophan found in the turkey meat used in the main dish amplified the effects of the Itis. Seconds later, the Itis claimed its second victim. As my brother and I slept peacefully on the sofa the TV blared.

Thursday, Friday, Happy Days.
The weekend comes,
My cycle hums,
Ready to race to you!

###

Mama arrived home from work around *12:45am* to find her two chil'ren huddled together on the sofa. She hated to leave us so often for work, but as a single mother with no family support in Miami, she had no alternative. When Songbird left us three years ago, she didn't know if she could go on: he was a provider, protector and her best friend. And he was also a babysitter. Their system was perfect, when one of them was off to work, the other would remain with us. It's times like this where his presence was missed the most. Ms. Denise could not deny that although her husband was everything a woman could want; his presence alleviated a tremendous burden placed on her. To commemorate her first and only love, she had some ink done to pay tribute to his memory. *Imagine that, Ms. Denise, the mother of two, creepin' up on 40 with her first tattoo.* I actually took her to the place where I had my tattoo done in Flea Market USA, Pepe's Piercings and Tattoos, Booth 128. They did the cheapest work and rarely asked any questions. I was only 13, at the time, when I had a Queen of Spades card image branded on my right calf for $70. A year after Songbird died, Ms. Denise decided do something her husband would never expect from her—get a tattoo. She asked Pepe to tattoo the silhouette of two songbirds perched side-by-side locked in a kiss, below them in script the sentiment "I need a little Songbird." and the date "August 12, 1997." Mama was hardcore; she decided to get it on her left forearm. Whenever she needed the strength of her best friend or wanted to share some excitin' news, she'd look at her forearm and he was there. This tattoo and her wedding ring which hung from around her neck  on a thin, 14kt Figaro gold chain were my mother's most-prized possessions. These were just small gestures to honor the love she had for her husband. But Mama always told us the greatest testament of their blessed union will always an' forever will be their chil'ren— Poo and Me.

2 MR. TOLLIVER

August 31, 2000
(Doral)

"**A**s a case manager or CPI, you must own these cases. Each one of the children on your caseload is now one of your own children. That's why it is imperative that you make sound, honest decisions. The actions you take will impact these children and their families forever!"

Mr. Dixon's last word resonated throughout the room. Eyes were fixed on him not because he had the build and stature of a linebacker for the Miami Dolphins, but because of his wealth of experience in South Florida's child welfare arena, 26-years to be exact. I scanned around the room attempting to make eye contact with anyone brave enough to remove their eyes off our instructor.

"As a case manager or CPI, you will serve various roles in these children's lives. You will become: a friend, a big brother or sister, an advocate in court, a guardian, a transporter, a liaison to their schools, their babysitter and their protector. You will be responsible for their physical, cognitive, and emotional well-being."

The room of 27-newly, hired child welfare workers were in awe. I couldn't describe the glow on their faces. All were eager to hop into the field, either to investigate cases of child abuse/neglect or handle foster care cases. But I've been down this road before and while my peers were eager to enter the game, I was happy to sit on the bench and enjoy this month-and-a half reprieve of training— if I could take another six I would. I continued to scan the room, until I spotted him, another human being eager to break out— tired of this harangue. And there he was. He sat in the front of the class next to the front door. He was around 6' tall with a semi-muscular build and short dark hair which was closely cropped. He also had the cutest smile. I could tell he was anxious to bolt by the way his leg bounced up and down as he sat.

During Mr. Dixon's speech, his almond-shaped eyes peered back and forth from his wristwatch to the Linebacker.

"Look to the left of you…" Mr. Dixon bellowed. "…grab that person's hand, and shake it because chances are that person will quit or resign by the end of next year."

The handshakes loosened at the gloomy, but truthful statement.

"If you cannot stomach any of these facts, it is best you walk out that door, the rest of you stay because I guarantee you that you will positively impact at least one family if continue to work in this district… you have my word."

Mr. Dixon was requisitioned by the Department of Children and Families (DCF) to provide training for the newly hired case managers and Child Protective Investigators (CPIs) in District 11 in Miami-Dade County, Florida. The Professional Development Program (PDP) was a crash course in child welfare practice. In two months, Mr. Dixon's task was to train Dade's aspiring child welfare workers in all their duties from drafting essential court documents to the handling of irate parents. Two other assistants helped with the training, Ms. Esperanza Ponce and Mr. Ely Tolliver. The trio would alternate in training the Fall 2000 PDP class, which met four days out of the week. On Fridays, the fledglings went back to their respective units and shadowed the veteran CPIs, gaining valuable on the job experience. After the two month training session was over, we had to take a written test and then pass an interpersonal field based exam in which our immediate supervisor and a PDP staff member reviewed our interaction with clients. If we passed, we would receive our Child Welfare Certification, which allowed us to operate as investigators and case managers for three years.

"Any questions"? Mr. Dixon calmly asked the class.

The handsome boy raised his hand, Mr. Dixon pointed at him and asked, "What's your name and what is your position"?

"My name is Jeremiah Abundo, I am a Child Protective Investigator in unit 808, Central."

Mr. Dixon smiled devilishly, but I couldn't fathom why.

Jeremiah then continued, "I was told that the police do not accompany us on all our calls. What do we do if we have to remove a child from a home and the parents become hostile"?

Although the question was a simple one, it had a majority of the class waiting for Mr. Dixon's response…even myself. In District 9, we always went out on our cases with law enforcement even to perform the most routine tasks like follow-up visits. I don't know how I'd fair in this wild Miami system.

Mr. Dixon and Ms. Ponce stepped back to allow Mr. Tolliver to retort. Mr. Tolliver had the most experience working as a CPI. He stood about 6' 3" tall around 160lbs and appeared to be in his 50's. Mr. Tolliver was an African American, who wore thin, wire-rimmed glasses and a receding hairline. I thought he had a striking resemblance to off-and-on Haitian president Jean Bertrand Aristide. He appeared timid, but I knew that wasn't the case if he worked in this field for over two decades. Mr. Tolliver slowly stepped forward and spoke:

"Jeremiah the fact is that you are on your own when you go to these homes. If you need the assistance from law enforcement, you are goin' to be waitin'… an' I mean waitin' a while because sometimes they do not respond to DCF dispatches right away. The fact is law enforcement has little respect at what Department of Children and Family does."

Mr. Dixon quickly intervened and stared hard into Mr. Tolliver face: Mr. Tolliver did not flinch.

"All right folks let's take a 15-minute break before we delve into Florida's juvenile statute Chapter 39, which governs our roles and actions as child welfare professionals. Please hurry back, we will be starting promptly at 10:30am."

###

I didn't smoke, but I stepped outside to join Jeremiah Abundo as he took a quick cigarette break. Since I was new to Miami, it couldn't hurt getting to know a few of my fellow case managers and child protective investigators. He pulled out a Kool Filter King from his shirt pocket, one of four loose cigarettes—or looseys he carried to last him throughout the day. He lit it and admired how beautiful the day was. A couple of days ago, August 23, 2000, Hurricane Debby came barreling down on South Florida, namely the Florida Keys. The residents of the Upper Keys had to mandatorily evacuate to the mainland. Thankfully, Debbie didn't do much destruction— a little rain and wind, but not much else.

"So you used to be a CPI in Collier County. What brings you to Miami?" He asked.

"I came to Miami because I needed a big change. Naples is a little slow for me and Miami is where it's at. I'm still young, I'm single and I like to have fun every now and then between cases." I replied.

Our conversation was slow going, but I knew he found me interesting. Between puffs, his gaze drifted from my face to my breasts… and I didn't mind one bit.

"What about you Jeremiah? What brings you to Miami? You mentioned you were from Palm Beach. Last time I checked there were abuse cases up there too?"

"Can I be honest with you Tamara"? Jeremiah asked rhetorically. "I came down to Miami for two reasons…first, is because I'm a mama's boy and if I didn't leave her nest. I'd be living with her forever…"

I let out a big laugh, but when I looked at Jeremiah and he wasn't smiling. After I composed myself, he continued.

"Secondly, I think Miami is one of the most challenging places to work if you're a social worker. The various cultures and languages will make for some interesting cases. I also want to make a difference in people's lives. You should know that feeling; you've been on investigations before. You've experienced the job first hand…I want what you have." Jeremiah stated.

I felt the compassion in Jeremiah's voice, but didn't have the heart to tell him the truth. It wasn't my place to crush someone's dreams, especially five minutes after meeting them. He would just have to find out for himself.

As Jeremiah flicked his ash, we heard a familiar voice from behind. The deep voice belonged to Mr. Tolliver.

"Hey Mr. Abundo, do you have another one of those?"

The aspiring CPI reached into his shirt pocket and gave the instructor one.

"Truth is, Mr. Tolliver I wanted to cut down on my smoking because it's becoming a very expensive vice." Jeremiah said. "Need a light"?

"No, I have a light thanks." Mr. Tolliver looked at the blue sky, took a toke of his Kool and expelled the smoke refreshingly.

"Mr. Tolliver, this is Ms. Tamara Norvil. She is a CPI transferring in from Naples and she has agreed to show me the ropes." Jeremiah stated.

Mr. Tolliver extended his bony, right hand outwards: it was like shaking the Grim Reaper's. Mr. Tolliver also enjoyed looking at my breasts too. He tried to play it off like he was fixing his wire-rimmed glasses, but the direction of his gaze was unmistakable.

"You know…sometimes we don't shoot it to you straight about what goes on around here and I don't think that's fair to you and those people in there." Mr. Tolliver stated then paused to collect his thoughts. He appeared as if he was in a daze. After a few seconds he spoke.

"Social Worker….right"? Ely asked Jeremiah.

"I just graduated with my BSW."

"Wanna change the world…right"? Tolliver blurted out.

"That's the only reason why I chose this profession Mr. Tolliver." Jeremiah replied.

"Child welfare work is the rawest type of social work there is. Often you do not get any respect— from the families down to the judges. Shit, even your own company doesn't care about you most of the time. I wanted to answer your question honestly before Dixon censored me. But you'll see for yourselves."

Mr. Tolliver looked at me and I gave him a quick nod. He described my feelings perfectly. Jeremiah would just have to see for himself.

"You seem like you've experienced a lot Mr. Tolliver." Jeremiah stated avoiding eye contact with the older man.

"Definitely, young buck, I've been to hell and back at this job." Ely eyed his watch before continuing. "If you slide me another square I'll tell you about one of my most memorable cases?"

"Ely, this case is ready to close, but you need to have mom sign-off on this daycare application and a copy needs to be included in the case file." Ms. Johnson stated as she handed me my thick case folder back. *Shit!*

I took the case file frustratingly and walked to my cluttered desk to get the phone number of Constance Diaz. I dialed the family's phone number and let the phone ring. As I waited, I eyed the massive case file which was before me. I couldn't help but shake my head, while thumbin' through the family's dysfunctional history. The mother on this case, Constance Diaz was only 24 and was the subject of 11-abuse reports. On the seventh one, we took her to court and ended up removing all six of her children from her care; five of her children came from different fathers. When Constance was 2-years old she was removed from her own mother due to substance misuse, Constance's little sister, Brenda was born with cocaine in her system. Over time Constance lost contact with her biological siblings while in foster care. Eventually, Constance followed in her mother's footsteps by smoking dope and neglectin' her own children. This family was a mess. I was so tired of dealin' with them: I prayed to God my supervisor would accept my investigation for closure. Cases like the Diaz Family leave you in a fucked up state—you go to sleep thinking about them and you wake up in the mornin' and they're the first thing on your mind.

After the eighth ring, a tiny voice murmured, "Hello".

It was Constance Diaz. Constance sounded as if she had just woken up and I was fuckin' livid since it was around 5pm in the afternoon. The first thing I thought when I heard her garbled speech was, *I hope this female ain't hittin' the pipe again?* Could you blame me? I knew another relapse would result in the removal of mom's kids instantly and would require a mountain of paperwork. I was already swamped with the forty-five or so cases on my desk. Besides, what did court and our system do for mom and her kids the first time around…absolutely nuthin'!"

"Hey Constance, this is Ely from HRS."

HRS (Department of Health and Rehabilitative Services) was the name the State of Florida used prior to creating the Department of Children and Families. At the time, I was frustrated more at the system then with the people I had to service. In Constance's case, her mother was a drug addict, and then Constance became an addict herself. Then, Constance was removed as a child, and eventually she had her own children removed from her care due to her drug use and negligence. *When would this horrible cycle end?* I felt the services we provided to the family were often ineffective and cookie cutter—just tools to get 'em outta the system. At the time, our nation's stance on drug prevention as a whole was so pathetic. When former First Lady Nancy Regan told people to *"Just Say No"* to drugs, I thought *"What the Fuck are they supposed to Say Yes To?"* To me, Constance never even had a chance.

"Oh, Hi Ely."

"How's everything"? I asked.

"Everything is fine." She replied

"Constance I need to come by your home this evening to have a daycare referral signed so I can close your case. Can I come by?

"Sure you can come by Ely…"

I wished she said no since Constance Diaz lived smack dab in Overtown, one of the most dangerous neighborhoods in Miami. Plus, it was gettin' dark earlier due to Daylight Savings Time. If she said no, I could tell my supervisor that she wasn't home, and advise Ms. Johnson that my follow-up home visit would have to be completed the following day. Even though I had some other tasks to handle— a child/parent visitation to facilitate and a trip to Kendall to drop off some medication at a foster home, I'd much prefer working an 18-hour day than going to Overtown at night. But with my luck, there was no avoiding a night mission to the ghetto. I was looking at reaching Constance Diaz's residence by 11:30pm. Irritated, I packed up my shit including the family's mammoth case file and trudged on.

###

At 11:48pm, I arrived in front on 785 Northwest 3rd Place in Overtown. Overtown is a small black neighborhood in the Northwest section of Downtown Miami. Overtown has a very rich history. In the post World War II era, Overtown welcomed famous jazz artists: Josephine Baker, Billie Holiday, Nat King Cole, Count Basie, Ella Fitzgerald, and Cab Calloway. It provided safe haven for these artists, when White-only hotels refused us lodging. Now Overtown was plagued by drugs, namely crack cocaine. The corners were filled with hustlers and drug dealers and their victims walked the streets like bony zombies. Last time I had a case in Overtown, I left my car to interview a family for 30-minutes and came back to a busted-out car window. The motherfucka stole all my cassette tapes and change outta my ashtray…. and had the audacity to break off my car's radio antenna. At first I thought it was a petty case of vandalism, I was later told that the crackheads often used antennae as pipes to smoke their rock. This evenin' I was shocked at how active the streets were for a Tuesday night— and I thought at the time that that was a good thing… more witnesses to testify just in case things go bad. I stared at 785 Northwest 3rd Place. The 3-story complex was comprised of a small gated courtyard where you had to climb steep, slippery concrete steps to reach the next tier. The safety railing looked ridiculously low and unstable. I wondered why HRS didn't get more reports from this place alone from little kids plummeting from these hazardous structures. The building reminded me of prison tiers.

It began to drizzle. I tucked my case file under my jacket and proceeded in my quest for the Holy Grail— Ms. Diaz' signature. I know, I could have forged her signature, which would have saved me some time and aggravation, and no one would know the difference. But in my 20-plus years of work, I never lied and wasn't going to lose my $19k/year job over some bullshit. Even before makin' it up the steps, I had to navigate my way past the drug dealers and thugs who congregated around the front of the complex and at the base of the steps. When, I finally made it to the top floor to Unit 314, I rapped on the door three times.

"Hello Constance!" I bellowed.

(No answer)

I knocked again. "Constance it's me, Ely!— C'mon now!"

(No answer)

I banged even harder on the door this time. But before I could say, "Hello" I was staring down the blue barrel of a 12-gauge Mossberg.

"Get the fuck in here nigga!" a deep voice ordered.

I felt the cold, wet steel on my forehead as I entered the pitch dark tenement. In the background, I heard the whimpering of Constance and her children.

Jeremiah didn't believe what he was hearing. But I'm glad he heard it firsthand from someone else. Working these cases is not some concocted fantasy you see on TV or the movies, things can go bad in milliseconds. Jeremiah's almond-shaped eyes were glued as he handed Mr. Tolliver the last of his looseys from his shirt pocket.

Ely Tolliver lit the cigarette and continued.

"The guy with the gun was one of Constance's baby's fathers. He just got out of jail three months earlier for beatin' her ass. He thought Constance and I were fuckin' around even when I showed him my ID and the daycare referral and he still didn't believe me. I think his name was Austin...Austin "Shorty" Diamond."

"How did you get out of that situation"? I asked

"Shorty made me take off all my clothes—drawers and all and then opened the front door of the apartment and threw them off the tier onto the courtyard. He ordered me out of the apartment and told me never to come back. As I ran down the flights of stairs, I couldn't escape the yells and the gibes. When I tried to retrieve my clothes those drug dealin' trash on the bottom floor ran off with them laughin'. I distinctly 'member some teenage boy playin' keep away with my Florsheims. A lady in unit 108 allowed me into her apartment; she gave me a bright orange beach towel to cover up with and she let me use her phone to call the police."

Jeremiah looked at Mr. Tolliver venerably and struggled to offer any words of conciliation. In some states, it is encouraged that child protection workers use the buddy system when handling cases. Michigan's Department of Human Services was exploring a bill to make it mandatory that child protection workers utilize this identical system. In other Florida counties, such as Collier and Broward, law enforcement accompanies workers on their cases. Mr. Tolliver's case reminded me of a statistic from my first PDP class in Naples:

A study conducted by the U.S. Department of Labor Occupational Safety and Health Administration found, "The Bureau of Labor Statistics (BLS) reports that there were 69 homicides in the health services from 1996 to 2000." The same study found that for every 10,000 full-time social service workers, 15 workers were victims of a violent assault   at   work.

Mr. Tolliver continued as the ash on his cigarette grew longer, "Did you know it took an hour-and-fifteen minutes for the Miami Police to arrive at the scene— and their headquarters are only five, fuckin' blocks away? I could've walked there...barefoot an' all in my orange beach towel lookin' like Fred Flintstone in 5-minutes tops!"

Ely shook his head and took the last pull of his cigarette, then exhaled a cloud of disgust into the air. He stared aimlessly at the blue sky. The sun's rays bounced off the thin lenses of his eyeglasses.

"When the police arrived, the officers were laughin' at me. I paged my supervisor to tell her of my situation and never got a call back. My wife—now ex-wife Michelle had to come to the scene and bring me some clothes and an extra set of keys so I could move my car. They even got me for my wallet! Do you think this story hit the papers the next day or made the 7 o'clock news? Do you think the Department sent me to counseling over this shit? The worse thing that came from this is when my boys were bullied after my story leaked out at their school. They thought their Papa was a soft-ass pussy...they never did fully understood the situation until they got older."

We stood there silently for a few awkward seconds. The 15-minute cigarette break allowed Mr. Tolliver to get years of anxiety off his chest.

Jeremiah eyed his wristwatch and smiled, then turned to the gangly man and said, "Thanks you for your honesty Mr. Tolliver. I really, really appreciate it."

Mr. Tolliver slowly emerged from his daze as he spoke, "No problem folks…I haven't shared that one in years. Just remember what you are in this child welfare system an' never forget this…you are a small, replaceable cog in this big machine. When they are done with you, they replace you with a newer—not necessarily better part."

I grabbed the Grim Reaper's hand and thanked him. His story and honesty made me think about my own life and vulnerabilities. We walked back to our PDP class with Mr. Tolliver's account fresh in our minds. As Jeremiah sat at his desk, he discovered a thick binder on it. He read the title to himself:

DEPARTMENT OF CHILDREN AND FAMILIES Resource Guide

He turned to page 1 and began to read:

Mission Statement

The Department of Children and Families is committed to working in partnership with local communities to ensure safety, well-being, and self-sufficiency for the people we serve

September 1, 2000
(Downtown Miami)

I stood anxiously at the entrance of the DCF Rohde building located at: 401 Northwest 2nd Avenue, Miami, FL. The building was separated into two towers, the North and the South. These two towers housed a number of the State's agencies. If you wanted to carry a concealed weapon or sell hotdogs you went to the South Tower, 7th floor. If you needed to check in with your probation officer (juvenile or adult) you went to the South Tower, 6th floor. If you needed to make adjustments to your food stamps case you went to the 2nd floor, North or South Tower. The ESS (Economic Self Sufficiency) Program was so big there was a breezeway that connected the two towers. I was headed to the South Tower, 5th floor where the child protective investigative units were housed. Before I entered the bland 15-story building, I adjusted my tie in a window reflection. My brother *(kuya)* Ronald had to teach me how to tie a Windsor knot because my father passed away just before that lesson could be shared. At first, I opted for a polo shirt and some khaki pants, but I wanted to make a good impression towards my co-workers on my first day. I chose to wear a navy pair of pinstripe dress slacks and a light blue dress shirt and a striped-blue tie. *There'll be plenty of casual Fridays to dress down.* I said to myself confidently.

Of the 27-people in my training class, only four were hired as child protective investigators, the rest were hired as foster care workers or family service counselors. I had three counterparts. The first was Brandon Russell, a 42-year old father of two, who worked as a CPI when it was still HRS. Russell left to work as a foster care worker for seven years, but grew tired of the job and wanted a less, prolonged interaction with the families so he chose to become a CPI again. Brandon worked in North Unit, 859. I always thought he was a boastful African American fellow trapped in some time warp; I got this feeling by having a few random conversations with him. *"Nowadays, workin' for the Department is easy compared to what we had to go through back in the days. I remember when I had 245-backlog cases alone!"* and *"Back in the days, we didn't have beepers or computers when I was comin' up, we did things by hand. Besides I don't trust technology!"* But when he talked I never responded, but in my mind I wanted to blast him— *"Back in the days?...245-backlog cases?...don't trust technology?"* *Sit your old-ass down Mr. Russell; I'm the new cog here to replace you.* Crazy, I was always taught to respect my elders.

Sara Rothschild, a single mother of a 3-year old son, Anthony Jr., applied for the job of CPI when she saw an ad for the position in the **Employment Guide**. The 31-year old never married the father of her son, Anthony Sr. He bolted out of their lives, shortly after he saw the two vertical lines on the pregnancy test. Luckily, Sara's mother who lived in Coral Gables agreed to watch little Anthony while Sara went to work for the State. I laughed the first time I saw Sara in PDP class after I saw her use half-a-bottle of antibacterial hand sanitizer to wipe down her desk area. In PDP, The Linebacker spied Sara in her futile attempt to disinfect her space and called her out: *"Ms. Rothschild, what are you going to do when you have to enter a roach-infested, urine drenched home and the clients ask you to sit down? A gallon of Purell ain't gonna help you Baby!"* She just chuckled and smiled. Sara Rothschild also stood out because she was the only White face in the Fall 2000 PDP class. Sara Rothschild was assigned to Central Unit, 802.

Tamara Norvil was a Haitian American woman who transferred from Naples, Florida (District 9). She's easily was the most beautiful thing I've seen since stepping foot in South Florida. Norvil a quiet young woman in her late 20's had a pretty face, a dark chocolate-brown complexion and was beautifully endowed. Norvil was initially hired by District 9 and was allowed to transfer to Miami Dade County prior to completing her one year probationary period because she spoke four languages: English, Spanish, Creole and French. Miami Dade County was always in desperate need of workers who spoke multiple languages. Of the three CPIs in my training class, I was closest to Tamara. Ever since our first day at PDP Training, we hit off well. We were young, single and childless and anyone who saw us together noticed the attraction we had for one another. Unfortunately for me, Tamara was detailed almost 30-something miles away to South Unit, 413.

###

I reached the fifth floor of the Rohde Building. To the right of the elevator, I saw a door with a Microsoft® Word generated paper sign on it which read:

District 11 Central Child Protective Services

Through the unlocked door I entered, which opened into a shallow corridor. At the end of the corridor, there were two hallways—one went left and the other went right. The hallways were actually connected and ran the perimeter of the floor. I looked at my wristwatch *8:50 am*—and noticed that most of the offices and cubicles were empty, just stacks and stacks of case files, some on office desks and others stacked neatly on the floor and some were in cardboard boxes. I walked along the hallway to the right until I found office S-525. I took a deep breath and knocked before entering.

"Hi, my name is Jeremiah Abundo; I'm the new CPI in Unit 808." I extended my hand to a fiftyish-or-so African American lady sitting behind a desk. The figure kept writing and analyzing the document before her.

"Oh…, Hi Jeremiah give me one second; this status report needs to be typed up and submitted to Judge Nielsen before the PM calendar." The figure blurted.

I waited a few seconds and reeled my hand back in and stated, "Take your time."

I took a seat in a wooden chair with red, Codura cushioning that flanked my new supervisor's desk. I stared straight ahead with my hands folded not before noticing the hodgepodge of mismatched furniture that sat on top of green, outdated Houndstooth-patterned carpeting. Thoughts swirled in my head; I felt a mixture anxiety and adulation. This was my first real job, and I wasn't sure how I'd fair. The smell of freshly brewed Café Cubano enticed me and brought me back to the present. After scanning the document, my supervisor pressed 'Enter' on her keyboard and the status report began to print on a local laser jet that sat atop her desk. She emerged from the desk to greet her new employee. She noticed my distinct race and ethnicity and noticed my overdressed attire. She fumbled over her introduction.

"Are you sure you're in the right area?'...MIS is on the 4th floor"?

"No, I believe I am in the right place, I am a new CPI detailed to Unit 808—Jamie Watkins is listed as my immediate supervisor." I politely replied; I was tickled by my supervisor's last comment.

"Actually, I'm Ms. Thompson, the unit secretary. Ms. Watkins is in court right now, I don't know when she will be coming back." Ms. Thompson replied.

"No problem. Is there something I can help you with?" I asked. I eyed a dozen-or-so boxes next to Mrs. Thompson's desk. "I have a strong back if you need some help with those boxes?"

"Thanks Jeremiah. But I don't having anything for you to do right now. And everyone in the unit is either out on a case or in court. If you want, I can call around to the other units to see if there are any CPIs you can shadow for the time being? While you're waitin', take these." Ms. Thompson handed me three manila case files— all distinct in size and weight. "...these are the cases that we received during the mornin' pull. The CPIs who are out in the field will pick them up and investigate them. Those will be your new co-workers."

I was giddy; it was my first glimpse into the life of a real child welfare worker. Just 10-minutes into the job, and I was so excited that I was being put to use. Mrs. Thompson led me into a vacant office adjacent to hers. Most of the offices were empty, but piles of paperwork strewn on desks served as evidence that they were inhabited. I opened the manila case folders one by one and read:

Initial Abuse Report 00-2514096 (Imm)

On August 26, 2000, Ebony was picked up from her mother's house and taken to her father's house for weekend visitation. While bathing the child, father noticed Ebony's vagina was red, swollen and irritated. It is unknown if mother's boyfriend is harming the child. Father refuses to give the child back to the mother.

Initial Abuse Report 00-2514515 (24)

Joe has been at the juvenile lock up since July 21, 2000, mother refuses to pick the child up from lock up. The child suffers from severe diabetes and DJJ staff is having great difficulty contacting/locating mother for medical consent for treatment.

Initial Abuse Report 00-2514991 (IMM)

On August 25, 2000, 17-year old mother Jessica was punched in the face by her 21-year old boyfriend/father Lester after Jessica asked Lester for $20 for diapers. This is not the first time Jessica was a victim of domestic violence. Lester fled prior to law enforcement's arrival. Their infant child, Irma was not hurt during the altercation.

I was floored after reading the allegations. Each one of these case allegations posed a unique set of issues. I kicked myself for prematurely critiquing my counterpart CPI Brandon Russell for having 285-backlog investigations open; I could now see how this could happen—but I still disliked him nonetheless. In early 2000, the Florida Task Force for the Protection of Abused and Neglected Children was hired to clean up 50,000 backlog abuse cases in Florida. The non-profit agency discovered that some of these case files originating from Lake County (District 13) were intentionally shredded, while some were hidden in office drop ceilings. As I thumbed through the case file contents I noticed an array of paperwork including: prior abuse reports, criminal records, birth displays, and multiple consent forms. Suddenly, a familiar voice drew my attention.

"Can't wait to get your feet wet"? Sara Rothschild inquired.

I closed the case folder I was examining and replied, "Oh…hey Sara…just looking over a few of my co-workers' new investigations. I haven't met anyone from my unit except for our unit secretary, Mrs. Thompson. Have you met anyone in your unit?"

"I met one CPI Andrea Paxton, she's been here less than a year, but she agreed to let me tag along when she hits the field. I can ask her if you can accompany us if you'd like?" Sara asked.

"That's would be grea…"

Before I could finish my sentence, I was interrupted by sounds that I haven't heard since arriving in Miami—the laughter of children.

I stuck my head outside of the office and saw a tall, thin black woman walking with a pair of twin, Hispanic boys. One of the boys was holding the lady's hand, while she clutched the other child in the crook of her arm. Both of the boys looked disheveled, and unkempt. The boy walking wore a pair of Lightning McQueen character sneakers, the headlights on McQueen illuminated each time the boy took a step. The boys appeared to be around three or four. As the CPI and the children passed Sara and me, the boy in the lady's arm smiled and said, "Hi." The smell of old urine singed our nostrils hairs. Both of the children appeared to be happy to be in the company of the thin investigator. Unsurprisingly, I turned to find that Sara crept back to her unit on the other side of the floor; I'm sure the threat of being soiled by the displaced children prompted her actions. I approached the trio. Before entering, CPI Rhonda Jackson's office/cubicle, I introduced myself.

"Hi, my name is Jeremiah Abundo, I'm the new guy in your unit? Need some help?" I stated.

CPI Jackson gave me a brief smile with her set of perfectly straight white teeth. She opened two 2.1oz Kellogg's® Frosted Flakes® cereal boxes and gave a box to each of the twins. Her natural shoulder length brown hair was pulled into a high pony tail. A few strands of hair draped over the frames of her tortoiseshell-colored glasses moved about while she continued to tend to Marco and Ronny Beltran. Automatically, I was smitten.

###

The sound of rushing sink water echoed over the muffled giggling of Marco Beltran. In just one hour after meeting CPI Rhonda Jackson; I admired her beauty— inside and out. The tender way she handled Marco and his twin brother Ronny was the way I wanted to handle my own clients as long as I worked here: no question was too trivial to answer and no spill was too big to wipe up. Rhonda had a thin face, her skin was a soft bronze, and when she directed her smile at you, she had you *whooped*. Rhonda asked me if I could give Marco and his brother paper towel wipe downs in the men's bathroom, and I immediately honored the request. For lunch, from her own pocket, Rhonda bought the children Happy Meals from McDonald's and outfitted the twins with some of her own children's clothes. Rhonda told me that many of the children we remove and place in care, enter the foster care system with literally the clothes on their backs.

(Giggle...Giggle...Giggle...Splash)

A grin plastered Marco's face as he ran his hands through the running water, splashing water on the plastic counter and also on me. I looked up at the large bathroom mirror and smiled, and Marco smiled back. The grime that once caked the boy's face was now gone. The boy appeared a shade lighter after the film of dirt was peeled from his skin. I combed through his brown hair which was amateurishly cut into a bowl style, watching the strands vanish through the gaps between my fingers; the gesture made me yearn to have my own children all the more. Wisely, I removed my silk tie, folded it and tucked it in my back pocket. My dress shirt was already splattered with water droplets and random finger print marks.

"Okay little man you're all done."

Marco just looked at me and giggled some more. He blurted something in Spanish, but I couldn't understand him. I whisked Marco back to his sibling; I knew Ronny missed the company of his twin. As I approached Rhonda, she was squirting ketchup onto Ronny's French fries from the way the boy was devouring his food, it appeared his nutritional needs were terribly neglected.

"Thanks so much Jeremiah." Rhonda said with that smile. "This case came in when I was On-call this morning. I thought I was all clear then I got a page from the On-call supervisor at *5:45am*. Fortunately, when I'm On-call I load up on Coca Cola and take an early nap, so I'm wired up. I woke up my chil'ren, got 'em dressed and dropped them off at their father's house in North Miami. From there, I picked up Marco and Ronny at the Miami Police station around *7:30am*. Then I tried to locate some relatives so the kids wouldn't have to go into shelter care— no luck. So here we are, I have so much to do, and so little time."

"Rhonda, I'm here for you, but I'm not sure what I can help you with?" I injected. "I'm a new kid with no skills."

The sound of Marco and Ronny rifling through there Happy Meal boxes broke the silence. The smell of French fries and hamburgers reminded me that I haven't eaten anything all day. From a distance we heard unit secretary Jessica Thompson approaching fast, as she loudly called out the overworked CPI's name.

"Oh Rhonda…Rhonda honey! I have a 24 for you!" The portly secretary exclaimed.

"Oh hell naw! How am I goin' to take this 24, I am in the middle of a removal. Get Jamie on the phone, this nonsense needs to stop!" Rhonda's smile vanished.

"Rhonda, Jamie's in court coverin' one of Daniel's cases. We received three cases this mornin': two immediates and a 24. I'm givin' you the 24…but you don't have to go on it right now!" The unit secretary stated.

I later found out that Daniel Diaz was a CPI who resigned two weeks ago after Customs and Border Patrol offered him a job. I also learned when a CPI vacated their position; their cases remained in their respective unit. The unit supervisor had the choice to reassign these cases to the remaining CPIs in the unit or work the cases for closure herself. Daniel Diaz stuck unit 808 with 31-live cases— 4 of them were court cases. Supervisor Jamie Watkins chose to work the cases herself rather than dole them out to the CPIs in her unit. My stomach began creaking and churning from lack of sustenance, but I was too into Rhonda's situation to think about food. I wanted to help, but didn't know what else I could do. I stared at Rhonda who took off her Guess eyeglass frames. She then rubbed her eyes for a few seconds before putting her glasses back on. I looked down to see that Marco and Ronny finished devouring their Happy Meals and were now playing with bouncy rubber balls included in their meal boxes. The balls were fashioned in the shape of eyeballs: the Beltran boys were not the least bit repulsed. Rhonda was livid at receiving her second case this morning, but soon realized that there was nothing she could do at this time, but pray some of her pending job applications would bear fruit. Rhonda looked down at her desk at a recent photograph of her and her two handsome boys, Theo and Jovan. The picture was taken at the 2000 Dade County Youth Fair. The trio was wearing matching blue denim shorts and gray, T-shirts with the saying "I Survived Y2K!" screen printed on the chest. Rhonda's eyes dropped from the picture, as she finally broke her silence.

"Mrs. Thompson, can you create a file on this Beltran case? I need to draft the shelter petition and get it off to legal before 4pm. I also need the name of the On-call attorney."

"Awright Honey, I'll have that case file for you in 30-minutes and I'll get you that other information." Mrs. Thompson stated.

"Thank you." Rhonda stated exhaustedly.

Rhonda thumbed through her new case file earmarking certain pages. She read the allegations to herself:

Joe has been at the juvenile lock up since July 21, 2000, mother refuses to pick the child up from lock up. The child suffers from severe diabetes and DJJ staff is having great difficulty contacting/locating mother for medical consent for treatment.

When she was done scanning the case file, she looked at me and said, "Hey new kid, I can use your help?"

When I cheerfully agreed, Rhonda's smile magically reemerged.

###

After reading the case file, Rhonda knew exactly her course of action. She would drop off and file her shelter petition at the Juvenile Justice Center around 4pm and then she would immediately meet with Joe at juvenile lock up. Luckily, juvenile lock up was in the same complex as the courthouse. Rhonda studied the case and determined there were no other children in the household, but there were several cases, which were similar in nature to this one. Most of these cases involved Joe's mother refusing to pick up the child from juvenile lockup and local police stations. CPI Abassi Okafor, a fellow member of unit 808, handled a prior case in 1998; his case involved Joe coming to school hungry and wearing filthy, ill-fitting clothing. In his case, Joe's mother refused to meet with school officials to remedy the problem. Rhonda, a 7-year veteran of the agency, knew there was a definite pattern of neglect. She determined that she was going to place Joe in foster care before this child ended up dead.

"Jeremiah, it's obvious that Joe's mother doesn't want this child and priors indicate this child has exhausted the good graces of all his known relatives." Rhonda stated as she adjusted her designer frames. "If the State deems Joe as an adjudicated dependent...simply put, the State finds that Joe's mother incapable being responsible for him, the State will take the responsibility for caring for this child until he turns 18. If he chooses, Joe will be able to go to a Florida run college/university free of cost and the State will flip the bill for his medical care also. If adopted, the person who adopts the Joe will receive a subsidy to care for him."

"What are the odds of this child getting adopted?" I asked.

"In Joe's case, it is highly unlikely he'll get adopted. 16-years old, two open delinquency cases, a high-school dropout, a diagnosed medical condition and a healthy hue of dark brown skin to boot, deadens his chances for sure!" Rhonda stated without censor.

"And what happens to the parents? Do they go to jail"? I asked.

"A dependency court judge can levy child support on the parents; however, this is rarely the case. If a parent is incarcerated, receiving SSI (Supplemental Security Income) benefits, or indigent, the parents pay nothing." Rhonda stated as she packed a clothing bag for the Beltran boys.

"So the parents are off the hook— what a system"? I added cynically.

"Rookie…we are here for the chil'ren. The Department wasn't set up as a punitive means. Just concern yourself with the chil'ren and you'll do alright here." Rhonda stated while she packed her work luggage—a pull cart with her laptop, case files and an accordion folder stocked with every departmental form imaginable.

I agreed to transport Marco and Ronny to their foster care placement for Rhonda and watch them until placement was secured. I wished I could do more to help, but since I wasn't a certified child protective investigator just yet; my roles were relegated to glorified babysitter and transport specialist. I quickly learned that due to budget cuts, the transportation department was cut from Child Safety's budget earlier this year. Essentially, a CPI was responsible for transporting a child to his doctor's appointments, court hearings, and visitations while bearing the responsibility to visit children/families on any new investigation received. In other districts, all children being removed from their parents/guardians were even brought to the Shelter Hearing/Detention Hearing. This hearing is held 24-hours from the removal episode of a child. Some judges liked seeing the kids they were actually impacting, while other judges felt the process re-traumatized the children by placing them in the same arena as their abusers, too quickly. Consequently, District 11 abandoned this practice due to its budget and lack of manpower. I would soon learn District 11 did things a lot different than the rest of the state.

Prior to her leaving the office to file the Beltran shelter petition with the On-call DCF attorney, Rhonda called the placement department and reminded them of her request for placement for the Beltran boys. She called for placement immediately after she picked up the boys at 6am from the precinct, since securing a foster home for them could take half-a-day. If a child had a mental health or a medical condition, the process could take even longer. As a reward for my babysitting duties, Rhonda agreed to take me out on a few of her cases in the future. She also allowed me to make a copy of her personal cheat sheet for CPIs. I was tempted to ask her for her phone number, but her cheat sheet would have to do for now.

"Here you go! Make a couple of copies for yourself and give it back to me on Monday and please don't lose my cheat sheet Rookie." Rhonda said hastily as she rushed off to her meeting with the attorney. But before she left, she slid me $30 just in case I needed something else for the boys. She left without a goodbye, but she did give me a smile.

I looked down to see the boys fast asleep on the office floor on a makeshift pallet; I split open a couple of cardboard boxes used for closed case files and laid them flat, so that the boys didn't have to lay directly on the grubby office floor. I'm sure these poor kids have seen their fair share of shitty sleeping accommodations in their lifetime; I'm just sorry that we weren't able to give them something a little more. Ronny had an impish smile on his face, while his brother had residual ketchup in the corners of his mouth. Their slumber allowed me to take a much needed cigarette break. I folded the cheat sheet, which looked like it had been copied a thousand times and stuck it in my back pocket. I then asked Mrs. Thompson to keep an eye on the children, while I grabbed some "lunch" from the hot dog lady on the first floor pavilion. The unit secretary agreed. I hated to lie, but I still had issues telling people I smoked. *Damn those TRUTH commercials!* They made me feel so guilty and foolish for continuing to indulge in this life-shortening habit.

To ease my conscious, I reluctantly stopped off at the hot dog lady and bought a smoked sausage sandwich and a diet Coke. There were several stone benches in the courtyard of the Rohde. I positioned myself on an empty bench farthest from the building. Under a lush Cabbage Palmetto, I ate half of my smoked sausage sandwich and washed it down with my diet Coke, then smoked my Kool to the nub. I reached into my back pocket to retrieve Rhonda's cheat sheet. The cheat sheet was basically an 8 ½" x 11" sheet of paper with: important contact information and phone numbers, steps/directions when submitting certain documents and crucial timeframes to remember during the course of a child abuse investigation. The page was crammed with info front and back. I made a promise to commit this entire sheet to memory before receiving my child welfare certification. As I read, a few pigeons began surrounding me— awaiting a handout I suppose. They edged closer and closer to me. Unfortunately, these birds didn't know I was Filipino, and we considered these little motherfuckers delicacies. In Tagalog, we call 'em, *kalapati*. I ended up ripping a few chunks of bread from my sandwich and hurled them in front of me. Seconds later, more pigeons joined the feeding frenzy. I crumbled up the rest of the bread and watched as the pigeons gorge on the ketchup soaked bread. I reminisced about the day's events and smiled. It was just my first day and there was so much to talk about. Mom wouldn't believe it. She politely opposed my career choice, but she was always supportive. She even had reservations about me coming to Miami. But I was glad I was here. I helped a coworker on my first day. I gave a couple of kids a little-needed laughter in their lives. And I was even glad I was here to feed these damn pigeons. As the supply of breadcrumbs dwindled, one by one the pigeons took flight. I stared at the ground until there was none. My mind drifted as a warm, endless breeze lulled me into a semiconscious state.

###

After dropping Allison off at her apartment, I entered the front door to the main house where I saw Mom wearing a border-print duster. The smell of *tuyo* (sun-dried fish) and fried eggs immediately struck me. This breakfast favorite was popular with our family and not so much with our neighbors— olfactorily.

"Long night Anak"? She questioned with a wry smile.

"Yes, Mom…you know I'm going to miss these morning chats with you. Thank goodness Miami is just an hour away." I said as my eyes burned from lack of sleep and hours of revelry.

Cynthia Abundo glimpsed at the clock and then looked at me. Everything about me reminded her of my dad. My quick wit, my patience, the way I held a cigarette— and this doesn't describe the physical similarities we shared. I was the same height as my dad 5'11", I possessed the same rounded jaw line as him and even shared same genetic predisposition for a lack of facial hair. I always found the latter astounding.

"I will miss you Anak and I am so proud of you." She said as her eyes-filled and dropped to the frying pan containing the eggs and fish. I wasn't sure what to think of the sight. Ever since Dad passed away, she was so fragile. I almost felt guilty to leave her in Palm Beach alone. Well, not totally alone, my *kuya* Ronald also lived in Palm Beach, but Ronald did not afford the same attentiveness as I did because he was too busy trying to start his own family.

"I made this *alumusal* for you. I'm just sorry it's going to be your last in this house. " She stated.

The pungent smell of the sardines and the eggs topped with fresh tomatoes served over a steaming bed of white rice captivated me and brought me back to a time and place when Dad was still alive. Mom made this same dish for him almost every day before my father, Jeremiah Sr. traveled to the Port of Palm Beach to work. Even though

Mom had a full-time job, she never had an issue preparing meals for her family. Born and raised in Cebu, Philippines, Cynthia Abundo came here to the US through a working visa on December 19, 1982 due to the shortages of RN nurses in New York City. She married her high school sweetheart in a town in the Philippines called Hagonoy in the province of Bulacan, a year earlier. Her decision to leave Dad and Ronald behind in the Philippines was a difficult one. But at the time, the US offered immigration incentives for foreigners who possessed certain skills. Mom was able to apply for citizenship in the US within two years of her arrival. Traditionally, she would have had to wait seven. When she arrived in the United States, she stayed with a few other Filipina nurses in a 2-bedroom apartment in New York. From the money she saved in rent, she allocated its use to petition Dad and Ronald to come to America.

Ravenous, I sat at the kitchen table and helped myself to the traditional Filipino breakfast or *alumusal*, Mom so thoughtfully prepared. Two empty chairs flanked me and I thought to myself, *Boy, life has certainly changed.* Yesterday was one of the happiest days of my life, and I was fortunate to have most of my family there. Both Mom and kuya Ronald managed to finagle some time from their busy jobs to make their presence. But Uncle Lonnie and his wife, Ingrid were no-shows. They were somewhere in the Caribbean on some sandy beach and unfortunately they couldn't make it. On June 15, 2000 at 11am— on the school grounds of Florida Atlantic University, 151-graduates received their Bachelor Degrees in Social Work. Mom was so proud of me even though she disapproved of my major. She made a point to remind me of this whenever possible. *"Anak, Social Work? Really?"* or *"The medical field is the wave of the future, Anak you can make twice the money as an RN!"* After seeing my determination to purse my career of choice and when she finally realized I was afflicted with the same Abundo hardheadedness –or *tigas ng ulo* which withstood generations; she relented. Although weeks before my graduation, she timidly suggested that I enroll in the accelerated LPN course at Rivera Beach Community College. I distinctly remember her actual words, *"Anak, I know you will do well as a social worker…but it's always good to have a plan B."*

I could have lived in Mom's house forever. While some parents can't wait until their kids graduate so they can empty the nest; in the Filipino culture it's different. You don't turn a certain age and you magically become an adult. My brother and I grew up in a happy household where both my parents worked hard to keep their boys without having to worry about much. I learned home is something you can always come back to. Our Palm Beach house was modest by most standards. It was big enough where each of the family members could be in a various parts of the house and never see each other the whole day. But I learned early, family is everything. I loved seeing everybody in our house share the same space. After my graduation, Mom almost tore my head off when I tried to surrender my set of house keys. Instead, she looked into my eyes, held my forearm and advised me of an old Filipino Proverb or Salawikain:

Aanhin mo ang palasyo, kung ang nakatira ay kuwago. Mabuti pa ang bahay kubo, ang nakatira ay tao.

When translated into it English it means:

What good is it to live in palace if its only inhabitants are owls. It's better to live bamboo hut inhabited by other people.

In the Philippines, my mother and her family of six grew up in a "bahay kubo" where she was actually birthed on its floor by my grandmother/midwife, Sophie. My uncle's home was just the opposite. Uncle Lonnie or *"Bayani"* (hero in Tagalog) and his wife, Ingrid lived in West Miramar, a city in Broward County just 18-miles from the City of Miami. Bayani and Ingrid shared a 2-story 5,000-square foot home— and the footage did not include a garage that was converted into an extra room, a practice adopted by a number of South Floridian home owners including my parents. Bayani's home was newly built in 1995 and equipped with an amoeba-shaped, in-ground pool with separate Jacuzzi and wet bar. The house sat on a one acre lot which allowed Bayani to dry dock his most-prized possession, a 23-foot Grady White Gulfstream 232 christened *"Mabuti"*, which means "good" or "fine" in Tagalog. I always thought Bayani was the complete opposite of my father. Touted as the braggart of the family, Bayani always called when he had some new trinket or toy. *"Kuya Jerry, you got to bring the boys and your asawa down here and check out my new boat."* Or *"Kuya Jerry you got to spend the weekend at this timeshare we just acquired!"* I always marveled at how my father never lost his cool or rebuffed, most often, Dad was excited and proud of his little brother. If Bayani didn't have anything to show off, he'd be absent in our lives for months.

Bayani thought he had to always impress his family, but we were very impressed with him already. Along with his boastful nature, Bayani was the funniest of the Abundo clan; he always had Ronald and me laughing. But regardless of his arrogance, his family members could not dispute his graciousness. After Dad passed away, he welcomed Mom, Ronald, and me to live with him bill-free at his Miramar home—forever. Mom politely declined her brother-in-law's proposition. But Bayani wouldn't take no for an answer, when he found out I'd be moving to Miami after I was offered a job with the Department. Consequently, my uncle and his wife never had any kids, but on July 1, 2000 I became Bayani's surrogate when I moved into my uncle's home. It was my first time away from home.

3 KIDS AND POLITICS

After calling the Placement Department at 3pm, I was miffed to hear that a placement was yet to be secured for the Beltran boys. Almost five-hours have passed, and the children were getting bored with their surroundings. I did my best to accommodate the children in this busy work environment; in desperation, I was relegated to building an indoor fort from a few office chairs and a large comforter that I found in the supply room. No TV, no sleeping arrangements, no toys, no cleaning wipes or food the children, I was at a loss for words. After an early lunch, the boys complained that they were still hungry, so I placed an order at a local deli. I ordered sub sandwiches, potato chips and fruit punch for lunch. I looked at Rhonda's office floor after the meal, and felt sympathy for the poor individual who had to vacuum up the remnants. In all honesty, these twins were a handful. You could tell these boys spent plenty of time alone with little to no supervision. When Marco escaped the confines of Rhonda's cubical and drifted into a nearby office space that belonged to Inspector General. One of the inspectors, yelled at me.

"You need to keep your kids over there and keep them quiet; we have people trying to work over here!'

I held my tongue and scooped up the wayward preschooler and took him back to "our side" of the office wing. I felt disjointed and confused. This was my first day at work, and I never envisioned it to be like this. I couldn't imagine what I'd have to do if I had my own court case or removal. According to Rhonda's cheat sheet, there's just so much to do in so little time. *How would I fill out the mounds of court documentation in 24-hours? When would I have the time to look for prospective relative placements for the children and conduct homestudies? How could I see to the removed children's needs if I was too busy doing data entry?* I made a mental note to discuss these questions with my new supervisor— whenever and if ever I get to meet her.

As I swept up some sub sandwich crumbs from my co-worker's desk, I heard the sound of men's dress shoes clacking towards Rhonda's cubicle. An unfamiliar voice spoke:

"And here we have another child abuse investigator protecting our youth." The tall, balding lanky White man gestured towards me eyeing me as if we were acquaintances. "Here we make sure the children are processed, clean and fed before they are taken to their respective placements."

The three individuals paused and looked at the makeshift fort fashioned from the comforter, and the crumbs that littered the floor.

"That's my juice!" Ronny interjected grabbing the juice box from Marco's loose grip. Marco began to cry. The trio ignored him. I picked up Marco and held him and remained silent while the trio confronted me.

"Mr. Griggs, FDLE". The gun toting individual said as he extended his hand out to me.

"Mr. Lance Archer, Director of the Abuse Hotline Tallahassee…you guys sure look like you're having lots of fun in here, I'm shocked to see you have time to build forts, seeing the amount of cases we send down to D11!" Director Archer chimed in.

Fun? If he only knew how long these kids have been here? I wanted to slap him back to the capital for such an idiotic comment.

"Mr. Parker tells us that the CPIs in Dade County are the best in the state. He says you guys work long hours and get the most difficult cases. Our numbers suggest that your district gets the highest amount of cases in the state and file the most detention petitions. Chet tells us, you guys like to do more with less and relish in that challenge." Mr. Archer stated anticipating my reaction.

Flattered, District Administrator Chet Parker replied, "Workers like this young man here keep our district going. In District 11, we do more with less, and we like it like this!"

Marco's wails became increasingly louder, I stood there bouncing him and rocking him back and forth. The office sounded like a factory. In the distance the sound of dot matrix printers buzzed incessantly while various rings and beeps could be heard from a myriad of devices: phones, fax machines and shredders. The garble of random conversations added to the sonic chaos. While the trio surrounded Rhonda's cubicle, people in the office avoided any contact with the trio altogether, they'd rather walk around the perimeter of the office than risk contact with the three men.

"Mr. Griggs and Mr. Archer are here to create a system so that you can get information from the abuse registry faster, this way you can go see your victims quicker and submit your reviews in a more, timelier manner. This all lends to helping us keep children safer. Administration is also working on getting you guys cell phones. So if you are in the field, we can provide you your case information over the phone. No more beepers or loose change to lug around... If you are On-call, we can stop calling you on your home phones and disrupting your entire household. We want to make you more efficient workers. What do you think about that?" Mr. Parker inquired while peering at my company ID which hung from my shirt pocket. "....Jeremiah?"

"Well...well Mr. Parker. Cell phones are always a good thing. They help us communicate faster..." I said stumbling over my poorly manufactured response. In truth, I didn't know what to fuckin' say? *That I've only been on the job for a day...and that I haven't been on my first case yet?* Maybe I shouldn't have opened my damn mouth. Feeling like an idiot, I wanted to crawl inside of the twin's makeshift fort and hide there forever. Luckily, before I could give any additional awkward comments, I was saved.

"Jeremiah. Pee...Pee...Pee...Pee!" Marco announced. The perfectly timed distraction allowed me to politely excuse myself from this pep rally. I bolted to the bathroom clutching Marco like a ventriloquist clutches his puppet. I held him out in front of me just in case we didn't make it. Ronny trailed close behind.

###

"Jeremiah! Jeremiah! Pick up on line three" Ms. Thompson bellowed down the corridor.

"Thank you Ms. Thompson. I got it!" I replied picking up the phone in Rhonda's cubicle.

"DCF investigations, CPI Abundo speaking…"

"Wow, don't you sound official! How's it goin' Jeremiah?" CPI Rhonda Jackson said jokingly.

"It's been an interesting day." I paused, surveying Rhonda's office and then continued. "The boys were good; they didn't cry or cause too many issues. Just kids being kids. How's it going with you?" I asked.

"I won't be in court tomorrow for Joe's shelter hearing."

"Oh yeah, why's that"? I asked.

"That crazy boy jumped outta my car and ran away from me a few minutes ago. We were waiting for a light to turn green on US 1 and Caribbean just listenin' to the radio, and when the song's chorus kicked in—*I'm sorry, Ms. Jackson Oooh…*' Joe smiled at me and opened my passenger car door, carefully closed it and bolted south on US 1."

"Damn, that is funny…."

"He always had a messed up sense of humor a few months ago he was arrested for peein' in his teacher's coffee while she took a bathroom break. **The Times** even ran a small piece entitled, 'Cup of Joe'."

We both laughed hard.

"…So you didn't have to chase him?" I asked.

"Hell naw Rookie! I'm a CPI not a bounty hunter!"

"So what do you do now"?

"I have to call Metro Dade Police and get a report from them. Call Jamie and tell her to place an alert in the system for Joe then write up an incident report. Then I have to go to the court house tomorrow and file a dependency pick-up order. Can't dodge court if I tried." Rhonda stated tiredly. "I do have some good news for you though. Placement called me with some foster homes for the boys."

"Homes"?

"Sorry Jeremiah, it's the best they can do for now. Marco's placement is going to be in Homestead, and Ronny's is going to be in Carol City. I want to help you transport, but I'm going to be here for minute waiting for Metro Police to arrive. But I owe you big time Baby!" She stated.

"That's no problem." I said as I quickly flicked on Rhonda's desktop computer and pulled up an internet site called Google to see how far Homestead was from Carol City. My eyes almost popped out of my head when I saw the distance—46.7 miles!

"So what do I do? Do I drop them off and just leave or did I need any paperwork completed for the drop-offs"? I asked.

"You're going to need some IPRs or Interim Placement Reports filled out and signed by the foster parent and the children will need to be fingerprinted and photographed prior to their drop-offs. Ask Ms. Thompson for help, she'll know what to do." Rhonda requested politely.

"I will make sure it gets done and I'll leave the paperwork on your office chair by Monday morning." I said.

"Thank you so much Jeremiah. If you need me you can page me at 305-952-7020. You're going to make a great CPI, just don't let the little things get at you or you'll go bananas here. I will see you on Monday Rookie."

At *5:35pm*, the random sounds of the factory were now heard infrequently, as employees headed out the door. In an hour-or-so, it would be me and the boys making any and all noises at the Rohde. Ms. Thompson rummaged through her office desk for a Kodak 35mm disposable camera. Marco and Ronny's energy waned as they sat patiently waiting to have their pictures taken. Just minutes before, Ms. Thompson and I struggled to attain a useable set of fingerprints from the twins. Due to the Department's financial constraints, I was relegated to using paper from the copier as a substitute for the normally studier card stock used for finger printing and I also had to use an ink blotter used for stamping mail; to my dismay the ink was lime green. The first set of prints I took was laughable; they looked like a preschooler's finger-painting project rather than instruments used to identify missing children. Before this day, I never fingerprinted anyone in my life— and it showed. After careful thought, I deduced that working here was going to be very challenging not because of the sheer danger of the job or the unpredictability of a client's behavior, but because of the internal mechanisms placed in a caseworker's way. Just like the ordeal I just experienced to get an extra car seat for the boys' placement. I had to literally beg, Mr. Steven Rigby, the supervisor in 425 for his unit's assigned car seat. When he finally opened his office after ten minutes of pleading and groveling, I couldn't believe what I saw. This guy had the fuckin' thing chained to his desk under lock and key. Apparently, car seats are hot commodities here! And when Rigby finally authorized the use of his car seat, I had to sign a contract stating I'd return it in 48-hours or receive a written reprimand. Fuckin' unbelievable—a rent-a-car seat operation at DCF. But overall my whole day working with the Department was a totally surreal experience…one I will never forget. *Can you imagine this was only my first day?*

At approximately *6:37pm*, the Beltran twins were finally leaving to their new homes. I caught a glimpse of myself in the reflection of a picture frame as I waited for the elevator to arrive. My new, Nautica dress shirt was marred in apple juice, ketchup and small brownish handprints. My dress pants were mangled. Perspiration saturated my short, black hair and rolled down my face while a backpack with the twins' worldly belongings slung over my shoulder. I looked down and felt the grip of Marco and Ronny clutching each of my hands as we waited for the elevator. In the few hours, I spent with the boys I noticed a considerable change: they seemed a little nicer and respectable towards one another. They affected me too. I left my first day of work so grateful to be raised by such great parents.

"Look it's going down! Twelve..........Eleven.......Ten........." Ronny observantly mentioned.

"Yes, it is going down. Good job Ronny. Good job with those numbers!" I replied back

Considering everything, I felt that I accomplished quite a bit today: I made two children smile; I nourished them, and put them at ease. And despite their situation, they reminded me of how much value the innocence of children brings to our busy adult lives. While filling out the IPRs, I found out why the Beltran boys were removed from their parents.

Around 3:45 am, neighbors found Marco wandering the streets looking for his mother and father. When the police arrived, Marco led them to his home. His twin brother, Ronny, was sleeping in a soiled mattress. The home was in disarray. There was no food in the refrigerator. This is not the first time the children have been left alone. The whereabouts of the parents cannot be determined at this time. Currently, the children are at the City of Miami Police station. Detective Bill Edwards requests an ETA from the CPI. (Imm.)

"Nine........Eight........Six........, it's almost here" Marco exclaimed.

I smiled at him acknowledging the comment.

There was a loud chime before the elevator doors slid open. We entered the elevator and Marco and Ronny jockeyed to mash the "L" button on the elevator's panel as usual Marco the bigger of the two won this exchange. The doors shut.

"Four…..Three……Two…." Marco and Ronny joined in chorus as the elevator descended.

I smiled, gripped their hands tighter and thought to myself, *It's going down. It's definitely going down.*

4 TAMARA

November 18, 2000
(Richmond Heights)

I scooped out dabs of Palmer's Cocoa Butter Lotion in my palms and worked the moisturizer into my ankles and eventually coated other crucial parts of my body: knees, elbows, arms and hands.

"Lotioned up. Check."

Then I slipped on a white midriff top that exposed my ample breasts and a pastel green skirt that hovered just above my knees. The green worked very well contrasting my silky mocha thighs, which were toned and firm from daily stints at the gym.

"Outfit. Check."

And even though the Department discouraged the wearing of heels while in the field, I ignored its advice and strapped on a sexy pair of 5-inch fitness model heels. At first I thought the heels were a bit too much—footwear a dancer at Club Rolexxx would rock during a set, but I was going for broke to ensnare him.

"Footwear. Check."

Since meeting Jeremiah Abundo at DCF's Professional Development Program (PDP) a few months ago, I was immediately attracted to him. Smart, funny, good lookin' and compassionate, I could see myself being with him. I could've been miles away in another city working in District 9 or in school working on my Master's in Criminal Justice upstate, but by sheer chance we met here and he reinvigorated my belief in men. Jeremiah is just what I needed at this point in my life. Today was more than an agreement to assist in a few follow up home visits, but my first legitimate date while in Miami—Jeremiah just didn't know it. Since graduating from PDP, we had a deal: I'd provide language translation services whenever he requested, in exchange for his help on some of my more "problematic" cases. In the few months of working, Jeremiah appeared to have a firm grasp of his duties as a child protective investigator. In fact, his ass never stopped talkin' about the job. Today, he promised to pick me up at my home around 11am to assist me with my mounting caseload. I was pleased to see he was a man of his word. Last week, he called me from a Cuban lady's home for Spanish/English translation. A routine homestudy for placement, which normally takes 30-minutes, took 1½ - hours. But I could never turn down any of his requests; I felt almost embarrassed to have this school girl crush on him at my age. Aside from his looks, his intelligence was just as appealing. I melted when he stood up in class and advocated for single moms:

Why do the media portray these single mothers in such a negative light? Where the hell are the fathers when these young women are being arrested for abuse or neglect? At least, mothers have the courage to stick around to take care of their children while the fathers get a pass!

After my last relationship in Naples, I needed a change—new job, new city, new relationships and a new start. I promised myself to really get to know people before allowing newcomers into my circle. Even though he was hundreds of miles away across the state, I was still afraid of him and still afraid to let down my guard. As I grabbed my keys and my purse and proceeded to slip out my front door, I caught a glimpse of myself in my parlor mirror. I balked and pursed my full lips, concealing my teeth. Manufacturing an open mouth smile was a difficult task nowadays. I slowly rubbed my upper lip in a circular motion having second thoughts about this date or even leaving my house.

###

"Oh I like this one; I can see this going in the living room. And it's only 35-dollars!" I stated holding up an abstract acrylic painting from some obscure local artist.

"A little too weird for me. My 3-year old can do a better job than this and he'll do it for free." Stevenson quickly replied.

Stevenson clutched my hand as we navigated through the maze of artists and exhibitors at the 21st Annual Naples National Art Festival. The Naples Art Association (NAA) organized this outdoor event in 1957. Their first effort showcased the work of 37 exhibiting members. Now the two day affair, hosts over 200 local, regional and national artists. We paused to watch a contortionist and a man juggling flaming torches performing to the music of the Bee Gee's "Staying Alive".

**Ah, ha, ha, ha, stayin' alive, stayin' alive
Ah, ha, ha, ha, stayin' alive**

I reached into my purse and did a two-step to the song's beat. I dropped two dollars in their glass fishbowl, which was overflowing with tips before offering up some well-deserved praise, "Good work gentleman! Good work! You made my day!"

Then I sang the chorus as I made my way back to Stevenson. From afar, I noticed he was impressed with my curvy, but tight physique. Stevenson loved my body. I started working out because of him: he must have hit the gym six days a week. The only day he refrained from working out was on Sundays. Sundays were reserved for church and watching football.

"That was a nice gesture Baby." His thick Creole accent emphasized stress on the last syllable of 'Baby' making it sound like 'Babeeeeee'. As a child growing up in Haiti, it was common for him to see street performers on the street corners of Port-Au-Prince. His favorite was Henri and his white marionette/sidekick Matisse, the two performed dance routines as heavy Kompa music thumped in the background.

"It's hard out here Stevenson, you got to help any little way you can." I said.

The smell of hamburgers and freshly grilled corn on the cob enticed me as we travelled deeper into the festival grounds. As you can imagine, the Naples Art Festival was also famous for drawing some of the best food vendors in the state.

"So what do you want to eat Baby"? Stevenson asked.

"Those foot long corndogs smell good. How about one of those?" I said as I pointed to a trailer, which specialized in fair food: cotton candy, pretzels, and popcorn. "You know I'm a sucker for fair food."

He rebuffed, "Since we're here, I think we should try something different, something we normally don't get to eat? How about some pinchos, fish tacos— or lobster rolls?" His voice deepened, while the tightness of his grip grew stronger for emphasis.

"Stevenson, I am not really feeling exotic right now, we're at a fair and I want fair food. It's a free country; you can eat pinchos, lobster rolls or deep fried escargot. And I'll take an ol' fashioned corndog." I stated.

Noticeably annoyed Stevenson barked, "Why do you have to be such a smart ass all the time? In three months of dating, we can never agree on what to eat. I say one thing, you say the complete opposite. Why can't you see things from my side once in a while?"

Shit. Less than an hour into our date and our first argument. It seems lately that our arguments were almost common place. The honeymoon phase was now gone. In the past, I'd hold my tongue and play the dumb-dumb role. But I couldn't conceal my true character— none of us can for long. Stevenson was right I was a smart ass.

"The increased bass in your voice and your augmented tone doesn't scare me Stevenson. We always do what you want. Every movie that we've been to is something you picked. You dragged me to **Battlefield Earth** and **Coyote Ugly** this past month alone and it was pure torture. I just kept my mouth shut and let you enjoy your movies. I spent almost 4-hours watchin' you fawn over John Travolta dressed up as an alien and watchin' you get back-to-back boners watchin' those bitches in **Coyote Ugly**. Stevenson don't tell me you never get your way…you always get your way!"

Stevenson knew arguing with me was futile. He knew I was just too clever and smooth with my delivery. Half of the time, I used big words that had him dumbfounded—scrambling for a dictionary. Words like "augmented" and "fawn" were a foreign language to Stevenson. *Let's face it, my boyfriend was a bonehead…but a fine bonehead!* His baby's mama, Olivia just cowered when he raised his voice. That shit didn't work with me.

"Forget about it. I'll just eat something when I get home." Stevenson fumed.

"No problem dear. No problem." I stated grabbing the crook of his muscular arm.

Stevenson said little to me during the rest of our journey. We walked side-by-side most of the way. He stared one way while I stared the other way. About fifteen minutes later, we reached Booth 223. A handsome gentleman with shoulder length dreadlocks with green eyes manned the booth. Prescott had several of his pieces up for display. His full name was Prescott Davis, but he went by his first name exclusively. Prescott was famous for his paintings of beautiful landscapes across town: Collier Seminole State Park, Naples Zoo and Naples Pier.

###

"This is a beautiful piece! How much for this one sir?" I asked as I ran my fingers across the canvas feeling every bump and depression on the oil-based acrylic.

"That one, I'm asking $150, but for you I'll let it go for $100…and forget the sir call me Prescott." The artist replied.

First, Prescott extended his hand to Stevenson who balked at the gesture and then he moved to extend his hand towards me. I shook the young artist's hand. From the look on Stevenson's face, the grasp was a millisecond too long.

"That painting took me a whole day to complete. That's a painting of Naples Pier. I made it on October 13, 1999 a couple of days before Hurricane Irene made landfall here. I call it **A Calm before the Storm**. You really appreciate the beauty of something right before its pending destruction. I'm glad the city recovered from that one." Prescott said politely.

"It looks like you put a lot of time into it." I replied as I handed him a $100 in twenties.

"Anything that's beautiful takes time to cultivate. You can't expect anything to grow if you don't take the time to feed it. Here…let me sign the back of the canvas for you." Prescott fished a black Sharpie marker from the front pocket of his tie-dye smock and proceeded to sign the piece.

"Is that Tamara with one 'm' ?"

"That's correct." I stated.

Seconds later, he passed me the canvas and I read the inscription aloud:
Tamara,
Never forsake life's eternal beauty and take time each day to bask in it.
                                         Fond Regards,
                                         Prescott,
                                         11/18/99

I smiled. But from the corner of my eye I saw Stevenson was fuming. Already pissed off from my comments about his movie and food selections, he thought I was flirting with another man just to spite him. *And he's goddamn right! I may not be able to beat you arm wrestlin'. But I'm gonna fuck you up in mind judo!* To top it off, the artist known as Prescott was bright skinned. The artist reminded Stevenson of that character Shazza (played by actor Gary Dourdan) from the TV series a **Different World.** Stevenson had some serious issues with light-skinned dudes. Firstly, he didn't care for them because Stevenson was blacker than Wesley Snipes' armpit. Secondly, these pretentious pretty-lookin' dudes with their pretty light skin an' their flowin' locks always went by a single name: Prince, Ginuwine, Debarge, Maxwell and Sinbad. *How dare they drop their last names and elevate themselves to the likes of Plato, Napoleon, Gandhi, Oprah and…even God!* I knew something was wrong when I ended up lugging the almost 4-foot painting to the car by myself, since Stevenson didn't lift a finger to help. He walked in front of me the whole way and never looked back. As I walked behind him, I became annoyed and irritated watching the fat humps on Stevenson's neck bounce up an' down…tauntin' me and talkin' to me all the way to the car. *How dare this 6'4", 240lb gorilla treat his woman like this?*

###

The sun was setting on Naples like the one on Prescott's landscape as we finally arrived at Stevenson's truck. Stevenson opened my door for me and placed my new acquisition in his back seat. But it felt as if his attempt at cordiality was forced. As we sat in Stevenson's red '98 Toyota 4-Runner, we were silent, I felt a pending argument approaching—a calm before the storm. Stevenson sped off. Minutes later he erupted.

"What the hell was that back there bitch? How dare you flirt with another man in front of me?" Stevenson yelled as his red eyes were fixated on me.

"Stevenson, what are you talking about? I just bought a piece of art from a struggling artist. I don't see anything wrong with my transaction—or that I behaved inappropriately!" I replied as Stevenson propelled the vehicle faster and faster, its driver paid little attention to the road.

"You know that's messed up Tamara, I just sat there quietly to see how you'd conduct yourself and you proved to me that you don't give a fuck about my feelings. What's up with that bullshit "…looks like you put a lot of time into it" and "…forsake life's eternal beauty". Just bullshit! All the while, you're doing the googly-eyed thing with that light-skinned asshole. I should have checked your ass back there, but I got more class than that. Too much class!" He continued to yell.

"C'mon Stevenson, it wasn't anything like that. It was purely platonic." I tried to laugh it off, but it wasn't working.

"And what's with you and all these big words…'platonic' and 'augmented'. You use these big words to confuse me. That's why I know you're a spiteful trick. You know I didn't finish school!" He blared.

Suddenly he broke hard to prevent us from barreling into a car in front of us. The painting and any non-secured items shot forward and ended up on the floor— including me. I've seen Stevenson mad, but not this mad before; I was getting a little concerned. I tried using my feminine wiles.

"Hey take it easy Babe…Take it easy…" I said as I reached over and tried petting his cheek.

"Get your hands off of me bitch!" He screamed as he aggressively brushed my hand away causing it to hit the rearview mirror almost dislodging it. Immediately, I reacted.

"Listen up Mon Cherie…" My Creole accent emerged only when I was angry. "…if you have a problem with big words, you should pick up a dictionary or a book and read a little rather than liftin' weights all fuckin' day and watchin' corny, imbecilic movies."

"See…there you go again with the big words… imbecilic."

"Yeah, imbecilic— foolish,…. idiotic,…. slightly retarded!" I slammed.

Just as I uttered the last syllable in 'retarded', Stevenson backhanded me in the mouth. The blow blinded me for a second and I was in shock. When I looked down, I found my two top teeth resting in my lap and my mouth bloodied. I didn't call the police, since I new most of them from my job, and I said nothing about the incident to family and friends. When I rubbed my upper lip, I remember feeling my top row of teeth, until I reached the center of my mouth, now there was an embarrassing void where my two front incisors used to be. I had to take an emergency two week respite from work for oral surgery so my mouth could heal. Now, I brush my upper lip when confronted with the least bit of stress; it's an incontrollable habit like nail biting, thumb sucking and teeth grinding. The pain of the blow was nothing compared to the injuries it inflicted in other ways. *How could I walk into the Collier County Office of DCF Child Protective Investigations a victim of domestic violence? And how could I protect others if I couldn't defend myself?* What choice did I have, but a fresh start in a new place where no one knew me?

###

Tamara and I cruised down US 1 to conduct another follow up home visit. Travelling on the weekends was ideal, since we didn't have to contend with the horrid Miami traffic. The last case we just finished involved a couple of children in the suburbs of Kendall in Miami; their parents got into a pushing fight, which resulted in the arrest of the father. Although this was Tamara's investigation, she let me handle a majority of the interviewing. It almost felt like this was my case instead of hers. While I interviewed the parents and discussed their situation, she remained in the front yard with the children. In District 11, Domestic Violence cases constituted almost 40% of DCF's cases and of these cases a majority involved alcohol. In this investigation, it was the parents first time in the system, so they got off with a warning and they were advised to sign our domestic violence notification:

If the Department continued to receive additional reports involving domestic violence and the non-offending parent failed to protect. the children would be removed from the home and a dependency court petition would be filed...

I found the notice effective most of the time. With hardened criminals, the notice was a joke. Legal documents even those signed by a judge— did little in preventing an offender from attacking a victim a second, third and even fourth time. By the fifth time, someone ended up dead.

"Thanks for handling that one back there." Tamara stated

"No problem. Where are we headed next co-pilot?" I asked.

Tamara thumbed through her stack of cases, until she located our next investigation.

"Keep heading south on US 1. This case is in Goulds, I have six victims to see." Tamara replied wiping the sweat off her brow.

"Wow, that's a lot of children. I hope they're all at home." I replied.

"Me, too." Tamara stated as she examined her case file.

"What's going on in this one?" I inquired as I reached into my shirt pocket to grab a cigarette.

"I got this Immediate On-call." She proceeded to read the report verbatim:

Initial Abuse Report 00-2514211 (Imm)
Mom Nancy Michaels has 4-kids from three different fathers. Billy Elliot, the father of her youngest child, Ezekiel was released from prison for sexual battery on a minor. This case alleges that Billy Elliot sexually molests mother's middle child, 9-year old Patricia White when mother goes to work. There is a fear that Mr. Elliot is a threat to the other children in his home due to his past history

"Who's the reporter T? I asked as I let the cigarette dangle from my mouth.

"The reporter is Samuel White, Patricia White's father."

In PDP training, case classification was one of the first lessons taught to us. An Immediate case requires an investigator to make an attempt to locate the child(ren) immediately because the victim may be in peril. A case is coded as an Immediate when: there is a child under the age of 5 in the home and the family has prior history with the Department, the case involves the egregious physical abuse or sexual abuse allegations, the case involves the death of a child, or there are no suitable caregivers available to care for the child(ren). I received my fair share of Immediate investigations while working in arguably the hardest coverage area in the State of Florida. I was detailed to cover District 11's Central Area of Miami Dade County which included impoverished regions: Overtown, Liberty City, Little Haiti, Little Havana, and Old Coconut Grove. Aside from the poverty aspect, the Central contained more people in its concentrated area than the other two regions combined, District 11's North and South Areas. We covered anything from Northwest 103rd Street to Southwest 40th Street (Bird Road). The Central also possessed all the counties major institutions including: Jackson Memorial Hospital (JMH), Turner Guilford Knight Correctional Center (TGK), the Dade County Jail, South Florida Evaluation and Treatment Center, and even the Miami International Airport (MIA).   Many of the State's Immediate child abuse investigations emanated from these institutions: from babies being born addicted to cocaine and heroin to female inmates giving birth while incarcerated to parents being detained by US Customs and Border Patrol after a failed attempt at smuggling illegal contraband into the country.

"T, this one is going to be interesting. What was your safety plan on this case?" I asked while steering my car closer to our destination.

"Billy Elliot agreed not to come around the children until he was interviewed by Miami Dade Sex Battery and Patricia was interviewed by the State Attorney's Office. He told me was going to stay with his mother up north while this case is ongoing. That was close to 30-days ago. I really need to get this case closed because my supervisor is on my ass. Denim gave me a list of cases that needs to be closed by Monday morning…." Tamara said as she held a checklist of about 12-cases scribbled with a series checkmarks and highlights. "…or he'll write me up. I love this job— helping the families is my passion, but it seems almost impossible to do at times!"

Watching a woman as beautiful as Tamara in anguish almost ripped my heart out. But I understood where Tamara was coming from. My eyes remained on the road.

"I hope you do something nice with all this OT you're making?" I asked.

"Overtime are you serious? Denim told me that I'm inefficient and incompetent if I can't handle my cases in a 40-hour work week. This jerk doesn't even stick around the whole work day, so you can't even ask him any questions. He comes in around 9am and leaves around 3pm then he goes home or gets in a round of golf. He's a total waste." Tamara stated while her face contorted as if she ate a rancid egg.

"My supervisor is cut from another cloth. Supe knows our breaking points. I've seen her go and make field visits herself and interview our clients in the office, if we get stuck in court or in the field. She's actually taken a case or two when we're really swamped. She even has a calendar on her desk and she remembers all the CPIs birthdays and sign-on dates and makes sure the unit never forgets any of them. I'm lucky I'm in the 808." I replied finally lighting my cigarette with a turquoise BIC.

(Beep. Beep. Beep. Beep. Beep)

The sound of Tamara's state issued pager interrupted our conversation.

"Speak of the devil, it's Denim. Please pull over at this gas station, so I can call him back." Tamara asked politely.

I pulled my Ford Taurus in to a Hess Station off Caribbean and US 1. I then handed Tamara 35-cents to use at a beaten up pay phone. From a few feet away I watched as she stood there using the payphone. She was the perfect package, intelligent, witty and considerate—not to mention she was drop dead gorgeous. I almost let my barely-smoked Kool burn my lips as I surveyed her silhouette. *With curves and a face like that, I could see myself going to the ends of the earth for her.* I was jostled from my sexually-charged stupor by Pierce Denim's harangue. Tamara wasn't on speakerphone, but I could hear Denim's loud voice clearly over the phone's headset. Tamara made sure not to tell her supervisor she enlisted my assistance to help her with her cases. She knew Denim wouldn't have allowed it.

"Okay, Pierce.......
I got it.......
I got it.......
I know I'm on probation....." Tamara replied in short bursts, and then remained silent. I listened as CPIS Pierce Denim ranted on:

"Norvil get it together!...You should have been finished with these follow ups last week!...Hope you don't think I'm authorizing OT for this extra work you manufactured!...There's a bunch of people out there that would love to have your job Norvil— remember that!"

"Okay…Pierce Okay, I'll do better and I'm going to have those cases for you by Monday." Tamara injected meekly after Denim's rant.

After a few seconds of silence, their conversation was over.

Tamara was visibly shaken. I spied her rubbing her upper lip during her phone conversation—*an odd habit I thought to myself.* Our remaining trip to Goulds was a quiet one. I did not utter a single word until Tamara initiated the conversation.

###

"I don't know Jeremiah? I just don't know? Maybe I should submit my resignation and head on back to Naples. I can join my sister, Karen in her home cleaning business." Tamara stated while rubbing her eye sockets.

"But you're a great investigator and you put so much time into this. Your documentation is impeccable and you have a way with the families." I said.

"It doesn't matter Jeremiah…Denim's right I need to get my cases in order. Maybe I'm just not cut out for this."

Later I found out the true reason for Tamara's unhappiness. Of the dozen-or-so cases Tamara shied away from, most of these had something distinctly in common— they either involved acts of domestic violence or one of the subjects on the case had some type of violent criminal past. When assigned an investigation coded **93T-Family Violence Threatens Child**, Tamara's demeanor changed instantly. Embarrassed and without the benefit of any counseling, she continued to remain a victim of her past. She walked into these cases lacking the heart and confidence to assert her authority. The White case was one such case; she never met with Billy Elliot, she just talked with him over the phone. From her take, Elliot just finished a bid in a state pen and wasn't too agreeable to DCF or its minions. As her head rested on the Taurus' passenger side window, she looked so hapless— almost a wreck. Her 2-minute conversation with her supervisor totally annihilated her. Now she was headed to one of the types of investigations she loathed and feared the most. To see someone so beautiful living in such a wretched state, prodded me into action: I couldn't remain silent any longer.

"Fuck your supervisor! Fuck Pierce Denim! He had no right to talk to you like that. You're the one going out on your day off to check on these children not him—and on top of it, you're working for free! If he wants to get some of these cases closed, he needs to get off his ass and help…or at least stay at work for a full 8-hour shift to help you guys out…" I blared swerving the Taurus a few times, since I couldn't help take my eyes off Tamara. "Your pigheaded supervisor has no tolerance or tact whatsoever!"

"Pig is right; he used to be a cop before signing on with the Department earlier this year."

"Well, shit that explains it all!" I stated as we zoomed down US 1.

We arrived at 22005 Southwest 113th Court Miami, FL. The pink 3-bedroom/2-bathroom appeared to be vacant, but signs of children were apparent. We observed trampled front grass, 25-cent potato chip bags and empty Capri Sun juice containers littered throughout the front yard and an indelible brownish/black blotch right under the front door knob, the mark created by little hands pushing the front door open, while turning the knob. After knocking a few times, tiny brown faces peered outside the home's front windows. Mother Nancy Michaels emerged and opened the front door.

"Hi Ms. Michaels. It's Child Protective Investigator Tamara Norvil and this is my fellow investigator, CPI Abundo."

"Oh Hi! How are you darlin'? You can come on in, but I'm about to head out to work in about an hour." Ms. Michaels replied.

Nancy Michaels had some hospital scrubs on, but she was not in the medical field, according to Tamara she worked in Deering Hospital's Cafeteria. A portly woman with a pretty, wrinkleless face and almond-shaped eyes, I wondered if she had some Asian in her. Ms. Michaels graciously offered us some ice cold sweet tea as she led us to the living room sofa.

"No, thank you Ms. Michaels. I was just doing a follow up visit to see your family. I also came to see if a detective from the Miami Dade Police has come to interview Billy and if the State Attorney's Office contacted you to bring Patricia in for a forensic interview downtown?" Tamara asked.

"No I haven't heard from no one, since you came. I haven't got any calls or received anythin' in the mail." Ms. Michaels replied.

"When is the last time you spoke with Billy"? Tamara asked.

"I spoke with him today; in fact, he's in the next room….Billy! Come on out here!" Ms. Michaels beckoned

Billy's heavy footsteps shook the house. Tamara felt each step in her stomach.

"Hello Ms. Norvil. I finally have the pleasure meetin' you." Billy Elliot smiled as he extended out a veiny hand.

Tamara waited a second before accepting the handshake. She was totally floored. Billy Elliot, the registered sexual offender was back in the house even though he promised that he'd remain at his mother's home. Her safety plan was shot to shit.

"Oh…Hi Mr. Elliot…how long have you been back in the house for?" Tamara said fumbling over her question. She then massaged her upper lip once again awaiting a response.

"Ms. Norvil, I came back three days ago. My mom lives in the Carol City and commutin' to and fro' wasn't practical. Carol City is 35-miles away an' my jobsite is 10-minutes from this house. My bossman ain't gonna' take too much of me bein' late, and wit' my history it's hard enough gettin' a job." Mr. Elliot replied.

I remained quiet; I promised Tamara I wouldn't intervene unless asked. I eyed the hulking A/P (alleged perpetrator), while looking for something to pick up and smash him with just in case things got out of control. I spotted nothing. I decided to take off my silk Tommy Hilfiger tie for my own safety. A smile blanketed my face as I held the tie in my hands, if needed I could use the tie as a garrote, should I have to choke Billy's big-ass out.

"Mr. Elliot I know this is going to sound inconsiderate, but that detective from Miami Dade needs to talk to you before you can be allowed back in this house." Tamara spoke.

Ms. Michaels quickly interjected, "But he didn't do nuthin'. This report was made by Patricia's daddy, Sammy. You don't even have to acknowledge this, I know that foo' called this case in. I put him on child support to recertify my food stamps and the next day you sho' up at my house with these sick allegations. Billy did his time and he ain't hurt no one."

Billy stood about 6-foot 5-inches around 250 pounds. He was 35-years old, but possessed a solid muscular build, fashioned from seven years of eating a shitload of starches and performing endless numbers of pushups, sit-ups, curls and bench presses. In my opinion, Billy had an uncanny resemblance to Miami Heat's starting Power Forward/Center Brian Grant. With tie in hand, I kept my eye on the convicted, sexual offender just in case I had to rush him. I hovered behind him ready to pounce as Tamara kept talking. But Billy remained calm. Watching this whole investigation unravel in front of me, made me realize how the Department could be perceived as inept by the public. Unfortunately, the public doesn't see the big picture as it relates to DCF and in that picture other agencies' cooperation and assistance are required for us to keep children safe. It's no secret; there is a lack of respect when it comes to the Department. *No other agency in the State of Florida could be summoned 1am in the morning by an anonymous caller and have an investigator knock on your door within a couple of hours. And try calling the State of Attorney Office after 5:30pm and see if anyone picks up the phone?* Just last week, I was told by Detective Bronson of City of Miami Police, that my client's forensic exam would have to wait a few days until he comes back from his weekend getaway. *Where was the alleged perpetrator supposed to go while Bronson sucked down mojitos while lying on some beach in Cozumel?* Moreover, what authority did the Department have in preventing an A/P from accessing his child without a court order?— just like in Tamara's case. Sometimes these unforeseeable gray areas in the Department's policy and procedures seem discombobulated, and as a result of this chaos the public remains ignorant. Through this ignorance, we are allowed to impose sanctions and manufacture rules on the fly and operate with little opposition. But sometimes—during the moments we least expect, we are challenged.

Billy put his weathered hands on Nancy Michaels' shoulders and she stopped talking immediately. He continued.

"Ms. Norvil you said this process would take a week and it's goin' on a month. I can't afford to lose my job." His tone grew stronger. "In fact, I refuse to lose my job 'cause the DCF can't get it togetha. I am not leavin' this house unless you have a warrant— a court order, or somethin' signed by a judge. If you have the power—go on an' arrest me." Billy proclaimed as he extended his thick wrists forward.

I finally interjected.

"Mr. Elliot? Got a smoke"?

###

I abhorred Newports, but withstood the agony to diffuse the situation. I ended taking off my dress shirt and donned a white, wife beater. While the sun slowly sank into the Everglades, we sat on the front patio utilizing two empty, plastic paint buckets as seats— remnants of Billy's trade. I listened attentively as Billy shared his tale…

"At the time was I was workin' for CSX makin' good money as a switchman. In two weeks, I could bring in $2500 after taxes. My partna had a great deal on tickets to the NBA All Star Game at the Miami Arena. It was the first time Miami hosted the All Star Game and I loved basketball. Jordan, Bird and Ewing represented the East while almost the entire Laker squad represented the West."

KEVIN L. RAMOS

Billy Elliot paused a minute to take a drag of his cigarette: the amber of his cigarette turned a bright orange for a second then returned to its temperate state. Then he continued his tale…

"Jordan and Barkley scored 17-a-pop and Magic had a game high 22. It was a magical night, the East won that game. I ain't gonna lie I was higher than a motherfucka on dat Jack Da Rippa and St. Ides and I was feelin' nice…real nice. I was wit' my boys, Rico and Jeff and after the game we headed to grab some chicken wings an' fries at Cotton's in OT. While we were walkin' outta the Arena, I heard a female voice callin' me out. She was bright skin, close to 6-foot tall, blond weave and she had ass an' titties all outdoors. I didn't pay that gurl no mind. But she kept chasin' us. She finally caught up wit' us at tha light on Northwest 2nd Ave and 8th Street. She approached me and my boys and said, *Y'all wanna' have some fun tonight?.* At first, we thought she was Five-O. But the way this chick was pursuin' us…this was entrapment all the way.   She grabbed my arm as we kept walkin'. My boys kept laughin' and talkin' shit like runnin' a train on dis chick. But trains were never my thing Mr. Jeremiah. My parents raised me better than that…plus I got sisters of my own!" Billy said. He paused and he closed his eyes for a second or two as he recollected, then continued:

"When dis trick thought she bagged the three of us, she went buck wild. She jumped out in front of us and blocked us from walkin' any further. Then said, *Ya'll niggas need to stop playin' an' get some of dis…*Then she grabbed her vagina outside her biker shorts and said, *See this… it's all meat daddy. This all you. What'chu workin' wit?* Then she made a quick move and yanked down my loose Champion® sweatpants—and my shit shot out like a Tomahawk missile!" Billy clenched his right fist and raised his veiny forearm perpendicular to the ground providing me a crude visual of his erection.

"Mr. Jeremiah did I tell you I was high as fuck? An' I ain't gonna lie I was rock hard too!   Outta nowhere, the Miami Police rushed us— jump out an' all. That Sunday— February 11, 1990 was the worst night of my life. Those corrupt cops arrested me and charged me wit' a bunch of shit: Lewd and Lascivious with a minor under 16—or L&L and hit me with a Resisting Arrest, Public Intoxication, and Battery Against a Law Enforcement Officer. They definitely knew how to fuck nigga. The cops knew what time it wuz— lettin' those outta town tricks post up in front of the Arena. Mr. Abundo I spent eight years locked up. Befo' that I was Mr. Clean— not even a parkin' ticket. Those crackas were just sore Lozano got seven for shootin' those two boys!" Billy stated before taking his semi-lit Newport butt and flicking it into the direction of the dark Everglades.

I, Billy's younger by 11-years, struggled with a response after hearing his tragedy. I gathered my words carefully:

"Billy that is one of the saddest stories I heard in my life. You lost a good paying job and spent eight years of your life incarcerated because you got high and an underage trick pulled your sweatpants down, but that doesn't change the facts. You're a registered sexual predator and the Department has an active abuse investigation listing you as a perpetrator. The allegations we received state you are inappropriately touching Patricia White, a child not of your own blood. Billy this case isn't going anywhere, until the powers that be feel you are not a threat. We're going to have to work this out and I'm here for your family until this is reconciled. But this has to be done by the book."

"So what do you want me to do, Mr. Jeremiah? I would never harm a child; I don't even be around Patricia like dat... " Billy stated.

"Let me see what I can do— I'll make a few calls and talk to some people. Just please be patient." I replied.

He gave me a nod as I eyed my watch, *8:13pm.*

###

"T, this one's gonna be an all-nighter. I spoke with a co-worker and she told me she has the hook up with Sergeant Ted Laramie over at the Miami Dade Sex Battery unit. He agreed to send over a detective tonight to take statements. I just have to wait on a police case number from a uniform—as you know that might take a minute. I still have to contact legal and see if we have sufficiency to file a dependency petition if Billy doesn't want to leave. I also have to write up all my notes. You can take my car, and start working on those other follow-up cases for Denim. Just pick me up in a few hours, and let me crash on your sofa or living room floor." I stated exhaustingly.

It wasn't the date she planned for, but she tells me it was one of the sweetest things another individual has ever done for her: I made her problems mine. By this time, Tamara was walking barefoot; she abandoned her 5-inch heals because they were awkward and forming blisters on the sides of her toes. She doubts I paid much attention to her heels or that knockout dress she had on during our busy day, but I did. Tamara was beautiful in anything she chose to wear, especially if it was for me. She handed me the file folder for **Abuse Case 00-2514211** in exchange I handed her my car keys. Tamara walked towards the Taurus, but before she could open the driver's side door, I yelled:

"Oh T… one more thing!"

Tamara swung around immediately to honor my request.

"Don't forget about me! I have no idea where I am!" I exclaimed with a smile.

She smiled back—open mouthed, I remembered that beautiful smile for the rest of the evening.

###

December 2, 2000
(Fort Lauderdale)

Lonnie "Bayani" Abundo watched as I limply held his most-prized fishing rod in my hands; Bayani knew if I got a bite from a moderately-sized fish, his favorite rod was doomed for the bottoms of the Intercostal Waterway forever. My uncle knew I was tired as hell and reluctant to go fishing. He almost had to throw me in his truck to get me to go with him. Every week it was one excuse after the other not to spend time with him. It's been just a little over five months, since I came to live with him and his wife, Ingrid. In this short time of being here, I could feel my uncle's anxiety lift from not being able to bear his own children. I was like the son he always wanted— one that he could smoke cigarettes with and drink beer with all night long. But I was also polite and helped with any household task without quarrel. In my first week of moving in, I offered to take over the landscape duties of the house by cutting the grass, pruning, and weed whacking, but he defiantly told me to "Save my energy!", he'd hire a company to perform those duties. I told him, "If you hire a landscaper, I am going to clean your pool." Bayani pressed the subject no further. He knew I was stubborn and I wasn't accustomed of having others do chores for me. My mother Cynthia always taught her children to take care of themselves. I cleaned the kitchen after I prepared food and washed my own clothes and folded them and stored them away. The other day Bayani came into my room to pilfer a cigarette while Ingrid was at the grocery store; he marveled at how tidy I was. My bed was always made and my desk was always in perfect order: 21-or-so manila case files stacked high, an assortment of highlighters and pens placed neatly in a wooden pen holder and my laptop. Bayani always harped, *"tulad ng kanyang ama"* or "You're like your father in so many ways." That always made me smile. As we floated on "Mabuti" his 23-foot Grady White, I stared into the greenish Intercostal hoping to catch a reflection of myself, but there was none.

"Pamangkin, may sigarilyo ka ba"?

"Sure, Bayani." I said as I reached into my pocket and fetched a cigarette for us both. I put one in my mouth and lit it with a silver Zippo, and then I lit one for my uncle.

"Thank you Nephew." He said as he grabbed the cigarette from me.

"It's so beautiful out here. I can see why Dad loved the water so much. When you're out here you can really think". I said as I eyed the multi-million dollar homes on Millionaires' Row. Each of the enormous mansions had a yacht docked in the back—some had two.

"I'm glad you like it. Casting off this monster is hell to do when you're alone. With you here, we can go out more often. Once you get the hang of casting off, you can use this boat whenever you like. Take your friends— or even a *magandang babae*". He stated as he gave me a wry smile, but I did not acknowledge him. Friends and beautiful women were the furthest things from my mind. Although I'd love for him and Ingrid to meet Tamara, this is the first time since arriving in South Florida I really had a chance to bond with my uncle. Truth is, I was seduced by my job, and it was my celibate mistress. If I wasn't coming home late, I'd be somewhere visiting a family, transporting a child, going to court, or on the computer doing some data entry. I always had something to do for her and I was on her time schedule. If I ever overslept or missed one of our dates, there would be hell to pay.

"How's the realty business, Bayani? Any new properties worth mentioning"? I asked, while I quickly glanced down at my Timex wristwatch, *11:13am.*

"Business has been really, really good. The banks are financing anyone and everyone. If you have a job and a bank account you can buy anything here in South Florida. *Anak ng puta!* You can work at McDonald's and be my neighbor. I just got this guy into a 4-bedroom/2-bathroom house in Surfside and he doesn't even have a job on paper."

A phantom gust of wind blew the Mabuti from side to side as if the gods disapproved of my uncle's shady business dealings. I took a swig out of my bottle of San Miguel Pale Pilsen, Bayani brought back four cases from the Philippines earlier this year. I enjoyed anything from my family's culture from the food to the beer. I also loved it when Bayani talked to me in Tagalog because I did not want to lose the little bit of my culture I still possessed. Of the handful of my Filipino-American friends none of them could speak Tagalog, but they could understand it when spoken to. I always believed that first generation Filipinos like my parents wanted to perfect their pronunciation and use of English language and practiced on their American-born offspring whenever possible. I vividly remember conversations with my parents in bits of English and Tagalog. *"How was school Anak? Great, makakuha ng aking tsinelas."* Or *"You said you wanted that dog Anak? Lakad ng aso!"* Even with all the practice, certain English words just never sounded right coming out of my parents' mouths. Like 'word' and 'world", if my mother Cynthia was talking you wouldn't know which one she was using because they sounded exactly the same. I did take pride that Filipinos felt compelled to speak the language of the land and was stunned to find out that 90% of native born Filipinos speak fluent English along with their local Philippine dialect: Tagalog, Cebuano, Ilocano or Hiligaynon.

"How does someone afford a $300,000 house making $6.50 per hour? I remember when Mom and Dad had to save almost $15,000 in cash to put down when they bought our house years ago. What changed all of a sudden?" I asked.

"You have to go with the flow Pamangkin. We'll cross that bridge when we get there as they say here in America. Until, the government says something, we're going to make as much money as we can while we can! *Anak ng pating.* When I started doing mortgages I closed on 2-3 houses a month. Now I do 15-to-20 a month. The money I make on the deals I use and buy more properties to rent or sell. At my office they call me Flip." He closed his last statement with a quick wink and a quick guzzle of his beer.

"Flip? Fine Looking Asian Person? You must pay your people well at your office for that gracious nickname Bayani!" I stated before letting off a brief chuckle. Face it, my uncle wasn't greatest looking guy. He ate whatever he wanted and he drank whatever he wanted, this resulted in his patented bowling pin-shaped physique. Add a skin hue that looks like he was encapsulated in a cryogenic chamber for eons and a serious comb-over and there you have my uncle.

"No—no, no, Flip refers to my business dealings. I buy low and sell high. You know Pamangkin, if things don't work out at DFC—I mean DCF you can come work with me?" Bayani countered totally disregarding my last comment about his appearance.

I thought about my uncle's gracious offer. I could feel the effects of the San Miguel infiltrating my system. My eyelids drooped and my legs were wobbly. The sun's rays sucked any energy I had left in my tired body. There are different stages of inebriation. Some people are extra chatty when they drink, while others get belligerent. When I drank more than four beers I got really sentimental. Until now, I never uttered a word to any of my family members about my job. I was taught social workers should always protect the confidentiality of their clients. Plus, I didn't want to burden my family with the truly sad stories of my clients. But I had my breaking point. Keeping it all bottled inside just wasn't healthy.

"Uncle"?

"What's that Pamangkin? Did you get a bite"? Bayani answered with his back turned.

I paused for a few seconds before answering....

"Bayani, shit is crazy over there. My job is fuckin' nuts. I didn't think people had it so bad...."

My uncle listened attentively as I spoke, but his eyes remained fixated on his line and tackle.

"The other day I had to do a follow up visit to see a 2-year old and ended up taking her to the Jackson's Emergency room after I found a rat bite on her leg that was infected. How the fuck does a rat bite you? I was there from 8pm to 2am waiting for treatment. We had to make sure she did not contract Rabies or Rat-bite fever. I ended up having to file it in court because the mother did not seek medical treatment quickly enough."

To my surprise, Bayani didn't flinch. He continued to bait his hook with a live piece of shrimp. He was careful to hook it in its last joint in its tail to keep it alive longer. His cigarette dangled from his mouth as the smoke blew into his eyes causing him to squint even more. He was silent.

"And the cases just keep coming. When you close one, another one comes in. Last week I got 10-cases and I'm still on probation. I should be getting 2-to-4 cases max! It's no surprise why they turnover people on a daily basis. The Department is so desperate; they are hiring anyone regardless of what type of college degree they possess."

Bayani popped open two more San Miguels and offered me one which I pushed away.

"There's another investigator that was hired along with me, who also works in my building her name is Sara Rothschild. She put in her resignation last Friday. They sent her to Liberty City on a dirty house case with eight children at 1am and she almost had a heart attack!"

"Damn, Pamangkin. If they sent me to Liberty City at that time, *Tae sa aking sarili*, then I'd have heart attack." The levity allowed me to smile for a brief moment.

"And the legal system is a fuc..." Before I could finish my sentence I felt a strong pull on my fishing pole which almost pulled me overboard. The buzzing sound from my reel's drag, sounded like a 50-lb bumble bee flying across the bow of the boat. Bayani rushed to my aid with a gaff in hand.

"Let out the drag Pamangkin! Let out the drag Pamangkin!"

I turned the knob on my reel from "5" to "1". This lessened the line's tension allowing the fish to run.

"Damn this is a big fish!" I yelled. I felt a surge of energy run through my body as if the fish and I were connected.

"Reel a couple of times then let him run".

Zzzzzzzzzzzzzzzzzzzzzzzzzzzzzzz

I reeled and jerked, reeled and jerked.

A silvery image appeared just below the surface as its dorsal fin knifed through the water leaving no wake.

Zzzzzzzzzzzzzzzzzzzzzzzzzzzzzzz

I pulled hard on 6ft Eagle Claw rod just as the fish surfaced a second time. The three-and-a-half foot Snook emerged from the green Intercostal as it leaped out of the water. The fish was large enough that Bayani could tell it was a keeper. The Florida Fish and Wildlife Conservation Commission deemed Snook a protected fish only to be taken certain times of the year depending on stock assessments. The Snook was one of Florida's greatest fighting game fish as well as the tastiest. It was cagey as well; it's rare that a Snook hit bait that wasn't alive. As I jerked the pole again, the fish shot out of the water, but landed awkwardly on its side, the sound and thud could be felt on the

Mabuti. Then, the Snook made its way to a stray dock pylon 15 feet from boat's stern.

Zzzzzzzzzzzzzzzzzzzzzzzzzzzzzzzzz

"*Anak ng puta!* Pull him away from the pylon! Pull him away Pamangkin!" Bayani knew if the monofilament line scraped across the sharp barnacles that grew on the pylon; the greatest catch of our lives would be a fleeting memory.

"Pull Pamangkin! Pull!"

A second later, the monofilament line whipped out of the water and my pole straightened to its original form. There would be no *Sinigang ng Snook* or *Inihaw na Snook* served at the Abundo's home tonight. I reeled up the excess line and stared at its mangled end. Emotionally and physically I was defeated.

"Just my luck, the biggest fish of my life and it gets away. What the hell else can go wrong?" I said as my chin sunk into my chest.

I looked as my uncle for consolation. He took his last swig of his San Miguel then tossed the glass carcass into the Intercostal, and then he approached.

"Listen Pamangkin. Shit happens. This one got away but you got to keep trying. Think about it. I hear you complain about your job. How you're overworked, the long hours, the piles of cases, the ridiculous recidivism and your goofball clients. Get over it. Take it for what it is."

"But Bayani, it's an unfair system." I rebutted.

"Unfair yes, but a job nonetheless. It's a job which you have to take pride in while you're there. Nobody is holding a gun to your head to be there. You chose this one Pamangkin it didn't choose you. If you got to deal with loads of bullshit don't take it personal because it's not—it's just business. I respect you because you want to help people and you care about others. But understand one thing *Kung di ukol, di bubukol.*"

"Uncle you're going to have to help me out with this one?" I asked.

"*Kung di ukol, di bubukol* is an old Filipino adage, *If it is not relevant, it makes no difference.* See that house right there?" Bayani pointed to an enormous estate outfitted with three waterfalls and a bell tower. "It belongs to Wayne Huizenga, the billionaire who owns Blockbuster Video and Waste Management. That guy has owned the Miami Dolphins, the Florida Panthers and the Florida Marlins— a real triple threat! He has money and power. That home is worth $15-million dollars. He matters in this society. That's what people care about!"

I lit another Kool and took a pull listening to Bayani's diatribe.

"Your clients are irrelevant in society's eyes. They do not have power or money. They are poor and uneducated. They do not vote— even though they have the numbers. Society sees them as blights— uneducated, drug-using, baby-making machines that suck up our tax dollars. To top it off, most of them are *itim* (Bayani ran his right forefinger across his left forearm.) I love this country, but it was still forged with years of untold racism."

"What do you think I should do Bayani"? I stated while expelling a cloud of smoke.

"First you need to be thankful you are working. Stop complaining about the things you can't control. Remember you can always walk away. Now, I wouldn't do your job if you paid me a million bucks, but I respect you for trying to help people less fortunate than you. You listen to their problems, give them advice, and send them on their way. It's like being a priest without giving up your fuck options!"

I laughed hard.

"That's the sound I like to hear. Speaking of which you need to find yourself a girl. Lord, you are in Miami and there are so many *magandang babae* here to choose from!" He said as he patted me on the shoulder.

"You know Uncle I am talking with this girl at my office. Maybe I'll bring her by sometime?" I replied

5 DA BEANS

December 15, 2000
(Liberty City)

Anxious eyes were transfixed at the clock that hung above the door in Mrs. Peggy Cantor's 11th grade English class.

"…And before we break for Christmas recess, I'd like to bring up one student and congratulate her for an excellent job on the Trust House's Wish-For-A-Day Essay Contest." After her students totally disregarded her announcement, Mrs. Cantor had to repeat herself more assertively this time. "Come on people, we have 10-minutes left before we break, and I want to share this fantastic accomplishment with you."

The class finally settled in.

"Quintavia Collins. Can you please come up to the front of the class?" Mrs. Cantor gestured to her not-so surprised student.

"Quintavia on behalf of the 11th grade English/Lit faculty, Mrs. Morris, Mr. Perdomo and me, we'd like to thank you for submitting this fantastic essay. Of the 30-or-so entrants in this year's contest we found yours to be the most original, heartfelt and unselfish. Now for those of you who did enter, what you write about is just as important on how you write it."

"What do you mean by that—my essay was just as good"? An anonymous male voice chimed from somewhere in the class.

"It means that if the contest's sponsor is Trust House, one of the most benevolent benefactors of college scholarships to inner-city youth, you don't write about wishing for Sprewells for your Caprice Classic or a new Hermes purse. Again, people the topic was Wish-For-

A-Day, if you wrote about something tangible—rims, purses, or a new car, after the day is over you would find yourself possession-less. So I do want to thank all of you who entered, but please understand the topic before you begin to write next time around."

Mrs. Cantor reached for a large envelope on her desk, opened it and rummaged through its contents.

"Quintavia here is a certificate of achievement signed by Principal Harvey, Mrs. Morris, Mr. Perdomo and me and a $50-gift card to Walmart—spend it anyway you like. And your essay will be entered at the Miami-Dade County Youth and Expo. Grand Prize is a $5000 College Scholarship."

"Good job white gurl!" This time the voice came from an anonymous female student, most likely one of the girls who despised me because I actually came to school to learn. Some students co-signed the epithet with their laughter.

"Alright settle down class. I'm not going to embarrass Quintavia by asking her to read an excerpt out of her essay, but I did include a copy of it in your holiday work packets. Please read it, I'm sure you'll enjoy it."

The clock struck and bells blared simultaneously.

"Okay, class…you may go."

The class stampeded out the door leavin' me and Mrs. Cantor behind.

"Hope I didn't embarrass you dear, but your essay was fantastic!"

"Thanks Mrs. Cantor. It's not embarrassing at all—anything dealin' with my daddy is far from embarrassing. That essay was homage to him. It wasn't a too difficult to write this one— that was inside of me for a long time." I stated while smiling.

"I wish I could have met your father. I would tell him how wonderful a student you are and how much of a joy it is to be your teacher."

"He would have liked you Mrs. Cantor. When he was alive he made it his business to meet all of my teachers and come to all my school open houses. He was a fantastic father—I wish he was still here today."

My last few words stung. Recently, my life took a dramatic turn. For the past month-and-a half, Archie "Lil Boy" Bedford squirmed his way into my beloved family circle; Lil Boy and Ms. Denise were now officially boyfriend and girlfriend. Even worse, I suspect that Mama is now sleepin' with the nasty ol' man. My Wish-for-a-Day Essay chronicled the day my father, Daryl "Songbird" Collins left this earth, August 12, 1997. I wished that I was by my daddy's side instead of being at our Auntie Belinda's house in California. I wished that I could have held his hand and whispered that I loved him that one last time. I wished I got his renowned recipe for chicken and dumplings. Now, things were so upside down, my mother's reckless decision to allow this lowlife into our home was almost unforgiveable. I eyed my plastic Hello Kitty watch, *2:40pm*; I still had to pick up Poo from Orchard Villa Elementary School which was 15-minutes away at 5720 Northwest 13th Avenue.

Mrs. Cantor picked up on the cue and asked, "Quintavia can I give you a ride home"?

"No, thank you Mrs. Cantor. I still have to pick up my brother from aftercare, and I know you got kids of your own."

"Alright dear, you have a great recess and I'll see you next year."

###

I adjusted my headphones and pressed play on my CD player as I walked out the front doors of Miami Northwestern Senior High. The old CD player was falling apart, there was a short in my headphones and every so often static interrupted the track I was listenin' to. When Mama came home, I promised myself to ask if I could use the $50 Walmart card towards a new MP3, maybe a Creative NOMAD Jukebox. Music always made the time go by quicker especially when I made my run to pick up my brother, since my school was over half-a-mile away from his. As I walked, I began to bounce to the beat of Sisqo's 'Thong Song':

Ooh dat dress so scandalous
And ya know another nigga couldn't handle it
See ya shakin' that thang like who's da ish
With a look in ya eye so devilish

I didn't know what was worse being beautiful or smart. If it wasn't hard enough havin' to deal with the creepas on the street, I had to deal with the same breed in school. At school I was often reminded of this on a daily basis. When I was in school, I heard 'em all— slews of lewd comments from all my peers. *"Damn gurl you got some big ol' titties!"* Or *"Damn gurl, you gotta a fat ol' ass!"* Or *"Damn gurl, when you finna le' me cut?"* And the aggression wasn't limited to verbal propositions. It wasn't a rare occurrence to feel the sting of some nigga slappin' or grabbin' on my butt as I transitioned from class to class. And the bitches out to the West…the bitches were no better. I almost got into a handful of fights when an attractive/cute boy came up and paid me a compliment— usually their jealous admirers were always in the wings. I found that these jealous girls always rolled in packs usually one pretty girl accompanied by a couple of mutts. I always traveled solo; I never needed a clique to make me feel whole. If I encountered aggression from these jealous females, I'd tell the boy that liked me to *"Handle Dat."*

Translation: *Tell that hoe to stop fuckin' with me.*

It never failed. The cute boys and ballers out to the West were commodities, and if you landed yourself either one; you upped your status. I was on the upper echelon because I had an abundance of fans: ballers, cute boys, D Boys, and even a couple of lustful bulldaggers — none of them I considered my boyfriend.

As I walked west on Northwest 71st Street, I eyed the beautiful track an' field to the left of me. Inside that 400-meter track, is the field where I tried out for the Golden Girls or G-Girls, the West's elite dance squad, in my sophomore year. After that fiasco, I decided to keep my focus on my academics. In the early 90's, as a little girl, I recall the school's main building sat smack dab on this track an' field and even then I knew it was in desperate need of renovation. It must have dawned on someone on the Dade County School Board that chil'ren need a clean, comfortable place to attend school. A place where the kids are not crammed in like sardines and where they're not afraid of contracting E. coli or Hepatitis from using the restrooms. Unfortunately in the past, the West has always been plagued with high drop-out rates and students suffering from substandard reading levels. Like most inner-city schools throughout the United States, the West had the same issues. *But what better way to initiate change than with a newly renovated school?*

She had dumps like a truck, truck, truck
Thighs like what, what, what
Baby move your butt, butt, butt
I think I'll sing it again
She had dumps like a truck, truck, truck
Thighs like what, what, what
All night long
Let me see that thong

I made a left and walked south on Northwest 12th Avenue. I saw Holmes Elementary on my left. Like the West, this school was also recently renovated. And like the West it had its fair share of issues like low test scores and students who lacked the most basic needs including adequate clothing and school supplies. To the right was Da Beans, I turned down the volume on my CD player whenever I passed through Miami's most notorious housing projects. Da Beans aka Pork 'n Beans formally known as Liberty Square was created in 1937, part of FDR's New Deal. Once a home for hundreds of middle income black families, Da Beans was now comprised mostly of single parent, welfare-dependent households. Drugs, violence and poverty ravaged this community. I eyed the mishmash configuration of 1 and 2-story buildings, which ran perpendicular to Northwest 12th Avenue. They were painted in pastels: blue, yellow, pink and beige and I even saw a few in burnt orange, a palette you could only pull off in South Florida. Each building appeared to be 200-feet long and contained around 5-6 units. I passed a courtyard between buildings and saw a few kids playing freeze tag while dodgin' clothes line poles, while freshly, hand-laundered clothes wafted in the wind. By one of the buildings, three boys eyed me as I passed them.

"A…A…A… Red! Come hur! Le' me holla at you fo' a minute."

I ignored the requisition from the boy with the shoulder length dreadlocks talkin' with his friends. They were posted up in front of one of the pink units to the right of me. I glanced at him and gave him a magnificent smile. *Instantly—a new fan.*

"Awright gurl. I'll get wit' ya tomorrow den."

The temperature was ridiculously hot for a December; some of the Beaners were runnin' their wall A/C units, which hung half-way-out their front windows. Other less fortunate Beaners who didn't have an A/C unit kept their front and back doors open which allowed for excellent cross ventilation, but they always kept their security doors locked. Every window in Da Beans was equipped with a metal grate, which was fastened from the inside of the window frame. As I approached Northwest 63rd Street and Northwest 12th Place, one of my favorite songs began playing: Destiny Child's 'Independent Women'.

The shoes on my feet, I've bought it
The clothes I'm wearin', I've bought it
The rock I'm rockin', I've bought it
'Cause I depend on me

I immediately fell in love with the song after I heard it on a bootleg copy of the movie **Charlie's Angels** which Archie brought to our house. Thus far, Archie's acquisition of the DVD was his most useful act since enterin' our lives. I glanced at my watch, *2:50pm* and felt relieved I was making such progress. I was just blocks away from Orchard Villa. I didn't mind the walk. Usually, when Mama asked me to pick up Poo it was for a good reason—usually it was work related. Today, Mama was contracted to clean a home on Miami Beach; she got these cleanin' gigs a few times a month. From the corner of my eye, I saw three girls approachin' fast from the right. The tallest girl, possibly the leader had half of her head braided in plaits, the other half of her head was a knotted mess. I winced at the awful sight and thought to myself... *Mama would never le' me out tha house wit' a head like that!* The leader wore an oversized Rocawear polo and some furry house slippers. The other two said nothing and looked no bigger than me, so I paid them little attention. I readied myself for battle. I loosened the laces of my Air Forces Ones, took off my jewelry a 10ct gold chain with a Hello Kitty emblem and my plastic Hello Kitty watch and I tucked these items in my back pocket. I didn't have to worry about hair pulling since I rocked a Halle Berry.

"Hey White gurl! Where you goin'"? The tall girl beckoned.

The song's chorus punctuated my reply:

All the women who are independent
Throw your hands up at me
All the honeys who makin' money
Throw your hands up at me

What irony? Throw your hands up is somethin' I was just goin' to have to do to reach my brother. I've done it so many times befo' since ignorant-ass people always wanna keep you down. Before my daddy passed on, Songbird taught us a few things. And one of those things was how to defend ourselves. I remember his wily self-defense lessons vividly.

Lesson One: "If you get in a scrap and you outnumbered, knock the biggest and tallest bitch out then break the hell out!"

"Ya heard me you stuck up saditty-ass trick. I asked you a question? Ya need to get permission befo' you roll yo' ass through hur!" The ugly bitch barked.

"Whose permission do I need"? I replied rhetorically.

"Mine bitch."

I recognized the face of the leader. Felisha Bennett was in my English class. Loud, disrespectful and an overall ugly person, Felisha always liked being the center of attention: my presence marred all that. She was dumb and ugly and I was the opposite.

"Listen Lisha I have no problem with you, please le' me pass?"

"No you listen Bitch! You may be a superstar hoe out to da West— pullin' niggas, storytellin' and what not, but I run shit ova hur babygirl— I run dis shit!" Felisha's nostrils widened as she snarled at me.

"What Girl? What do you run here? You run these projects? You run Da Beans? You run this goddamn sidewalk. Girl, what you need to do is le' me pass." I pleaded trying to talk some sense into the trio.

"Yeah bitch, we run dis. DBB fo' life hoe!" Felisha screamed as she flashed a horribly done tattoo inscribed on her left forearm that read 'DBB' in New Time Roman font. It looked like it was handcrafted with a single sewing need and some India ink.

"Dem Beans Bitches!" One of Felisha cronies chimed in.

I heard about these hoes, jumpin' people throughout the projects and robbin' them and gettin' high with their proceeds, and actin' as lookouts and jumpoffs for the dope boys.

"I read that bullshit-ass essay about yo' ol' boy and le' me say dis hoe, you ain't shit and yo' ol' boy ain't shit!" Felisha screamed.

The mere mention of Songbird's name incensed me especially comin' out the mouth of this trollop. I cocked back and clocked Felisha with a right cross that landed flush on Felisha's neck. Felisha fell back and gasped for air. I pounced on her grabbing the girl's semi-completed hairdo and slapped and clawed at her. A few seconds past before DBB girl #1 came to her leader's assistance and knocked me off Felicia. I crashed to the ground landing on my CD player crushing it. DBB girl #2 immediately went for my legs in an attempt to pin them. I retracted my left leg and scissor kicked it up catching DBB girl#2 square on her chin causin' the girl to reel back and scream. Felisha regained her composure, mounted me and rained down a hail of hammer fists. A loud booming voice ended the altercation almost immediately.

"Lisha get off that gurl! Tonya, Bertice....kick back!"

The shirtless muscular figure extricated the combatants from one another.

"Y'all need to stop with this foolishness. Look how much attention you bringin' to da spot...And Lisha if mama has to snatch your butt outta DJJ once mo', you gonna wish they never let yo' narrow tail out!" The unknown boy stated.

The DBB girls cringed at the peacemaker. Felisha's brother helped me off the ground and picked up the mangled CD player, while the trio retreated back into the depths of the projects.

"A man...I'm sorry for my sista's behavior. Let me pay you for yo' CD player dat those bitches broke." He stated.

The hero reached into his back pocket and pulled out a knot of fives, tens and twenties bundled in a rubber band.

"Here's a yard. Go buy yo' self a new CD player and cop that new Lil' Wayne."

I smiled and balked before accepting the money.

"I don't take money from strangers." I said.

"Okay, my name Antwon, I'm no longer a stranger."

I reached out and accepted the restitution.

"My name is Quintavia, but my friends call me Queen."

"Awright Queen, pleasure to meet cha. I feel so bad fo' this situation, I finna accompany you to yo' destination and see no one else messes witcha today." Antwon stated.

I acquiesced.

We slowly made our way down Northwest 13th Avenue. I easily kept pace with Antwon as he slowly peddled beside me. In truth, I welcomed Antwon's company. I had so many fans that liked me, but it was rare I had a genuine attraction for somebody else. He had a nice clean, bald fade which complimented his handsome face. I also marveled at his chiseled physique. From behind, his shirtless dark body revealed a canvas of his life—tattoos of fallen comrades and loved ones. The biggest one he had was a "305" in gothic lettering covering his back. Most of his tats looked like they were done by a professional.

"Sorry again fo' my sista, she's been a mess since our gran' daddy passed earlier dis year. He neva let that gurl get outta line or eva let her run wit' those dumb little girls. I did see you got a good lick in… punched that chick dead in the throat!" Antwon said as he smiled at me flashing his full-gold grill.

I laughed. "Yeah, my daddy always told me to go after the biggest and loudest one. I was just followin' directions."

"Is yo' father still around?' He asked.

"No he passed a few years back. He was a good man. He worked hard for us. He fed us. And he made us laugh. He's the type of man I want in my life."

"Can I be in your life"?

"That all depends…are you a good man? And do you work?"

"I'm a good man and I have my own business?"

When I saw that wad of money, I knew exactly what this boy's occupation was. A horn honked at us as we walked closer toward Orchard Villa Elementary. A voice bellowed out of a blue '73 Chevy Donk, "Whud up Twon?" Antwon stuck his hand up acknowledging the rider. It was the first time in my pubescent life, a car's honk wasn't for me.

"So what kind of business do you own"? I asked suspiciously.

"I own a mobile car wash." Antwon reached into his back pocket and gave me one of his business cards. I read it aloud:

Dirty South Mobile Car Wash and Detailing
Antwon (305) 947-7170
The dirtier the better!

"Pretty impressive. If you have a mobile car wash where's your truck or work van?" I asked.

"My partna got it. He doin' some work down south. We rotate days. Yesterday was my day. I worked from 7am till 8pm; I cleaned fourteen cars and detailed two. Those detail jobs are my bread and butta. I make at least fiffy a pop on those jobs, but they take time. I wanna open up my own stand and get a couple mo' trucks." He said proudly

"So you have it all planned out. What's your plan if you get sick or what you finna do when you're 60-years old and gotta bad back and you can't bend down to spray Armor All on those tires?" I inquired.

"Damn Gurl, you are saditty!"

I chuckled. I thought Antwon was cute, but I was no dummy. I was hip to all these games these men played. If it didn't happen to me it happened to a friend or to a loved one. The other day some man tried to mack to me at Bucky's Washhouse. He pulled up in 2000 BMW 528i and told me he was 21. I suspected game from a mile away. As he talked shit, all I could think about was one thing...*anyone who drives a $38,000 whip to do their laundry at a ghetto washhouse— ain't about shit.* An' I was right, the other day I saw Mr. BMW drop his son off at the West. He didn't recognize me when I waved an' tried to say "Hello" though.

"So what's yo' plan Gurl? Since you can read me so well, do you even know what you wanna do in life? Where you gonna be in 10-years?" Antwon stated now on offense.

I caught myself with nothing to say. Antwon dumbfounded me with a series of simple questions that I never bothered to ask. I excelled in school, I was polite, and I did what was told, but I never thought of my future…at least not the specifics. All I know is I wanted to do something that allowed me to utilize the "Dr." prefix in front of my name.

"You know Antwon. I'm gonna have to get back with you on that."

It was Antwon's turn to laugh.

"I may have been born and raised in Da Beans, the bastard son of deadbeat, a high school drop but I don't intend to be here the rest of my life. I have aspirations and goals. During yo' life, never stop dreaming. No one can take away yo' dreams."

"…Hold up Antwon, did you steal that last line from 2Pac?"

"Yeah I did."

We both laughed as we approached the entry gates at Orchard Villa Elementary. It was 3:20pm and I was a few minutes late, but I was still thankful for Antwon's intervention.

"Well Antwon, thank you for your company and gettin' those crazy girls off me." I stated.

"No problem gurl. I'll make sure Lisha and her lil' crew don't botha you no mo'. Shit, I'll make sure no one messes with you as long as I'm around. Dis bike ride was a good work out, we might have to do this more often." He said as the sun's ray glistened off his grill and the sweat off his dark skin.

"Yeah, workin' out is good for you."

As I entered the gates into Orchard Villa's school grounds, I heard the sound of knobby bike tires pressed hard against concrete driftin' off into the distance.

###

As Mama stared at her boyfriend, Lil Boy from outside of the front window, she felt something she hasn't felt since her beloved husband passed away years ago—security. Although she missed her husband immensely, she couldn't deny that she longed for companionship of another man and the touch of another as she lies down at night. She also welcomed the financial assistance he provided when bills needed to be paid. In her eyes, Archie Bedford was no Darryl Collins, but for the time being, he'd make due. Her family was happy, especially me. She couldn't recall seein' me this happy since Songbird passed away. I was always responsible and never had any issues doin' chores, but now I did them with a smile ear-to-ear. I floated around the house with my new MP3 player handling the duties of the house effortlessly. From folding piles of clothes to helpin' Poo with his winter recess homework packet, I was simply amazing. Ms. Denise hinted I found a new boyfriend which could explain the phenomena. But I never told Mama about Antwon. Mama was proud of me, and she let the world know it, especially her co-workers at Rainbow. "My daughter has a 4.0 GPA and she goin' to be a doctor!" "Queen is so dang responsible an' she fine as hell just like her mama!" Still, it was her duty as a mother to assess the caliber of any individual involved with her children platonically, romantically— and even more so sexually. Mama couldn't see herself a grandmother at the ripe age of 37.

"Mama please pass me the tape." I asked as I stood on a metal folding chair holding a string of Christmas lights.

"Here you go child."

"Thank you Mama." I replied.

Poo pulled up another folding chair next to me. Even standing on a chair he was vertically challenged.

"Queen le' me help. Le' me do a couple." Poo asked.

"Poo you can string the lights on the bottom of the window and decorate the tree and then I'll help you hang up the wreath." I said.

It was a three days before Christmas, December 22, 2000 and the Collins Family had extra decorations to hang thanks to Old Man Archie. When Mama told him that the family was goin' to erect our 6-foot plastic Christmas tree this year—a Collins family tradition, Lil Boy stepped in and purchased a real, 9-foot Douglas fir. He also bought some extra lights, ornaments and garland to hang on the tree and around the house. He promised, "That this Christmas would be one we'll never forget!" For an old guy, Archie was strong for his age. The way he manhandled the tree and lifted out his old Ford Econoline van impressed the whole family.

"Awright it's up family, Come inside an' take a look see!" Archie bellowed.

We entered the apartment; the smell of the freshly-cut tree thumped us as soon as we stepped through the front door. The bare Douglas fir stood erect as could be, Lil Boy stood next to it just as erect and proud as if he planted, watered, fertilized, and then cut the tree down himself.

"It's all ready for y'all to decorate." He said.

Poo made a dash for the tree and started hanging red and green glass ball ornaments on one of the limbs causing it to droop down.

"Listen Baby, You can't stick 10-balls on one limb… you gots to spread 'em out Poo. And make 'em stretch. Mama said as she corrected my brother's sloppy technique.

Lil Boy maneuvered his way behind Ms. Denise and gave her big bear hug; Mama immediately felt his arousal. She also smelled the pungent One Man Show cologne which did a poor job masking the smell of his drinkin'.

"Archie thank you for the nice things you bought for us this Christmas. We're glad you're here to spend it with us." Mama said.

I looked at Mama, but didn't say a word, I let her continue.

"We hope that we can grow together as a family." Mama stated as she turned her head and gave Lil Boy a peck on his mouth.

"Denise, I know you've been without a man hur for some time, but now that I'm around, you and the kids are not gonna have to want for nuthin. If somethin' breaks, I'm gonna fix it. If there's no food in the fridge, I'm gonna go out to Top Value and get some food!" Lil Boy let out a tremendous yawn mid-speech, which took everyone by surprise. "I just need y'all to trust me and gimmie my respect as a man. Back in Palatka, we used to go huntin' for wild boar while the females waited for us to clean our catch. Just le' me be the man and exercise my God-given rights while I'm around hur." Lil Boy advised.

Simultaneously we all made eye contact after listenin' to Lil Boy's babble. I couldn't tell you what Mama and Poo were thinkin' exactly... but I'm sure as hell it was probably congruent to what I had rollin' around in my head...*Not only is this old man's speech noticeably slurred, but his thoughts make absolutely no sense whatsoever.*

After pepperin' the tree with ornamental balls and a few candy canes, Poo took a stretch of garland and began wrapping the fir from top to bottom, he couldn't reach the very top of the tree so he began wrapping from the mid-section of the tree. As he made his way around the tree, a piece of garland snagged on one the fir's limbs. In an attempt to free it, he tugged too hard causing two of the glass orbs to plummet and shatter on the tile floor. Poo was mortified.

"Awww ww shit! Look at this fuckin' mess Malcolm! Why you have to be so goddamn fast all the time? This shit don't make no goddamn sense. You know how much these things cost! Go fetch a broom from outta tha kitchen and clean this shit up!" Archie yelled.

His sudden change of tone surprised us. He went from bein' Jolly Ol' Saint Nick to Ghetto Scrooge in a matter of seconds. Terrified, Poo retreated into Mama's arms. Lil Boy's outburst had me perplexed— *what happened to the 'If somethin' breaks, I'm gonna fix it' proclamation?* At that very moment, I would forever despise the old man—drunk or not. I shook my head then headed to the kitchen for a broom and a dustpan.

"No Quintavia that lil nigga need to clean up his shit since he made this mess. You can't go runnin' to yo' Mama when you get in a fix. Malcolm needs to learn how to man up if he wants to be anythin' in this world!" Lil Boy yelled as spittle drizzled over his full-length salt and pepper beard.

Seconds later, I exited the kitchen and hovered toward Lil Boy with broom in hand. Mama separated the two of us.

"Listen up Archie you ain't comin' up in here and yellin' at my lil brother you sorry-ass motherfucka. Go yell at one of yo' own damn kids, I know you gots at least eight of those bitches in the greater Miami area alone. But what you need to do is stop drinkin' so much bitch 'cause you can't even get his name right, it's Marcus. M....A....R....C....U....S! Dumb bitch!" I barked back.

"Quintavia you need stop bein' so mannish and respect your elders gurl! Respect the man of the house. You still a chil…"

Mama managed to push her inebriated beau out the front door. I shook my head. From the window, the two silhouettes bantered back and forth, until the larger one eventually vanished into the night—off to one his other baby mama's houses or off to the A-rab store for another fifth of Rose. Mama came back inside to find me sweepin' up the broken glass as Poo continued to haphazardly decorate the fir.

"Poo—Baby, can you please go to yo' room so yo' sister and I can talk? I'll be in there in a minute and I'll read you a book." Mama requested.

Mama waited for Poo to enter our bedroom then Mama continued after she heard the bedroom door shut.

"You know he isn't so bad dear, you just got to get to know him."

"Mama I don't like him and never will. How can you lambaste a child over a 50-cent ornament from Family Dolla? Could you imagine if Poo broke somethin' of real value? He was outta line for that…way outta line!" I said defiantly.

"Queen, life ain't black and white, child. You have to take the good and the bad. Believe me child, yo' father had his demons just like the rest of us. Lil Boy has his ways, but he got a good heart. He don't have to help a single woman with two chil'ren. He don't have to chauffer us around town but he does. He didn't have to spend the lil money he has on us but he did, so please child give the man a chance, I'm sure he'll surprise you."

"Mama it's just that…that…"

"C'mon child, speak yo' peace girl. I'm a grown woman and I value your opinion 'cause you almost grown yo'self." Mama requested while she held my hand. Mama's pretty smile never left her face.

"Mama it's just that I can't believe you went from a man like Songbird to that. You're too beautiful a person Mama to settle. An' being with Lil Boy settlin'. I know Songbird liked his beer, and got flip out tha mouth, but he never disrespected you or his chil'ren eva. He never went into Poo like Lil Boy did. And the messed up thing is that Lil Boy been around us for a few months, imagine him in a year or two?"

Mama took the broom and dustpan from my hands.

"I promise you I'll talk to Lil Boy about some of his ways. All I ask Baby is that you give him a chance."

I took a second before I responded. I never disobeyed my parents and regardless of my feelings, I wasn't goin' to start today.

"For you Mama…I'll try."

Mama gave me a bear hug similar to Lil Boy's

"I wanted to ask you somethin' else child"?

"What's that Mama"?

"Do you got yo'self a new boyfriend that I don't know about"?

"Why you ask that Mama"?

"'I see you bouncin' around here with a smile on yo' face, I haven't seen you this happy in a while now. The way you talk, the way carry yo'self got me thinkin' you got somethin' new in yo' life and it's probably a new friend boy."

My cheeks reddened and my palms moistened, my body snitched me out and I was nabbed.

"It's a boy that I met on my way home from school a few weeks ago. He's just a friend and his name is Antwon. I wouldn't consider him my boyfriend. He's just an associate... we're really just talkin' right now." I blushed.

I felt prettier when I was happy, and Antwon's presence in my life made me happy. You know when you in love 'cause that person makes you wanna do better. Antwon had me taking better care of myself. I never let a day pass where my nails needed a fill or my Halle Berry and brows weren't trimmed up. I did leave out a few minor details about my friend though— like the fact our relationship began after he saved me from a DBB ass-whoopin' and the fact that we had sex at least four times so far — quick hits before pickin' up Poo from Orchard Villa. I hated lyin' to Mama, but I knew Mama wouldn't approve of Antwon for a number of reasons: Antwon was from Da Beans, he dropped out of school in 9th grade, and I suspected that my friend served drugs out his mobile detailin' van.

"Oh yeah... I'd love to meet him one of these days." Mama stated.

"I will have to find out his schedule next week since he got his own business." I replied.

"How about you invite yo' friend over for Christmas dinner? Hopefully he isn't workin' on Christmas."

"Okay Mama I will invite him over for Christmas dinner, all I ask is that you give Antwon a chance befo' you judge him. Just like I'm finna give Lil Boy a chance." I stated truly wanting to make amends for this evening's craziness.

"That's fair Baby. I'm lookin' forward to meetin' your new friend."

6 CHRISTMAS DAY

December 25, 2000
(Da Beans)

It was a sweltering 88-degrees in Miami. By midday, it was the hottest Christmas ever recorded. Da Beans was alive, its residents flaunted their newly opened gifts. The younger men proudly donned their Ecko denim outfits and the women rocked UGG boots ignoring the record setting temperatures, while the children zipped around on their Razor scooters, the hottest toy of the year. Like anywhere else, Christmas afforded budget-minded parents an opportunity to splurge on their kids for a day and the ghetto fabulous to dig deeper into financial ruin. In typical fashion, Antwon peddled his green, 18" Huffy BMX bike while I walked alongside him.

"My mama is gonna like you Scrub, just be yo'self." I stated.

"I don't know Queen, I don't wanna mess up yo' family's Christmas dinner." Antwon replied cautiously.

"You gotta come…I told her you'd be there. Plus, it's important that you meet my family in a proper manner. I also cooked so you gots to be there!" I said touching his hand as he steered.

"Oh yeah Gurl? What's fo' dinner"?

"Seasoned roast turkey, giblet gravy, cornbread dressin', green peas and limas with turkey necks, sweet potato casserole—and Mama even came outta retirement to make her famous pound cake." I said proudly.

We walked down Northwest 12th Court. The sound of Donnie Hathaway's 'This Christmas' played over an old boom box. As we approached Northwest 62nd Terrace our path was interrupted by a small mob of people gathered around the front door of one of the 1-story apartments. The mob was angered—oblivious it was Christmas.

"Whud up cuz? What's goin' on here"? Antwon asked one of the mob members.

"Cuz, HRS is in there, they about to remove my lil cousins." A middle-aged man with a head of freshly-done cornrows grumbled.

"Damn, sorry to hear that bruh. DCF on a Christmas day! Ain't dat sum shit." Antwon said as he gave the unknown man a dap as we kept walkin'.

###

My lips were dry from talking and I did not dare ask for a sip of water. My white, DCF polo shirt was soaked with sweat. But that was my stupid decision to pick the worst color shirt to head out in the field in. I was more concerned with fashion before function— a typical rookie mistake. The heat was stifling at 6306 Northwest 12th Court, this particular housing unit wasn't equipped with an A/C unit and I regretfully requested that the family keep the doors closed to prevent any additional family members from entering the tiny dwelling. Ironically, my current investigation, **Abuse Case 00-2526321**, proved to be one of my most heated cases I received thus far. Mother's prior dependency case history, the sheer number of participants involved, and the volatile location all added to the tension. Around 25-people waited in the next room and outside of the apartment for me to make my decision. It's amazing where this job takes you. Three hours earlier, I was sitting at home in my underwear plopped in front of a 32" TV waiting for the Dallas Cowboys to play the Tennessee Titans in the NFL's 2000 Christmas Day offering. Now I was in the projects, sweating my ass off, wishing I could spend a little time with my own family in Palm Beach— or better yet making love to my new boo, CPI Tamara Norvil. We did get to spend yesterday together before she went out of town, since Tamara promised her big sister that she'd spend Christmas with her family in Naples. I wasn't so lucky; as a rookie and the least-tenured in my area, my holidays off were now an afterthought.

I decided to interview the mother, Ruth Jenkins, first. As in most of my cases, I felt dealing with the most irate participants head-on was the best practice. It allowed them to blow off steam and it gave them a sense of control—even though I knew otherwise. After providing the mother a copy of her Rights and Responsibilities Form (the R&R), I read mother the allegations. Then, I watched in disbelief as this lady stormed out of the house yelling, *"Oh Lawd! HRS is tryin' to snatch my chil'ren! Somebody help! These crackas tryin' to take my chil'ren."* After I convinced the frantic mother to come back inside the home, she proceeded to call every living relative on her family tree. Relatives came from as far as Homestead so none of the children had to enter foster care. From grandparents to baby daddies to great aunties, they all came. Now they were all outside a bedroom door waiting for me to render a decision.

I re-read the allegations of **Abuse Case 00-2526321** to myself before interviewing my target child, Coretta Jenkins:

Mother Ruth Jenkins had two of her children; Albert and Alberta removed from her care in 1994 for substance abuse. Since mother's reunification with her children in 1995, mother gave birth to three other children Ricardo, Corretta, and Diane. There's concern that Barry Pierce, mom's boyfriend and father of said child Diane physically abused Corretta. Ruth Jenkins allows Barry to discipline the children. On 12/22/00 Diane was observed with unexplained bruising to her arms. (Imm.)

As I opened the bedroom door which spilled directly into Ruth's tiny living room, a burst of heat enveloped me like a nuclear blast. The intolerable heat was generated by 18-or-so irate family members and an apartment void of any air-conditioning or fan. Consequently, the smell was just as leveling. The smell reminded me of my high school locker room after our infamous, mid-August Suicide Practice Sessions with the Palm Beach Prep Wildcats. Some of the family members were in their Sunday's Best drenched with sweat: their Christmas Dinner plans were shot.

"A HRS Man, Ruth is a good mother! She wouldn't hurt any of her chil'ren!" An unknown relative yelled.

The mob muttered affirming the statement. Even as the mob surged, consumed by Ruth Jenkin's diversionary theatrics, I remained level headed and polite.

"I'm sorry folks, I don't want to keep you but these allegations are serious. The State of Florida wouldn't send me out here on a Christmas if this wasn't important. Please just be patient, I'll give you a decision after in a few minutes."

I gestured towards Corretta and escorted her into my makeshift interviewing room. She sat on the edge of the bed while I sat in a gray folding chair.

"How are you doing Corretta"? I asked.

"Fine."

"My name is Mr. Jeremiah, I work for Department of Children and Families and I protect children. I'm here because we got a report that someone was hurting you. Is it okay if we talk?"

"Sure." Corretta wiped a few braids of hair from her face.

"What do your friends call you"? I asked.

"They call me Retta for short. It's okay if you call me Retta."

I looked at Retta, the child cringed and turned to escape my gaze, but wasn't fast enough. I immediately knew something was wrong when I spied the child wearing a long-sleeve sweatshirt in this fuckin' sauna.

"Retta, what we talk about is gonna be between you and me. I'm not going to runoff and tell your mom or Barry anything. I just need you to be honest with me." I waited for a response before I continued.

"Can I see your arms Retta?"

Corretta was apprehensive, and tugged her arms back as I reached for them.

"Hold up a second Retta. Out of all the relatives outside that door, who is your favorite one of all…Please it has to be an adult? I asked as I leaned forward in my chair.

Retta paused a second before responding. "My cousin Keisha. She my favorite."

"I'm gonna bring her in. Would you mind if I did that?" I asked.

Retta raised her head and squared her shoulders. The suggestion definitely appealed to the 6-year old.

I opened the bedroom door and walked into the family room. The heat and smell thumped me once more. Through the front window, I saw family members on the front porch smoking menthol cigarettes and I was in envy. In milliseconds, I was peppered with a barrage of questions, comments and scowls.

"DCF Man! What the hell takin' so long? You need to make a decision about these chil'ren. I have to be to work at 11!"

One of the relatives retorted. "You know if this was some White child on the Beach, we woulda been done by now. It's only us Black folk that get put through dis!"

I scanned the room looking for a particular face, but the individual was not in sight.

"DCF always in people's business, that's why yo' agency's a hot ass mess! HRS ain't no good." A portly lady blasted.

I raised my voice to stifle the haranguers. "I'll be just a few minutes. I just need Cousin Keisha's assistance. Cousin Keisha! Is there a Cousin Keisha here?"

A slender 20-something year old black female methodically arose from the sofa. Keisha's nose piercing and neck tattoo caught my eye. I admired her for her bold individuality, so I smiled at her and said "Hello". She didn't say anything, but the stare she gave me froze my rookie-ass almost immediately.

"Ms. Keisha can you please step into the room? Retta asked that you be by her side. Thank you." I said as I held the door open for her.

Keisha walked through the door. I continued to scan for the face I was looking for earlier, but I abandoned my search. I reached in my pocket and thumbed the text message, "**911-6306 NW 12 CT**" into my newly-issued Nokia 5110. I mashed 'Send' and went inside the bedroom.

"Keisha, I'm going to examine this child for marks and any other indicators of physical abuse. She asked that you be in here. We will have to totally disrobe this child, but it is necessary." I said.

Cousin Keisha looked at Retta who began crying, and wiped the tears from her eyes with the hem of her shirt.

"It's awright Cuzo, you can trust Mr. Jeremiah. He a nice man." Keisha said.

I nodded at the affirmation.

Keisha continued hugging and holding her younger cousin, but directed her question at me, "What can I help you with Mr."?

"Keisha I need you take Retta's top off we need to look at her arms."

After the long-sleeve sweatshirt was removed. Keisha was surprised to find a loosely wrapped Ace bandage on the child's right forearm. Keisha touched the bandage and Retta winced.

I slowly removed the loosely-wrapped bandage—unfortunately it was the only "unwrapping" done this Christmas at the Jenkins residence, since the home was totally devoid any Christmas presents or holiday fanfare. After the bandage was fully off, Keisha responded...

"My Lawd who did this to you Retta! Who hurt my baby cousin like dis!" Keisha let out a scream as tears rolled down her face. Relatives from the next room rushed towards the bedroom door, but I prohibited them from entering with the wave of my hand. Keisha nodded to them signaling she and Retta were okay.

Under the Ace bandage was the worst case of physical abuse, I have seen since signing on with the Department. Retta's entire left forearm was a welted pulp. Retta's dark chocolate pigment couldn't mask the abuse, her dark-purplish forearm was swollen beyond belief, and it was easily bigger than my own. The welts that wrapped around the little girl's forearm looked like toy train tracks branded onto her skin. A quick glance at the ghastly abuse immediately brought Keisha to tears again.

"Retta I know this hurts and I've never met a child braver than you. But I need for you to answer some questions for me?" I stated.

I softly cupped Retta's right wrist and I was in disgust at what I saw. Retta had welt marks on her right forearm as well from the savage belt beating. I suspected they were glancing blows—collateral damage sustained as the child raised her forearms to shield herself. I immediately reached into my back pocket and began snapping pictures with my Nokia phone. After my interview I would have to call CPT (the Child Protection Team).   Any case involving physical/sexual abuse, medical neglect or case involving a substance exposed child requires a call to this unit. If the child exhibited physical injuries, CPT would send a trained physician or nurse to meet with the abused child or a consultation would be scheduled to have the child brought to their office. CPT are the experts; they could tell you what a child was hit with and how long ago a child was hit. When you went to court, it always helped to have one of their reports as evidence to reinforce your shelter petition. Their role in protecting children throughout the State is indispensible.

"Retta, Who did this to you? 'Member I'm here for you and nobody else is goin' to hurt you." Cousin Keisha asked.

The child clammed up.

"Retta, I know this isn't the first time something like this happened to you. I don't want this to happen to you again or your brothers and sisters." I stated softly as sweat rolled down my face.

"Go ahead Retta, ain't nobody finna hurt you no mo'." Keisha chimed in

"Barry hit me."

"Okay Retta, Why did he hit you?" I asked.

"He hit me 'cause I spilled juice on the flo'."

"…And when did he do this"? I asked.

"He whooped me two days ago."

"Retta, where was your mom when he hit you"? I asked.

"She went to the sto'… gettin' the baby milk."

"Who put this bandage on you"? I asked.

"My Mama…Mama put dis bandage on me."

"When you do something bad who punishes"? I asked.

"Barry."

"You don't have to worry about Barry hitting you ever again Retta." I whispered in Retta's ear, while drops of water rolled down my face once more and it wasn't from my sweat.

Our interview was interrupted by the sound of police sirens blaring outside the front of the home. *It's been less than 15-minutes. It couldn't be that fast? I must be fuckin' dreaming.* The cantankerous ringtone of my Nokia 5110 followed; the annoying sound jarred me back to reality. I excused myself and retreated into the bathroom:

"DCF, CPI Abundo speaking. How can I help you?"

"I got your text Jeremiah, Miami Dade should be dispatched to your location in couple of minutes. I spoke with Sergeant Pratt and she told me she'd get a uniform out there ASAP."

"Yeah, thanks Supe. They're here already I can't believe it. That was faster than Dominoes!"

"What's going on over there are you okay? Don't tell me you are removing people's children again!" Supe stated jokingly.

"Supe, I wouldn't take them if I didn't have to. I'd rather be watching Dallas beat up on the Titans, while sippin' a beer in my underwear."

My Supervisor Jamie Watkins laughed as she always did. She respected me even though I was old enough to be her son. And she loved my hardworking and dedicated spirit, but equally admired the levity that I brought to the unit.

"How long are you going to be there Jeremiah? Tallahassee called me with another Immediate for the Central and I have no one else to give it to. I gave Ferguson from the South two immediates and Caldwell from the North also has two Immediates— one of them involves a child that was poisoned, it might end up a being a death case."

"Damn sorry to hear that. What's my case about? Maybe you can downgrade it to a 24 if the case is not that serious." I asked.

"Jeremiah I looked at this one and it could have been downgraded, but the hospital social worked called this one today. The child was born four days ago—cocaine exposed, now the child is ready for discharge and placement. Jackson is not going to let that child remain at its facility a second longer than it has to—they're not going to flip the bill."

"Shit, my case involves 5-children. Mom's boyfriend beat the shit out of this child with a belt. It looks like this bastard took it to the child with the buckle. I still have to observe the rest of her body for injuries, and contact CPT. She told me that he's the disciplinarian in the house. I sent my text after I saw that the A/P fled. That motherfucker was here when I got here, but bailed after I started my interviews with the children and other family members started arriving. I'm filing against the mother because she allowed Barry to beat this child egregiously, and then had the audacity to wrap an Ace bandage around the injury and think that it's okay. You know how much pain this little girl must have been in the past two days?" I stated rubbing my neck.

"Wow….I got some more bad news Jeremiah. Administration instructed the supervisors that we need to better manage our units, and this includes doing a better job monitoring of our unit's overtime. I know you're working Jeremiah, but anything over 40-hours, I'm going to have to flex you out."

"Damn, Jamie what is this bullshit? I'm here doing the State's bidding—keeping children safe and now I'm not even going to get paid?"

"You can pick any day you want off this coming week, you might even get two days depending how long you spend on this removal."

"Supe, that's not the point. I still have 30-day and 60-day reviews that will be due on my days I'm scheduled to be off, and you know I'm going to turn on my laptop and submit them to you. But it's the principle. I'm here on Christmas caring for other people's children, but I'm not afforded a holiday…some time with my own family?"

"You know how Administration is Jeremiah. It's about the bottom line for them; they're so estranged from you and me they don't know what it takes to do this job from the frontline. From one social worker to another, you can never put a budget on what we do— keeping families together. Unfortunately, this backward state wants to deal with the issues after the fact."

I listened to my supervisor, but my mindset was on the State and its archaic practices in dealing with child welfare. Instead of teaching people about safe sex, the conservative doofuses in Tallahassee think people are going to do the right thing. *Yeah right!* Instead of allowing the Ruth Jenkins' of this world to have a gaggle of children…at the very least, give them the education and means to make alternate choices. I also directed my venom at the Administration of District 11. None of which I respected, since a majority never touched an investigation in their lives and were totally out-of-touch with the needs of its line staff and our clients. Now they want to put limitations on overtime? *What did District Administrator Chet Parker say a few of months ago? "In District 11, we do more with less, and we like it like this!" Bullshit! "In District 11, you want more for less, and Jeremiah don't like it like this!"*

"Jeremiah, are you still with me"?

"Yeah I'm here Supe. Sorry about that. My mind was just floating, plus I haven't even eaten since breakfast."

Jamie was one of the many supervisors at the Department that really cared. She'd pick up the phone at 3am and help any investigator out regardless of what area. If need be, go out on the case herself. If a CPI needed to vent she had her office door wide open. I had the utmost respect for my 'Supe'.

"Tell you what I'm going to do. My sister is going to be hosting Christmas dinner, and she lives in Brown Sub that's a few minutes from Da Beans I can help you with the home studies or with placement. I feel so bad you have so much work to do. Let me help?" She said.

"Supe that's okay. I don't have any kids or a spouse and at this rate I don't see me getting either of the two anytime soon. Spend time with your family...enjoy them, enjoy your Christmas. The Department can't substitute for family." I stated as memories of my own family came to mind.

"Thank you Jeremiah. I'm going to call CPI Kaye Hudson in Unit 915. She's scheduled to work the On-call tonight. I'll see if she's willing to handle this Immediate for us. If need be, I'll go out on the case myself. Can I do anything else for you?" Supe asked.

"No you been great as usual Supe. Thanks for calling Metro for me. Speaking of which, I need to speak to them before they drive off. Take care Jamie, it's always a pleasure and Merry Christmas to your family."

"Merry Christmas officer and thank you for coming out so quickly." I said.

"No problem I don't want anything happening to you guys on my watch." The tall Hispanic officer said as he held out his hand.

As I grabbed it, I eyed the silver shield on the officer's shirt pocket, engraved on a platinum name tag just below it read, 'R. Ruiz'. Officer Rene Ruiz's large hand enveloped mine. One twitch of his gargantuan biceps and his shirt sleeves looked like they'd rip into shreds. Ruiz was accompanied by two other patrol cars. The lights spinning atop their cruisers seemed to draw more and more people to the Jenkins residence.

"Officer Ruiz it's a pleasure to meet you…CPI Jeremiah Abundo of the Department of Children and Families. We will need a detective out here since the injuries to the victim child are egregious. It appears that mom's boyfriend beat the crap out of the child with a belt buckle. Actually, I noticed he left the residence when he realized the outcome." I stated.

"Okay no problem I'll call it in. How long have you been out here CPI Abundo?"

"I got here around 3pm and been here for the past 3 ½ hours. I still have to place the children, do a homestudy or two, and then I have to type up my notes and draft the shelter petition. This case captured my entire Christmas."

"You should have called us earlier. These situations can turn volatile quickly. I know this firsthand because I used to be a CPI back in the days." Officer Ruiz stated never taking his eyes off the incident report he was filling out.

"Is that right… who did you work under?" I asked.

"My supervisor was Pat Turner. Wally Baker, Thelma Tillman, Grace Hanson, and Abassi Okafor were all CPIs in my unit."

"What a coincidence! Abassi is in my unit, 808 Central. Great guy and a helluva a CPI."

"Tell him Cuban Rene said hello next time you see him."

"I'll do that. Can I ask you a question Officer Ruiz?" I asked.

"Sure, go right ahead CPI Abundo."

"Why did you leave the Department"?

Cuban Rene paused from his writing before answering.

"I left DCF because it became too much. You've been here going on 4-hours, I'll probably be here 40-minutes max. When you go home you have a crap load of paperwork that you still have to complete. When I go home I just relax—play with my kids, my dogs and make love to my wife. You have to put these worthless parents back with their children and hope they do not re-abuse or neglect them; I just throw these good-for-nothings in jail— if they get out, I arrest them again. To top it off, you're probably not getting paid for half the shit you are doing. The paperwork, the headaches, the lack of resources all take a toll on you, I did almost two years before putting in with the academy—most brutal two years of my life if you ask me. I really respect you guys because of the job you do; I loathe the crappy, unrealistic system you have to contend with though."

I was stunned. Hearing these sentiments coming from someone who worked both sides was refreshing, but posed some real questions about my future with the Department. *How long can I work at this pace? Where will I be in 10-years? How much of myself am I willing to sacrifice?* I didn't have to mention anything to the Cuban Rene and he identified with my frustrations almost immediately. Polite and insightful, my chance encounter with Cuban Rene was definitely a highlight of the evening. It also questioned my whole attitude regarding cops. *Maybe there are some good ones out there?*

Officer Ruiz's walkie-talkie chirped. He excused himself to answer the call. But his conversation with dispatch couldn't be ignored.

"Ruiz, QSL."

"Ruiz, Would you like us to send relief to your location? Shift is over in 10-minutes." The dispatch officer asked.

"QRU, I'm almost done here. Just giving DCF a copy of my prelim incident report."

"QSL. Have a good evening Officer and Merry Christmas."

Cuban Rene holstered his walkie-talkie.

"See there's another thing that separates us from you. When we are on a case, and the shift is over we get relief and get to go home. You guys have to see a case though from start to finish—and a case can take 10-hours or more, if I'm not mistaken."

"Never thought of that Officer Ruiz, you made some valid points."

"Here you go CPI Abundo." Officer Ruiz handed me a copy of his preliminary incident report and a business card with the police case number and a general telephone contact number printed on it. I marveled at the 1-page incident report— nothing in size comparison to what I was expected complete before day's end.

"CPI Abundo one other thing, I'm at your disposal until you say leave…even though it seems you got everything under control. The real officers at the precinct respect what you guys do. From one CPI to another, you can call on me for anything."

"Thanks Officer Ruiz. Thanks for everything and Merry Christmas."

After exchanging handshakes, I headed back inside of 6306 Northwest 12 Court to deal with the Jenkins family, while Cuban Rene trailed closely behind.

###

Unlike the Jenkins residence, every square inch of the Collins residence reeked of Christmas. The tiny apartment was transformed into a festive wonderland. From the smell of the oven baked turkey and pound cake to the plastic set of musical bells that hung from the fir that played random Christmas tunes, the Collins family was truly anointed with the Christmas spirit. Lil Boy Bedford had a lot to do with this. The extra money he brought to the house allowed our family to splurge a little more on frivolous items we wouldn't normally purchase like the new, plastic nativity scene at the base of our Christmas tree. Mama decided it was time to throw out the old one, and get a historically correct one with an all Black cast.

Dinner was wonderful. As promised, I cooked a feast to make Songbird proud: Seasoned roast turkey, giblet gravy, cornbread dressing, green peas and limas with turkey necks and sweet potato casserole. Mama was unable to make her famous pound cake because she was downtown at The Camillus House helping serve Christmas dinner for Miami's homeless. When she took inventory of all her blessings this year, Mama immediately signed up to help at the shelter. The Camillus House provided her family a Thanksgiving and Christmas dinner or two right after Songbird died. Even my boyfriend, Antwon "Scrub" Bennett brought an offering for tonight's feast, some homemade souse that his cousin prepared. After Mama saw the pig feet, snouts and tails floating in the semi-clear fluid, she made an excuse to save her portion for tomorrow's lunch. Her choice to abstain from pork was not dictated by religion, but from Quentin Tarintino's movie **Pulp Fiction.** After

Samuel L. Jackson's convincing denunciation of pork consumption, she hasn't eaten the "filthy animals" ever since. Lil Boy was surprisingly sober; he promised Mama he'd refrain from drinkin' before and during dinner. However after dinner, he was goin' to hang with the fellas down at Ol' Hickory Package Store on Northwest 17th Avenue and play some Spades and have a few beers.

"Quintavia, this dinner is fantastic. I wish yo' Mama cooked like this fo' me mo' often".

I detected some sincerity in Lil Boy's compliment before I responded, "Thank you Archie. I'm glad you like it."

"So how did you get the name Scrub"? Poo asked.

"Yo' sister gave me that name 'cause that's what I do for a livin'. I have a mobile detailin' business. I wash cars and trucks all ova tha county."

Up until now, Mama didn't know very much about my boo. She was intrigued to find out more about Scrub.

"So what school did you graduate from the West, Central, Edison, Jackson"? Mama asked in an attempt to delve.

"No Ms. Denise, I didn't graduate from neitha." Scrub said.

I looked at her and sure Mama wasn't pleased with his response. Shockingly, she remained composed.

"Do you plan on goin' back to get your GED?—it could help you with yo' business"? Mama asked.

"Never really thought about it. Business is doin' well. I'm makin' mo' than some adults wit' college degrees. School ain't for everybody. I told Queen about my dreams about expandin' the business and I'm on my way."

Even after hearing Scrub's sentiments, as backward as they seemed, Mama admired his gumption because the smile on her face never wavered.

"I wanna' scrub cars too. Do you have one of those machines that shoots out water like a canon?" Poo inquired.

"Sho 'do...got two big ol' compressors!" Scrub responded.

"No Boy, You finna' stay in school and get yo' education!" Mama said vehemently. "Lord have mercy, Scrub you rubbin' off on my baby already!"

"Naw, lil man you need to stay in school, Queen tells me that you' killin' it at Orchard Villa." Scrub wisely stated.

"You know Antwon...if yo' business don't work out, you can always go into the services. I did a few years in the Army and it made me a better man." Archie added.

Lil Boy loosened the button fly on this pants, he was stuffed from the good food and wanted to get his drink on. His attention was fixated on the clock that hung on the living room wall. During dinner earlier, Lil Boy swore up and down that he's met or seen my new boyfriend somewhere before but couldn't pinpoint the time or place.

"Mama... Scrub's Uncle Ricky got this Box Chevy that he's basically givin' away fo' free. Scrub said he's willin' to talk to him to see if he could put us on a payment plan. If we pay him $60-dollars a week, it will be all ours by March." I said excitedly. As I smiled a dimple formed at the left corner of my mouth.

"That's good Baby and thank you fo' thinkin' about us Antwon." Mama stated.

"Mama, we gettin' a car? I wanna drive!" Poo said childishly.

"Yes baby, you can drive." Mama responded.

"Antwon, where yo' people from son"? Lil Boy asked.

"My mama is from Adel, Georgia, but I was born and raised in Da Beans. My daddy left when I was one so I don't know much about 'im. I neva been outside Florida. You got me thinkin' about the military Mr. Archie. When you were enlisted did you get to travel?" Scrub asked.

"Uncle Sam allowed me to see a number of different countries on tha house. You should really give it some thought. I don't see the US gettin' into any wars anytime soon. Get that military experience while you young boy!" Archie said now combing his teeth for stray matter with a toothpick.

15-random gunshots rang outside somewhere in the City, the noise briefly interrupted an off-key version of 'Silent Night' being played on the plastic set of musical bells that hung from our Christmas fir.

"Yeah boy think about the military life." Lil Boy reiterated.

"Yes sir, I'm finna look into that, but I have to jet right now, and pick up my mama from work. It's dark and she don't drive at night no mo'. Thank you fo' havin' me over. I told Queen that you might not care for me since I'm a dropout from Da Beans, but I was wrong. I wanna wish you all a Merry Christmas and thank you for havin' me." Scrub said politely.

"Antwon, I'm finna make you a plate for your mama. Tell yo' peoples thank you for that delicious pot of souse." Mama stated.

"Yes ma'am I will."

I smiled at Scrub's amicable gesture towards our family. As Poo wiped pie residue with the handkerchief that hung around his neck, Lil Boy smirked after he finally realized where he met Antwon before. A devilish smile washed over his face.

"Was I good today baby? Did I behave appropriately enough fo' the almighty Queen"? Lil Boy asked.

"Yes, you done good baby. Thank you for everythin' you did for us this Christmas." Mama replied.

Lil Boy bear hugged Mama while she fixed a to-go-plate for Antwon's mother. Then, he quickly turned her so they faced one another. She felt his arousal at the top of her stomach. A Cheshire cat smile blanketed his face, but his happiness emanated from a place other than a sexual one.

"You know baby. I did this for you. I still feel chil'ren need to remain in their place. Panderin' to a teenager is somethin' I would normally never do, but I kept the peace and didn't take a single sip 'cause of you. When I come back from Ol' Hickory, I'm finna show you how much I love you gurl." Lil Boy stated.

Mama had to arch her back escape Lil Boy's stiffness. Lil Boy proceeded to exit out of the galley-style kitchen. Then he stopped abruptly at the entryway. With his back turned he spoke, "Baby, I know where I seen Antwon befo', but I didn't want to ruin yo' daughter's Christmas."

Mama froze. She tossed the ladle-full of lima beans back in the pot.

"Archie, if it involves any of my chil'ren, I need to know."

Lil Boy turned to face Mama, then spoke, "Baby one thing I don't want to do is interfere in yo' relationship with yo' daughter. Blood is thicker than water. And she was here way befo' I started comin' around, but I feel it is my duty as yo' boyfriend that I warn you of things befo' they come back to bite you."

"Go ahead Archie."

Lil Boy made his way back into the narrow galley-style kitchen. He made sure he was beyond ear's reach of the dining room before continuing.

"A couple of months back, after work, I was at Ol' Hickory playin' tunk and havin' a few drinks with the fellas. Some young boys in a Ford F-150 came by and cleaned the cars for a few of the customers. If you've been to Hickory on a Friday, you know it's packed with all sorts of people—longshoremen, tradesmen, county workers, retirees an' a few off-duty police every now and then. The men at Hickory would sit under a tree have drink or two, an' get to talkin' while watchin' these young boys bring these dirty cars back to life. Business was so damn good, they started comin' every week…usually on Fridays 'cause it's payday. I later found out from my partna Rudy, that the boys were doin' things other than cleanin' cars."

"What 'other' things were Antwon and his boys doin'"? Mama naively asked.

"Well if you asked for the #1 Workin' Man's Special—they'd clean yo' car in-an'-out, hand dry it, then leave some reefer in yo' ashtray fo' later. For others that wanted a thorough cleanin', they asked for a #3, The Works, they'd clean yo' ride in-an'-out, vacuum, buff on a coat of Turtle Wax, then leave somethin' major in yo' glove compartment… some Heron or some soft white. The owners at Ol' Hickory ran these cleanin' boys off 'cause it was bringin' too much heat to our spot. It was bad enough the police came by hagglin' us for drinkin' in public. Fo' sho they'd shut us down for any type of drug activity!"

"My baby got herself messed up with a drug dealer, I'm gonna have to talk to her." Mama said anxiously.

"You need to do that Denise. You don't want that boy messin' up that girl's life, regardless of how much she fancies him."

"Thank you Archie maybe it's best you go so I can have a talk with her.

###

"Awright now. See y'all later. Merry Christmas again!" Lil Boy said loudly as he exited the front door.

"Merry Christmas." We replied jovially.

"Do you think yo' ol' girl likes me"? Scrub turned and asked me.

"If she didn't care fo' you, Ms. Denise will tell you what's on her mind right then and there. If she didn't like you, you wouldn't of made it to dessert." I affirmed.

"Dang, that's a relief." Scrub said relieved.

"I think she likes that you got your own business even if you dropped out of high school. That really impressed her." I said.

"I hope it did. You'll see. I'm finna show Ms. Denise another side of me. But fo' now I need to get outta here and pick up my mama up from her job." Scrub stated. He rose from the table looking dapper in his off-white, woven linen short sleeve and shorts set with a matchin' pair of crocodile print closed toe sandals. He winked at Poo and hit him with a quick smile partially showing off his grill. I walked him outside and we exchanged innocent pecks, before parting ways. Scrub then cranked the ignition of his F-150. The vehicle's loud muffler set someone's car alarm off.

"Tell Ms. Denise thanks fo' the plate!" He exclaimed hanging out the pick-up truck's window as he puttered off into the night.

I was smitten. Scrub was a little rough around the edges, but sincere. Over time, maybe I could smooth some of those edges out. But for now, I was happy and that's all that counted. I walked back into the apartment where Mama sat waiting on me on the sofa. Judging Ms. Denise's affect, I immediately knew there was a problem.

"Hey Mama everything okay"? I asked.

"Yes baby everything is okay, how about with you"?

"Everything is great, just about to do some tidyin' up before goin' to bed." I replied.

"Okay we can clean up together an' talk a little." Mama offered.

I smiled confirming my satisfaction at Mama's proposition. Although Mama may be disappointed with my choice of boyfriends, Mama would never embarrass Scrub in front of everyone. She just had too much class for this.

"You get the table and I'll sweep the flo'." Mama stated.

I nodded. Anything that involved physical work or sweating had Poo heading for the hills. As Mama and I talked, Poo sprinted to the bedroom to play his newest Christmas acquisition, a Playstation 2 with a copy of Madden NFL 2001. The system came at a hefty price, but Lil Boy did not mind making the investment, since he dabbled in video gaming himself from time to time.

"So Mama, what did you think about Antwon"?

"Queen he seems like a nice boy, but I'm not so sure about him droppin' out of high school. It's hard out here if you don't have an education. Look at me; I have to work a few jobs just to make ends meet." Mama said as she swept. Her gaze was fixated on the little piles of dust and debris she collected every few feet.

Mama was careful with the words she chose and the method how she conveyed them. She didn't want me to think she disapproved of my boyfriend over trivial reasons. And she didn't want indict Antwon because I would ask for evidence. Ms. Denise knew me and Lil Boy didn't get along and this would just deepen the rift between the two of us into a chasm.

"Mama school ain't for everybody. Songbird made a way and he didn't' finish school; he joined the Navy and made a life for himself and created a good family. Antwon even told us that he was thinkin' about the military if his business doesn't work out." I stated as I calmly stacked the Collins prized dinnerware into a pile and collected the flatware by hand.

"Queen school ain't for everybody, but it's definitely fo' you! Please understand the sacrifice yo' father and I made fo' you so you and yo' brother didn't have to want fo' much. We always gave you a safe home to come home to. I'm just afraid that Antwon might...might...might..." Ms. Denise stammered.

"What undermine me! 'Cause me to live my life in mediocrity, just another poor, needy female outta tha ghetto. I tell you Mama that is not happenin'! If I choose to be with dat boy or not, that's not happenin' to me!" I said loud enough, where it drowned out the sound of Poo's Playstation 2 heard in the background.

I was frustrated at Mama's train of thought. Since I met Antwon months ago, my grades have not slipped a bit. In fact they've gotten better and I never neglected my housework or my obligations to my family. To me, I was the same responsible Quintavia Collins; the only difference is that I lived life a little happier and did things with a smile my family hasn't seen in years. But Mama was not impressed with my theatrics. One thing you never do in our household as a child is lose yo'self because Ms. Denise will gladly help you get back on course.

"Hold up young lady! Remember who's the mother and who's the child. If I tell you somethin' and you don't care to hear it...that's just too bad! Just remember it's comin' outta a place of love. Get hot and bothered but you ain't finna disrespect me because at the end of the day, nuthin' can supersede the love a parent has fo' a child— and I mean nuthin'!" Mama stated as she pointed and wielded the broom like a scepter.

I was venturing on to foreign ground. I never challenged Mama's authority or outwardly defied her wishes. Last time I did so I was 6-years old when I refused to take a bath. Luckily, Songbird was alive to save me from Ms. Denise's wrath. I eyed Mama holding the wooden broom and didn't hesitate for a second that Mama wouldn't physically castigate me even at the ripe age of 15.

"Mama there's gotta to be somethin' more to this. Your whole demeanor changed from the time we ate dinner to the time you prepared Scrub's mama a plate. If there's somethin' more to Antwon you can tell me 'cause I'm really startin' to care for this boy. Just tell me the truth, I'm a big girl… an' I can handle it." I pleaded as my eyes grew big and watery.

Mama loosened the grip of the broom handle after she saw my eyes and the heard the cracking in my voice. She knew me all too well and my amazing resolve. And Mama knew tears didn't flow often when it came to her eldest.

"Child, this boy is not good fo' you. I have firsthand knowledge that he isn't tellin' you the whole truth about himself. If you continue to associate yo'self with this boy he will take you down with him and jeopardize all what you've strived fo'." Mama pleadingly.

"Why don't you let me be the judge of that Mama? Let me make that decision." I could not contain the pools that filled my eyes. A second later—a deluge.

Mama spoke softly because she knew I was hurt. She remembered brining Songbird to meet her folks for the first time and asked herself— *What young girl does not butt head with their parents over a boy?*

"Quintavia, Lil Boy has seen Antwon at Ol' Hickory servin' drugs out there in his lil pickup truck. He told me that he uses his car washin' business as a front. Antwon hasn't been straight with you from the get go." Mama stated.

"Lil Boy? You get yo' information from that deadbeat and you believe him? You know Lil Boy don't care fo' me and would be pleased as punch to see me unhappy. Where yo' man right now? Out there, sittin' under a tree, one o'clock in the mornin' gettin' drunk, or maybe he's fuckin' one of his baby's mamas. I don't care what you say; I'm goin' to make my own decision who I'm goin' to be wit'. I suggest you reevaluate yo' own situation befo' trying to better mine!"

I stormed into my bedroom. I'm sure, Mama had thoughts of hurling that broom at me like a spear, but her better judgment got the best of her. Normally, Mama would not be so forgiving, but she knew I was in agony. And even though she knew I was outta line, Mama provided me a pass because there was some truth to my statements about her new man, Lil Boy.

###

"Hello, who's this?" Tamara answered half asleep.

"Hi Baby, Sorry to call so early, but I'm trying to place a couple of children on my removal, but the foster parents do not speak a lick of English." I said exhaustedly.

"Damn, Jeremiah it's 2 o'clock in the morning. You got that case yesterday around 3pm, what happened?"

"There were five kids that needed to be placed. I placed one with his biological father and the other two went to a relative's home, a paternal great aunt. I had to complete homestudies on both placements. I couldn't find relative placements for the other two. I tried leaving them with a maternal uncle, but he had a disqualifying hit for a drug conviction in '94. Between the drive, the fruitless homestudy on the uncle— that ate up two hours of my day, and the tremendous wait time for placement…it's been a Christmas to remember. I just got a shelter placement for the kids and it's here in Hialeah."

"I see your point J. Sorry you had such a rough one. I wish I was there to help you." She said comfortingly.

"No problem Babe. Can you tell the Ms. Toledo, the foster parent, that Bryant is lactose intolerant and Byron is asthmatic and takes Albuterol? I'm going to have to contact Children's Medical Services to see if they can refill Byron's prescription. These kids are coming here with just the clothes on their backs".

"Put her on the line."

I placed my cell phone on speaker mode and held the phone in front of me so Ms. Toledo and I could hear:

"Buenas, Señora Toledo, Mi nombre es Tamara Norvil, y soy una Investigadora de Protección de Menores le estoy hablando de parte de el Investigador Jeremiah Abundo!"

"Buenas Señora Norvil, estoy sorprendida que el investigador Jeremiah no hable Espanol- Su apellido es Abundo?"

"Los padres de Jeremiah son de las Filipinas, que fueron colonizado por los Españoles hace mucho tiempo."

"O! Ya veo."

"Gracias por recibir estos niños a esta hora tan tarde. Bryant es intolerante a la lactosa y Byron es Asmático. También, el investigador Abundo se pondrá en contacto con el Servicio Medico para Niños, a ver si se puede rellenar la receta de Byron mañana. Byron esta tomando Albuterol. Desafortunadamente, los niños están viniendo a su casa nada mas con la ropa que tienen puesta."

"No hay problema, Ningún problema en absoluto. Me asegurare de que Bryant se mantenga alejado de los productos lácteos y que a Byron se le de sus tratamientos para el asma. En cuanto a la ropa, tengo bastante que le servirán a estos niños."

"Gracias por toda su ayuda, Señora Toledo. El investigador Abundo le dejara una copia de el Informe de la Colación Provisional con mi numero en el. Por Favor, deme una llamada si tiene algún problema."

I took my cell phone off speaker mode and then placed it to my ear…

"Jeremiah, I told her that you'd leave a copy of the Interim Placement Report with my contact info on it if she has any questions, so don't forget to jot my number down on it." Tamara said.

I scribbled Tamara's number on the IPR form that was completed in triplicate; I tore off the last page and gave it to Ms. Toledo.

"Thanks Babe. Sorry to wake you, I wouldn't bother you if it wasn't important." I said.

"I know Jeremiah... I know Jeremiah. Plus, you missed that sound of my voice." She said.

"Yeah Babe, I do miss your voice and some other things about you too. How's your family? Are you having fun in Naples?"

"Definitely, it's nice seeing my niece and nephew and great getting away from the Department for a couple of days. We just came from the Naples Christmas Boat Parade and we had a blast. I'm scheduled to work New Year's Eve so this is wonderful break."

"I'm actually off for New Year's Eve...I'll probably visit Mom up in Palm Beach. I've been such a horrible son since I started working here. But let me call you later. Ms Toledo looks like she needs to get the boys settled in. And I must say my goodbyes."

"Do you need anything else Jeremiah"? She asked before letting out a big yawn.

"No that's everything Babe. Thanks for picking up." I said then she hung up.

7 AFTERMATH

I awoke early at 6:30am, this Tuesday morning and it wasn't because I had to get ready for school—it was Christmas recess and I could have slept in. I didn't get much sleep after my argument with Mama. I tossed and turned in my bed restlessly and barely got any sleep. All night, Poo kept on askin', *Are you awright? Are you awright?*, which added to my guilt. I knew some of the awful things I said couldn't easily be mended. In my heart, I knew there had to be some truth to Mama's disclosure, even if I loathed its source. There was just too much attention to detail and too much coincidence for it to be false. I decided to cook the family breakfast to atone for my behavior—a minor penance. It's something Songbird did when he was at odds with Mama an' like my daddy, I love participatin' in the act itself. It's somethin' about providing your loved ones life-giving nourishment with your own two hands that makes that act cathartic. Like Songbird, I liked to surprise the family by making a truly homemade breakfast— nothing packaged or processed. Today's menu included: homemade biscuits, grits, eggs, fried chicken and waffles. One thing I could not replicate was Songbird's beautiful voice as he pleasantly wakened his family. Last night, the second I closed the door to my bedroom, I prayed that God would right things. Nowadays, God was so foreign to our family since Songbird past. On Sundays after breakfast, our family would venture to First Baptist Antioch on Northwest 22nd Avenue and Northwest 44th Street. The church was a small, storefront approximately 2000-square feet which was formally a dry cleaning business. Pastor Willie Wilkins made a deal with the owner to lease the space in as-is condition in exchange for a break on the rent. The owner welcomed the deal since it was more expensive to remove some of the more permanently mounted/fixed equipment. When Pastor Willie gave his sermons on Sundays everyone ignored the dry-cleaning hooks that hovered from above and the two mammoth-sized exhaust fans situated right above the alter. Songbird always joked that we attended the most-blessed church in Miami citing the adage "Cleanliness is next to godliness".

The smell of the home-cooked breakfast permeated the air as the sound of our plastic silver bells played Hark! The Herald Angels Sing. After listening to the playlist for the past 30-days, I committed the list to rote memory: Hark! The Herald Angels Sing, The Twelve Days of Christmas, O Little Town of Bethlehem, The First Noel, O' Come All Ye Faithful, Jolly Old St Nicholas Away in a Manger, Deck the Halls, and We Wish you a Merry Christmas.

I wore an extra-large Gloria Estefan Concert t-shirt which commemorated the American Airline Arena's inaugural event January 2, 2000. The shirt fit like a sleeping gown due to my short stature. The shirt was another perk from Mama's job. My pink-polka dot headwrap kept any strands of hair from falling into my cooking. I fished three Styrofoam plates out of the pantry and doled out equal portions of food on the plate. I gave Poo an extra waffle due to his sweet tooth. As I began plating the food, I could feel my spirits lift. I couldn't wait to see Mama an' Poo's faces after they got their first forkfuls of my Day-After-Christmas Breakfast. As The First Noel blasted from the off key bells. I sang the lyrics:

The First Noel, the Angels did say
Was to certain poor shepherds in fields as they lay
In fields where they lay keeping their sheep
On a cold winter's night that was so deep.
Noel, Noel, Noel, Noel
Born is the King of Israel!

While in the kitchen, I heard steps approaching as I continued to plate the food from the stove. One more dollop of grits and a piece of crispy piece of fried chicken and waffle, then the plates were complete.

"Mama, I wanted to apologize for my behavior…." I blurted eyeing my ladleful of grits trying to keep them from spilling over.

"Quintavia I don't know what's mo' delightful, yo' singin' or the delicious smell comin' outta this kitchen? What did you prepare for us this mornin'"?

I turned to find a Lil Boy at the entryway of kitchen. He wore one of Ms. Denise's robes, which was obscenely tight fitting; his lower thighs and forearms were exposed. He looked like he hasn't slept in 36-hours.

"Archie, what'chu doin' here? Where's Mama"? I demanded.

"She went to clean a house on Key Biscayne—I drove her there myself. As for me, I live here. I'm the head of the household— or don't you 'member? I'm the king of this hur castle an' right now yo' highness is hungry!"

"Okay wait outside the kitchen and I'll fix you a plate." I said.

Lil Boy didn't budge; he knew better 'cause if he did I'd slip somethin' in his shit so quick I'd change his whole life around--possibly D-Con grits with a side of Drano Eggs.

"Quintavia, yo' Mama told me how you went off on her last night an' it really hurt her feelin's. I had to console her all the way to work. I owe you an apology though…I didn't want to cause no problems between you and yo' mama. It just broke my heart to share that information with her. But that boy you messin' with is gonna cause you some real heartache. It's best you stay way clear of him." Lil Boy said in a garbled tone. The whites of his eyes matched the pink polka dots on my headwrap.

"Archie, I know yo' ol' ass received immense pleasure at tellin' Ms. Denise about 'Twon….you a spiteful ol' man! You come into people's lives and leave destruction everywhere you go!" I yelled.

"See Gurl, there you go again, gettin' flip out da tha mouth. You gonna have to learn some respect for yo' elders lil gurl." He said.

Archie moved closer towards me cutting off any possible escape route out of the narrow galley kitchen. I eyed anythin' I could get my hands on to use as a weapon, but before I could pick up the empty sauce pan used for the grits, Archie pounced on my and subdued me with one of his smotherin' bear hugs.

"Don't move Gurl…just enjoy tha moment." He whispered in my ear. I felt his penis on the small of my back. I tried to escape his hold, but his grip was inextricable. The smell of stale urine and cheap liquor was inescapable and making me dizzy.

"Get the fuck off of me Archie, or I'll tell Ma…"

"What? You finna tell yo' mama. Yo' mama ain't gonna believe you not after the way you carried on last night. Plus, I got mind control over yo' mama Gurl. I don't know if she'll ever look at you the same way. Now fo' yo' fuckin' mouth, I got somethin' to clean that filthy mouth out wit' an' it ain't soap!" Archie spoke calmly in my ear. From behind, I could feel his bushy beard grazing across my smooth face.

I couldn't move. My screams went unheard in the windowless galley kitchen. The more I struggled, the tighter his grip. I almost vomited as Lil Boy cupped my breast under my loose t-shirt. Then, his other hand slowly moved down to my panties. The second I felt his genitals touch my bare skin, my body went limp.

"Please Archie just get off me. Just get off me. I won't tell anyone."

"Damn right you ain't finna tell anyone about this! Just 'member that I'm the king— and I'm hur to stay and you just a lowly servant, here to serve me. Next time you raise up, 'member how this feels…an' 'member how I can take you anytime I want!" Lil Boy growled as he grabbed my neck and pushed it down towards the kitchen counter.

He released me from his hold just as Poo entered the kitchen.

"A what'chu doin' in here? Queen you made waffles! I love your waffles!" Poo said oblivious to the events that just transpired. His exhilaration blinded him from seeing tears streamin' down his big sister's face.

"Poo go wait at the table, and I'll bring you a plate." I said trying to regain my composure, but failing miserably.

Lil Boy pulled the hem of the ill-fitting robe down and retied its belt. You could see he was still on hard as he walked to the dining table to join Poo. But before he left, he gave me a wink an' a quick smirk before he bellowed,

"Yeah Poo…I'll be there in a second Boy! We finna eat good this mornin'!"

I couldn't control my hands from shaking as I realized I was minutes away from the unthinkable. But what just happened was more than enough. The instantaneous shift in power blew me away: I went from being Lil Boy's young nemesis and adversary to his underling and slave to his sick desires. His words would haunt me for weeks to come… *'member how this feels…an' 'member how I can take you anytime I want!*

8 THE 808

January 5, 2001
(Downtown Miami)

"**R**honda— honey can you pass me another glazed"? Mrs. Thompson asked as she collated paperwork for Unit 808's Monthly Meeting.

"No problem Ms. Thompson." Rhonda replied as she passed the unit secretary a warm Krispy Kreme doughnut.

I looked at the meeting's agenda and eyed my wristwatch, *9:45am* and turned to my supervisor.

"Hey Supe, are you keeping us long? I have an Initial Review due before 12:30pm"?

"Jeremiah you may need to bring your laptop to this meeting since we've got quite a bit to cover. This is the first unit meeting of the New Year and it's always packed with information." My unit supervisor Jamie "Supe" Watkins answered. "Oh….and Jeremiah when you come back from your office stop by Abassi's and tell him to come on. We need to start this meeting and finish so we can go about our day."

"No Problem Supe!"

I grabbed my laptop and headed two offices down to the one belonging to CPI Abassi Okafor. I saw the bald, Nigerian Black man tilting his head as he peered through his thick bifocals at a monochromatic computer screen. CPI Okafor was updating the demographic information in FAHIS (Florida Abuse Hotline Information System). Even after his lengthy tenure with the Department, Abassi was limited to hunting and pecking on his

130

keyboard; his keyboarding prowess— a whopping 19-words per minute. Since supervising Abassi for almost seven years, Jamie invested both time and money at enhancing her senior investigator's typing skills through the procurement of the PC program **Mavis Beacon Teaches Typing**. But Abassi abhorred the program's use of arcade games and novelties to teach the frustrating skill. I fell out when Jamie told me of Abassi's most recent review of **Mavis Beacon Teaches Typing Deluxe Version 11:**

"One minute you are drag racing then the next minute you are playing Missile Command using the alphabet. This is just bullshit Jamie! I have to update my FAHIS and close cases. Mavis Beacon can go fuck off!"

If Bassi only knew Mavis Beacon was a fictitious character! I admired my mentor's exemplary work ethic, since he knew he was slower, he came to work earlier. While I was just rolling out of bed, Bassi had coffee brewing 7am each work day.

"Hi Bassi? Hope you had a good Christmas and a Happy New Year." I exclaimed. The salutation startled him from his computer work.

"Christmas… you know I don't believe in that Santa Claus Ho Ho Ho Shit. I'm Muslim brother. Did you forget?" He said stoically as he turned in his chair and looked up at me.

"Yes I did. As-Salamu Alaykum Brother Okafor!"

"Wa laikum As Salaam! Brother Abundo. Happy New Year and a Merry Christmas to you and your family, I hope you had a blessed one!"

Abassi arose from his office chair and gave me big a hug. I received similar receptions from most of the Nigerians who worked for the Department and was flattered at the friendly gestures.

"Our unit meeting is about to start and Jamie said it's going to be a lengthy one." I said

"Okay, I'm right behind you."

As Abassi trailed me, he placed his hand on my shoulder and then whispered in my ear.

"Brother Jeremiah, I'm going to need your assistance tonight, if possible"?

"Sure Bassi, What's tonight?"

"Tonight is Friday Boss. It's Friday night." Bassi stated vaguely.

Child Protection Investigator Supervisor (CPIS) Jamie Watkins paced in her office waiting for her unit meeting to start. In 15-years of working with the Department, Jamie Watkins' office was filled with various trinkets and mementos of her topsy-turvy career. Numerous plaques and certificates adorned her wall, some of significance and most used as filler. Jamie chose to memorialize anything that impacted her while she worked at the Department—both good and bad. She framed an article in **The Post** titled DCF Imposter Tries to Steal Children printed January 1990. The article describes how an imposter tried to use Jamie's name and likeness to remove a sibling group in Little Havana—they never caught the imposter. To the top of that article hung another, Jealous Boyfriend Kills Mother and 2-children printed May 1988. The article chronicles the brutal murders perpetrated by paramour Derrick Sullivan who after released from the Dade County Jail, walked straight to the home of Rachel Stanford and her two children Wyatt and Wilma and shot and killed the entire family. Jamie had an open investigation with the family alleging 'Family Violence Threatens Child', the Department's maltreatment code for domestic violence. Consequently, the initial investigation was generated by law enforcement after Sullivan was first arrested for punching and biting Rachel weeks before the tragic incident. When the media found out about DCF's open case, Administration attempted to scapegoat

Jamie for the deaths, claiming she didn't do enough to protect the children. Only when relatives came to Jamie's defense in the Press did Administration halt its inquisition. Apparently, Jamie spoke to so many of the relatives trying to convince them to cajole Rachel to enter a domestic violence shelter with her children; the family members knew the young CPI did her very best to help the Stanford family. Her proudest achievement came in the form of a clear 1-foot by 1-foot acrylic plaque engraved **Child Protection Worker of the Year** which was issued at the 1993 Dependency Summit in Orlando. The annual event attracts dependency professionals throughout the state of Florida: including investigators, supervisors, case managers, administrators, attorneys, and even judges. When Jamie became the recipient of this prestigious award; it was one of the most joyous days of her life. Now, seeing the dusty plaque reminds her of her co-workers…trampled, mangled and spent. The same co-workers, who may never receive a single accolade in their tenure, internally or externally, but continue their heroic efforts to protect Florida's children on a daily basis. She stared at the plaque which was in desperate need of a good cleaning. Using a damp Krispy Kreme napkin she wiped away a thin film of dust, instantly rejuvenating it to its original state. She ran her fingertips over the plaque's engravings and was instantly transported.

"Hello Ms. Nunez. My name is Jamie Watkins; I am a Child Protective Investigator for the Florida Department of Health and Rehabilitative Services. I'm calling to speak with Antonio Fajardo?"

"Who?—" Then the caller quickly hung up."

I moved to the next row on my list. The list contained 52-or-so entries— all scattered throughout Miami Dade. Each of the columns contained: the parent's name, alleged maltreatment, number of children in the home, address and phone number. After my attempt at contacting a person, I marked a "√" next to the entry if phone contact was made and an "X" if contact was not made. I went through twenty-three names so far and managed to mark only three "√" on my list.

This storm was a doozy. Over 145,000 people lost phone service and millions were without electricity. After the storm, we spent our days yearning for a glass of cold water and at nights praying that God would deliver us from the uncertainty of South Florida's darkness. I moved to the next name on my list.

Joel Shapiro	Physical Abuse	2	15601 Howard Drive, Miami, FL	305 256 6558

I dialed Joel Shapiro's telephone number. After half a dozen rings a man answered.

"Hello"

"Hello, I am looking for Mr. Joel Shapiro."

"This is Mr. Shapiro, How can I help you?"

"Yes Mr. Shapiro, My name is Jamie Watkins; I am a Child Protective Investigator for the Florida Department of Health and Rehabilitative Services. I'm calling to see if your family needs any assistance from my agency. I know this storm has caused a lot of stress..."

"Are you kidding me? HRS is calling me about my children? Right now we have no power! No ice! We're short on food and I have half-a-fucking a roof! Why are you guys trying to complicate my life anymore than it already is?"

"I understand your frustration about the Hurricane Mr. Shapiro, but I just don't want you to get frustrated at your children because it is not their fault. Please, just be patient with them. That's all we ask."

In the background, I could hear the muffled sounds of children crying...almost wailing. After Mr. Shapiro barked at them the sounds ceased instantly.

"Ms. Watkins of HRS…you can't do anything for me or my family if your name isn't FPL, State Farm or Glacier Ice. I live in Country Walk and this is not the ghetto, I suggest you help some needy family in the Hood!" Mr. Shapiro blared sarcastically.

I attempted to employ a different tact to diffuse the situation.

"I can hear you are frustrated Mr. Shapiro…"

CLICK

I could have marked my fourth "√" on my list, but I didn't. Before Joel Shapiro hung up on me I heard the children wailing again, this time I distinctly heard a tiny male voice begging for "Help." I tried calling back a few times after, but nothing. Turning a deaf ear to crying children is something I couldn't do, especially if these children lived a stone's throw from me.

After Hurricane Andrew, the Category 5 monster the leveled South Florida on August 24, 1992, a majority of South Floridians did without lights, clean water and roofs for months. The damage sustained from Andrew totaled over $27-billion. The Florida Department of Health and Rehabilitative Services still manned calls to the abuse registry after the hurricane and since gas was in such short supply HRS altered its policy requiring its CPIs to make contact with their families by phone. Consequently, the Hurricane created a slew of issues for children due to the chaos. Kids were being left home alone and not being fed, domestic altercations were rampant and some parents could not keep their cool when their children whined about being "sticky", "hot" and "hungry." I talked to my supervisor at the time, Patrick Dutton, and apprised him of my conversation with Mr. Shapiro. After pleading with him, he gave me the green light to visit the Shapiro residence to check on things since it was just walking distance from my home. His only caveat, "As long as you're not wasting the State's precious gas— proceed with your investigation CPI Watkins."

The Shapiro residence was about one mile from my home. I packed a knapsack which included a flashlight, some Twinkies, some potato chips, a few bottles of water, mosquito repellant and my first aid kit. Attempting to drive my car through the maze of downed trees and power lines didn't make much sense so I decided to walk. On August 30, 1992 around 7pm, I began my mission down Southwest 157th Avenue which intersected with Howard Drive. The streets were somewhat clear. As I walked, I was surprised some of my neighbors took the initiative to use chainsaws to cut fallen palms which blocked streets and stacked the cut pieces in their swales. I smiled when I saw a 70-foot Royal Palm cut into quarters neatly stacked in front of someone's house; I knew it must have took a collective effort to handle that task. Almost every home had some type of roof damage, while others had windows blown out. Some residents spray painted their claim numbers with their home insurance carrier right on their garage doors: "State Farm #FL52523", "Geico #5452", "Progressive #x254276" and "All Stare #8583647". The hum of portable gas generators filled the air. Many families camped out in front of their homes to guard against looters. While the zealous hovered on rooftops—shirtless men strapped with bandoleers of ammunition and Mini-14s. I passed a 2-story townhome, and I waved at a family who looked like they were tailgating in their front yard. Their setup included a: 50" projection TV, beer, barbeque and patio lounge chairs. I couldn't blame them; you had to do anything to escape the stifling heat inside of your house. As I approached the Village Homes at Country Walk, a small housing subdivision, I almost feinted when I saw these homes were totally obliterated by Andrew. For most of these homes, there was no where to spray paint claim/insurance information, just giant mountains of wood, drywall, wires and bent metal. The homeowners looked like zombies rummaging through the destruction hoping to find bits and pieces of their pasts still intact.

After walking another five minutes, I finally arrived at 15601 Howard Drive, Miami, FL, the Shapiro's residence. From the sidewalk, I could hear the yelling and the cries of children over the noise of the loud generators. It was almost 8pm and almost pitch dark so I fished out my flashlight then I approached the door and banged on it.

"Hello Mr. Shapiro I need to see your children." I yelled flashing my identification.

Mr. Shapiro cracked the door, while tiny faces cowered in the distance.

"Boy you guys are persistent, I'll give you that. But like I told you before I don't need your damn help. My boys are just fine, and I wish you would just leave!" He screamed.

"I'm afraid there's a little more to this than you think Mr. Shapiro. I am not leaving until I'm sure your children are safe. I heard you screaming at them from the sidewalk and you did the same thing over the phone." I said aiming my flashlight inside the pitch dark house.

"You better call the police then because you are not entering my home!" Mr. Shapiro stated as he proceeded to shut the door. But before he could fully shut it, I chocked my right foot between the door and the jamb to prevent it from closing.

"I guess that's what I'll have to do. Just remember one thing Mr. Shapiro, the County Jail doesn't have A/C either and the gentleman down there don't take kindly to child abusers." I calmly replied as I freed my foot from the door and the jamb.

I made half way down the front yard before Joel Shapiro begged me for forgiveness. Later, I discovered minor evidence of physical abuse on both of his children, Isaiah and Ishmael. But what landed me the coveted **Child Protection Worker of the Year Award** is that I recovered two missing children from California: the Shapiro boys were victims of an interstate parental abduction according to the National Center for Missing & Exploited Children. Their poor mother was separated from her boys for three years.

###

"Glad you can join us gentlemen. Please take a seat." Supe Watkins stated.

Unit 808 gathered in CPIS Watkins' office like we did every first Friday of the month. At one point, the 6-chairs that surrounded the circular desk in Jamie's office were filled but for the past few months, recidivism in our unit— and the agency as a whole was at an all time high. It was almost impossible keeping a full unit. Watkins had 6-FTEs (full-time employees) detailed to her unit; Mrs. Jessica Thompson held one those position numbers as the unit secretary. Currently, 808 was down two CPIs.

"Firstly, I want to thank you for all being here; it's always wonderful working with such a talented bunch of people. I hope each of your families had a wonderful holiday season and a Happy New Year. I wanted to start our first unit meeting promptly because I know you want to prepare yourselves for Monday. On Monday, all the kids will be back in school. Let's see if we can make it 'till summer break with our core intact" Supe stated.

I was happily chomping on a cruller. I always liked Supe's meetings because she fed us, plus she took the time to convey essential information needed to do our jobs. She always kept us abreast of changes in judicial procedures and protocols, provided us information on any new client services, and kept us aware of the state of our agency as a whole. Many supervisors didn't have these meetings with their investigators, which meant CPIs had to fend for themselves like

Tamara. She drafted a 12-page shelter petition and was mortified when she had to re-do it over again because it was completed in an obsolete format. Her supervisor, Pierce Denim failed to relay the news of the change. One of the key reasons I lasted this long with the Department is because of Supe.

"**Item 1: Status.** Currently we have 108-CPIs allocated to District 11. Of these 108, 85 of these positions are filled. Basically we are operating at 78%. The 2-vacant chairs next to you indicates Unit 808 is operating at 60%. There is temporarily a hiring freeze, that's why our FTEs are yet to be replenished."

"Excuse me Jamie... but why is there is freeze? We need every able body catching cases." CPI Rhonda Jackson inquired.

"We have a freeze because Administration has to offset the costs of any overtime with hiring dollars." Supe replied. Her eyes never lifted off the agenda.

"That's bullshit!" Abassi exclaimed in his clearest English.

"I concur, straight bullshit." I added as my attention remained focused on my cruller.

"How does anyone expect to function is this working environment? We're getting a case a day...sometimes two and then we're expected to handle these tasks in forty hours? Why doesn't anyone from Tallahassee bring their asses down here to see how dangerous and difficult it is to work child abuse cases in Miami?" Abassi added.

CPIS Watkins allowed Abassi to vent before intervening.

"Abassi, we go back forever and what has ever changed?" Jamie stated rhetorically. "Correct, absolutely nothing. Keep doing the fine work you are doing because only you, your families, and God know how hard you really do work."

The statement quelled CPI Okafor.

"**Item 2: Time and Attendance**. You must sign-in and sign-out utilizing the unit's log—no questions. If you go on a case and you spend an evening in the field you have to log your in-and-out times the following day. District Administrator Chet Parker was down here the other morning around 8am and found the cubes and offices empty. He somehow equates that with us being non-productive..."

Now it was Rhonda's turn…

"When we're with families till 11pm and updatin' cases till 1am, does he still think we're non-productive. He will never understand 'cause he never did this job before." CPI Rhonda Jackson stated as she kept her eyes transfixed at her laptop. "The disconnect between line staff and Administration comes from respect. We have to respect them and they have never earned ours. 95% of the almighty Administration has never worked a child abuse case in their lives. Let's not even talk about the racial composition up there. Let me shut up now befo' I get myself in trouble…"

"Good points Rho!" I chimed in as I reached for her hand to provide tender consolation. Rhonda smiled and brushed me away. *I think she likey me.*

Supe quickly responded, "Don't you guys worry you will have a chance to speak your peace, Chet Parker is going to have his first meeting of the year on February 19th—so mark your calendars. It will be a district meeting so all the CPIs will be in attendance. I suggest that you speak your mind because nothing will change unless you are the catalyst. He wants to know why recidivism is at an all time high. He will then choose a few of you to form focus groups to come up with ideas to fix some of these issues."

"If there is no struggle, there is no progress." Rhonda quickly followed.

"Beautiful quote Ms. Jackson is that you?" I asked.

"No Jeremiah. That's Frederick Douglass." Rhonda gave me a look that melted me in my seat.

"**Item 3: Performance Evaluations**. The beginning of 2001 marks the start of your performance evaluations. Your evaluations will be heavily weighted on the State's seven-performance indicators which include: Cases Commenced in 24-hours, Victims Seen in 24-hours, Initial Child Safety Review Submitted in 48-hours, Cases Submitted for 45-day Disposition, and Cases Submitted for 60-day Disposition…the other two performance indicators are supervisory based. Remember if you can close a case without any safety issues within 30-days the last two performance indicators do not come into play. But you and I know that this is next to impossible the way these cases are flying in and the limited staff we have to receive them. The commencement of your case begins after you make a good faith effort to see your child. So everyone should be at 100% regarding this indicator. The Initial 48-Hour Review Submission is something you can also can control. Just give yourself ample enough time to complete your Child Safety Assessment…and I do not want to hear about system outages or broken laptops. Always expect the unexpected…and I almost forgot after you spend all that time inputting your Safety Assessment remember to hit 'Send'. It's still a missed CSA if you don't hit 'Send'." Supe methodically explained.

"Boss, we do our best to keep these families together. We keep good numbers, we come to work every day, unlike malingers in other units. What is the incentive for us to maintain this feverish pace? I haven't gotten a raise in seven years. I have been told some CPIs who graduated PDP are making more money than me!" Abassi stated while looking at me.

The truth caused me to almost gag on my cruller. I thought of finding words to console my friend, but I figured it was best to keep my mouth full. As co-workers and friends I have grown to love, I could imagine how awful Rhonda and Bassi felt to be slighted for so long. Truth is, they never had any animosity towards me or withheld any of their precious knowledge to undermine me because I was new. It seemed the longer you worked at the Department the less value you had. What did Mr. Ely say? "…*when they are done with you, they replace you with a newer—not necessarily better part.*"

"Bassi, I've known you for how long? And even though the Department can trample on you, you still continue to remain one of the finest CPIs in the district. This goes for you too Rhonda. Without you guys, CPIs like Jeremiah wouldn't have anyone to model after. For this I thank you both." Jamie replied.

Like always, CPIS Watkins knew exactly what to say to pacify her staff. Supe taught me that a few kind words like "Thank You" and "Please" can go a long way, not only with your staff, but with your clients.

"As for our Victim Seen in 24-hour Percentage, it's at an abysmal 65%. This is one stat we need to continue to work on. We are one of the one of the lowest ranking units in the district. However, I don't want you to sacrifice your integrity for good numbers. If you didn't see 'em, you just didn't.'"

Now it was my turn to speak, I raised my hand to ask a question like I was in third grade. Ms. Thompson shook her head.

"Go ahead Jeremiah." Supe stated.

"I know I've only been here for a few months, but I know my issue with the Victim Seen Percentage. On almost every 24 I receive, I'm given hours to see the victim—sometimes I only get three or four hours. Mondays are the worst; I got a case last week that came in on a Sunday at 11am and it was rolled-over and given to me the following day, Monday morning! I had an hour an-a-half to see four victims." I stated.

"A very astute observation Jeremiah. Your performance and professional standing are predicated on mechanisms destined to fail…" CPIS Watkins stated as she gestured at Ms. Thompson to close her office door. When the door was shut she continued.

"…Since you came to the 808 months back, you've helped everyone in this unit. You helped Rhonda during a removal your first day stepping foot in this office. You went on cases for Bassi. I saw you the other night after work helping Ms. Thompson on the 5th floor of the South parking garage plugging her tire after she ran over a nail. Your dedication to your co-workers speaks for itself, I cannot even expound on your dedication to our clients. Why do you choose to do these things Jeremiah?" Supe asked.

I was thrown by the question. I was never at a loss for words, but the question had me stymied.

"I guess my parents raised me well?" I replied.

"Yes, your parents definitely did raise a good boy." Jamie stated as Rhonda rubbed my deltoid for confirmation.

"…and I guess I just care about other people." I added.

"Exactly, you care Jeremiah. You care about everyone and everything. Our beloved Department does not care. The system does not feel—it has no heart!" Supe stated passionately. Her last sentence caught everyone's attention— our eyes were fixed on CPIS Watkins as she spoke.

"Bassi just did his 20-years and I just did my 15 and we did not receive any acknowledgement from the State— or even from our own Administration? Not a card, not a call, or even a Lotus Note. Jeremiah, I know you don't have any kids, but for those of us that do, we have to spend an arm and a leg on daycare. For goodness sake, DCF licenses every daycare in Florida and even provides temporary subsidized daycare vouchers for most of our clients…so even after we spend countless days and nights caring for other people's children, why can't the Department give its own employees a break on daycare?" Supe questioned leaving the 808 silent. She continued:

"How many cases do you have open?" Supe asked as she pointed to Rho…

"30"

…and then to Bassi.

"33"

…and then to me.

"25"

Supe continued:

"I know there are some nights you stay awake hoping nothing implodes on any of your cases even though you did everything in your power before you left that family's house. Pray nothing happens because you're only good as your last case around here. The Department cares little for its employees when a tragedy occurs because you are expendable. When a child dies, they fire you and me…then they attempt to fill every vacant position and pump every resource into this district trying to pacify the media and quell any public scrutiny. Little by little as our budget dries up, those resources and FTE position numbers vanish into wind, until the next tragedy takes place. Jeremiah, you've witnessed these disservices to the employees, one day you will see how it adversely affects our service to our clients."

CPIS Watkins gazed at the framed article **Jealous Boyfriend Kills Mother and 2-children** hanging on the wall beyond the vision of her unit members. A loud chime from Gesu Catholic Church's Bell Tower off Northeast 2nd Street jogged Supe from her daze. The noon chime also reminded me of my own Initial Review that was due in 30-minutes. I cracked open my Dell laptop and began hammering out my Initial Review to submit to my supervisor. The rapid sound of my keystrokes provided a strange background track for the rest of our meeting.

"Mrs. Thompson it's noon. How many cases has Screeners given the unit thus far?" CPIS Watkins asked.

"We have three Jamie, one for each of the CPIs. This is Screeners first pull. It's likely that the CPIs will see a second case before day's end." Mrs. Thompson held the freshly pulled cases in a fan like a hand of Three Card Poker.

"Are we breaking this meeting early Ms. Watkins"? Our unit secretary asked.

"No…not just yet. We have a few more important items to cover and then we'll be done." Supe replied as she scanned her agenda.

"**Item 4: Documentation**. You must have two relevant collateral contacts on each of your cases. One of these collaterals must be from an unbiased source (teacher, pediatrician, therapist, etc). Please clearly document the collateral's name, title, and contact information and the time and date you spoke with them. If services are put in the home to prevent the removal or displacement of the children, you must document that a service provider is engaging these services with your clients. And if you remove a child and place the child in shelter, you must document any efforts you made to locate and place the children with relatives as your first option. Any questions?"

My unit remained reticent.

"**Item 5: Transfer Cases from CPI to CPI which require shelter court involvement**. This one was a hot topic in our last supervisors meeting we had before the end of 2000. The topic was tabled because of a transfer we received in this unit. Last month, Rhonda received one of her prior cases back from CPI Preston Hall who commenced the case and then transferred the case back to Rhonda. The case alleged that the mother was leaving her three children with random relatives for days and sometimes weeks. The last time she left, the relatives were having great difficulty locating mom, so a report was generated. Preston found out the mother was arrested on a possession charge and was being detained at the Women's Annex... Instead of filing a shelter petition and giving the relatives legal custody of the children, right then, a petition was not filed and court action was not taken. Preston allowed the mother to scoop up all of her children from these relatives including a 3-month old newborn after the mother agreed to take a drug test. Preston knew this case was coming back to Rhonda so he threw a band-aid on this one and sent it back to us. Consequently, there are 6-priors on this family. The last case was also drug related, but mother was compliant with her substance abuse counseling before we closed our case. When this case was transferred back to Rhonda, it was a powder keg. Unfortunately, I was in Broward for the Infant Mental Health Training when this case entered our unit, so I didn't have a chance to review the case. To make a long story short, the mother didn't go to her drug test and now she can't be found or any of her kids. Point blank, a petition should have been filed by

Preston Hall rather than leaving this powder keg to blow up on Rhonda's watch. When I called Preston's supervisor…"

I quickly turned to Rho and whispered, "Who's Preston's Supervisor"?

"Some new guy Pierce Denim…seems like a very unhappy person if you ask me." Rho replied as she cleaned her glasses with the sleeve of her pink DCF polo.

"…he told me that our unit should have done a better job with our case when we had it the first time around, then hung up on me. At our last supervisors meeting, Denim and I had it out, we had to take an early lunch because it got so intense. As a result of our skirmish, a new protocol has been drafted and it goes as follows: In the event you remove a child for another CPI, prior to the transfer of this case. You must: complete the Initial CSA, add all children to the HSN database for the service component, make sure any parental/sibling visitations are completed if the children are in shelter placement, attend the shelter hearing, fingerprint and photograph the children, and staff case with Services for transfer. Basically you do everything, so the clients do not suffer and safety is not compromised. Any questions?"

"Boss lady, what is the policy regarding prior cases for veterans? Is it still at two years"? Bassi inquired.

"Yes, Mr. Okafor. If you worked with a family in the past and a new case comes in, you will receive the new case on this family if the hotline intake date is within two years of the hotline intake date of the last prior. If the new case's intake date is past the two year mark, the case will be assigned to a new investigator. However, you still must have a staffing with the previous investigator who worked the last case…and as always please document your exchanges with these investigators in your notes." Supe advised.

"Last Item: the Holiday Schedule and Upcoming Events Please mark these dates in your calendars. After the fiasco we had this past holiday season filling coverage spots, Administration has decided to assign a particular units to cover the district during the holidays. We are assigned to work these to holidays in 2001:

Labor Day, 9/3 (3pm-11pm)
Christmas Day, 12/25 (3pm-11pm)."

"Damn another Christmas!" I cursed aloud.

"No skin off my dick brother, I don't celebrate that shit." Bassi laughed while jabbing me with his finger.

"Sorry folks we drew numbers out of a hat and it's pretty much etched in stone. If it's any consolation I will be your supervisor during these coverage periods." Supe added.

"Maybe we can bring our families to the office and have a Christmas/Office party here?" Mrs. Thompson injected.

"That sounds like a nice thought Mrs. Thompson, but we'll be out on cases leavin' our loved ones trapped here in this hot-ass building. At least at home, there are toys for our chil'ren to play with and a television to watch the football games. Even the Capitol Police are taking the day off, so security won't even be present in the building. We're just scarred." Rho stated.

As the unit meeting concluded, we started gathering our belongings, preparing to disperse. Jamie stopped us and provided a few more bits of information:

"Remember on February 9th which falls on a Friday, we'll be taking CPI Rhonda Jackson to dinner at the restaurant of her choosing to celebrate another great year of her life. Hopefully by then we will have a couple of these empty positions filled so they can join us in our celebration and our case catchin' bonanza. Also, please mark your calendars for February 19th, we will be having our district meeting with Mr. Parker and the entire CPI staff. This meeting is mandatory and clerical and support staff will also be in attendance. The exact time and venue will be announced at a later date. As always, it's my pleasure to work with all of you. Again, continued blessings and happiness to you and your families this coming year. This meeting is adjourned if there are no more questions?"

###

I stared at CPI Abassi Okafor as he drove his black, 1990 Toyota Corolla; his eyes were glued to the road. Then I looked down at his car's instrument cluster, the odometer reading was stuck on 185,240; the vehicle's bedraggled appearance and rough ride were testaments to its years of services for the Department. I wondered how many children were actually transported in the backseat of his sedan. *Hundreds? Possibly thousands?* The Corolla's backseat was wrapped with industrial plastic and duct tape to make for easy cleaning. Abassi's own children complained of the Corolla's uncomfortable seating and aesthetics, but after a few bouts with some enuretic and encopretic children, he couldn't give a rat's ass about the complaints from his offspring.

"So what did you think about our first meeting of year"? I asked.

"Same shit, nothing new since I've been here." Bassi stated without taking his eyes off the road. "I've seen this agency's policies fluctuate so frequently— too many times to count if you ask me? The only thing that counts around here are numbers and keeping the Department out of the headlines."

"Damn, you don't sound too cynical old man?"

"It's not cynicism Jeremiah. It's the truth. This year's agenda is keeping as many kids out of foster care system as possible and what guides this agenda?—usually money. Understand there are big bucks generated each time a child enters the system. Everybody gets paid from the foster parents to the therapists to the judges— even us. And when the money well dries up, the agenda changes once again— now we're a more family-oriented and family-centered agency. When a child dies that paradigm is abandoned and everybody's children are placed in foster care. It's economics— not a true free market model because we control the variables." Abassi stated. His statement exposed his background in business and finance.

"I didn't think of it that way Bassi; I'm so caught up in my own caseload. I guess I fail to see the big picture sometimes." I said as I stuck my hand out his car window feeling the wind flap it every which way.

"Oh yeah, politicians also dictate agenda. The new one for this coming decade is Privatization. Mark my words, it's coming and Governor Jeb Bush is its biggest proponent. In a year or so, you'll see the State's entire foster care system doled out to private companies and believe me— they're going to get paid some major bucks!" Abassi stated this time peering at his rearview mirror. "When it's all said and done it is all about money. Who do you think is going to get the million dollar contracts?"

"Shit, I see your point."

"There's nothing we can do, but keep going out on these cases. So those meetings we attend are just fruitless even the one coming up on February 19th with Administration. It is just a show...Damn, let me take that back. I did discover something in our unit meeting earlier—
I did notice that Rhonda was really fawning over you. I think you have a chance with her." Bassi stated.

"Oh? Yeah?"

"Hell yeah brother, I was trying to make her my second wife, the day she joined the 808. She's smart, sexy and doesn't take shit from no one. They say us African men prefer a more docile, submissive woman, but that shit isn't true brother. We like to break girls like Rhonda; we enjoy taming their fiery spirit and breaking their backs!" Abassi took his eyes off the road for a second to give me a quick wink. "...You need to get it together young brother and read the signs and give her a shot— you're young, single and having nothing to lose."

"Well, you know..."

Abassi cut me off before I could utter another word.

"What? That you're fucking that CPI down south— the entire department knows that shit. You don't think Rhonda doesn't know that shit? She still flirts with you despite your involvement with your other girl? So what are you going to do about it? My dad had six wives in Nigeria and look how I turned out? I'd have my share of wives here if it wasn't illegal." Bassi stated excitedly.

I reclined in the Corolla's worn passenger seat and smiled at the thought of breaking the backs of Rhonda and Tamara. My mind drifted. *Maybe they'd fight over me and then reconcile by agreeing to have a threesome? Shit, why stop there! Maybe there's a chick in the North area that would complete my stable! Bishop Don Juan Abundo!* Feeling good, I lifted down the passenger-side sun visor to look at myself in its vanity mirror... but to my dismay it was missing, so I used the reflection from my Nokia phone instead. I loved checking out myself in the mirror after a fresh haircut and shave: my Caesar was on point and my face was smoother than a baby's bottom. For the New Year, I decide to take casual Fridays to a new level. I sported a royal blue Lawrence Taylor Mitchell & Ness Throwback Jersey, blue jeans and a clean, white pair of K-Swiss. The $265 jersey was a belated Christmas gift from bottom bitch, Tamara. My girl gave me and taught me a lot. One thing Tamara taught me is that this job seemed easier to do when you looked good...because first impressions mean everything.

"Bassi, where are we headed to?" I asked as I peered out a cloudy car window.

"We are heading to North Bay Village on a dirty house case. It should not be anything major since the family has no priors and youngest child in the home is 13."

"13? Shit, my dad would whip my ass if I didn't sweep the floor or handle my chores. What's going on in today's society when you can't tell you kids to get off their asses and help out?" I added.

"In my country, if you don't follow the instructions of your elders, anyone...and I mean anyone can place their hands on your children. If your child disrespects a teacher, they have authority to punish your child. If you're away and your neighbor sees your child behaving poorly, they can whip them too. A couple of years ago Hilary Clinton's wrote a book **It Takes a Village** which subscribes to the community methodology of raising children. We all need to put our pride aside and accept that we need each other." Bassi stated in his thick native accent.

"I get a lot of that when I go on cases. Parents dislike DCF because we come into their homes and tell them how to raise their children. I understand their frustration Bassi, but some of these parents don't have a clue. The other day I had a case with a 17-year boy who wanted to take his new Acura CL to his girlfriend's house, but his parents refused to let him take the car because of his poor grades. Mind you, his parents bought him the car and the parents drive a fuckin' raggedy 1988 Dodge Caravan. They sacrificed so much so they can give their kid the best in life. Well, the 17-year old attempted to choke his dad out when he refused to furnish him the keys, so the dad picked up the closest thing to him—a metal ladle, and whacked the child on his bicep. The blow caused a bruise to the child's arm. So what do you think happened next?"

"The boy called the Hotline"? Bassi said shaking his head.

"Yeah! The boy called the damn case in on his dad after he tried to choke him out. Can you believe that shit?" I said looking at my mentor. A big smile washed over his face.

"…When I got to the house the father didn't want to talk to me. He told me DCF had no right to tell him how to raise his child. I took him aside and I broke it down for him Bassi. I told him that he was a fool for buying an eleventh grader with a D+ average a $32,000 car. And if his son could negotiate a deal like that with his parents, he never respected them. That's when the dad started crying. I told him you don't have to buy your child the world, just earn his respect."

"That's an interesting angle Jeremiah, but shouldn't children already respect their parents?" Bassi countered as he turned east on to Northwest 79th Street.

"When I say earn…I mean teach. Teach your children the value of waking up in the morning and going to work. Teach them that life at 17 with no job, no responsibility and fucked up grades is a Dodge Caravan— if you're lucky… not a fresh from the factory Acura!"

As I discussed the Rodriguez case with Bassi, I thought of my own parents and the sacrifices they've made. I remembered the days Dad woke up at 5am to have his plate of *tuyo* with eggs and rice then headed out to work. Most days he'd be back later that night, but there were many times he'd be gone for days until his ship reentered port. Then thoughts of my mother Cynthia emerged—pulling doubles and doing extra hours at the hospital, so the family house didn't perish into foreclosure after Dad passed.

"Well what happened with the boy, he had a mark on him right? Did you take it to court? Did law enforcement take the father down"? Bassi asked.

"No, none of the above. I had to talk to Dr. Tanner of the Child Protection Team and explained that the father was trying to defend himself. I also had to speak to the Detective with the Sweetwater police and advise him of our stance and that we had CPT's backing. They did not arrest the dad or take it to court. However, I did refer the family for intensive in-home services."

"So you advocated for the parents on this one?" My mentor asked.

"That I did."

"Good man. Good work CPI Abundo."

I took the compliment to heart since CPI Okafor spent almost the same amount of years protecting children as I've been drawing God's air. Through all the chaos, scandals and madness, Bassi held fast and remained steady: he never lost his cool—ever.

"Bassi, what's that hanging from your rearview mirror?" I inquired.

The turquoise string of beads hypnotized me as they swung side to side as Abassi drove. Even at idle, the string jiggled due to the Corolla's need for a tune-up.

"They're called misbaha. They are my prayer beads I use when performing Dhikr."

"Nice. It's good that you find time for God even with the rigors of this job." I stated.

"You have to brother. You always have to allocate time for the Almighty."

"Funny you say that, I was raised Catholic and I used to go to mass frequently." I lamented.

"I did not peg you as a Catholic Jeremiah? I mean look at your name…it's so Old Testament!" Bassi stated.

"Yeah I was baptized and performed my first communion and the whole nine. Is there a problem with me being Catholic Bassi?"

Abassi remained quiet.

"Come on Abassi, I think we're mature enough to have a healthy discourse on religion. If you have a problem with Catholics I'd love to hear your rationale why?"

"Jeremiah no offence but your religion is the worst religion in the world."

I guffawed. Then, shot into defense mode. I maybe a bad Catholic—even a downright horrible one, but I couldn't sit idly by as some guy disrespects my religion…no sir.

"You're kidding me right? How can Catholicism be the worst religion? Explain that ludicrous statement Bassi."

He took a second, and then fired off a response…

"If you look at history there are multitudes of examples on how the Catholic Church subjugated people and exploited its power. Take for example the Spanish Inquisition. Many Jews, Protestants and Muslims were put to death or forced to convert based on the Catholic tenets. Here is another example that hits closer to home— at least for your parents. Look at Ferdinand Magellan, he attempted to circumnavigate the world backed by the Catholic Church of Spain, each stop he tainted native cultures with the virtues of Christianity. When

Magellan attacked the island of Mactan in the Philippines, he was killed by a Filipino native and Muslim, Lapu-Lapu."

My Nigerian buddy's knowledge of Philippine history impressed me and now I respected him all the more. But I still remained focused in our debate. I deftly countered...

"Bassi, every religion has exerted their authority in one form or another—if not physically then mentally. Look at your Muslim brothers. They strap bombs to one another and will blow up a plane or an innocent crowd of people. Look at your people in the Middle East, they just don't seem like they can ever be at peace. Your religion seems quite fanatical if you ask me."

Abassi took a second and volleyed back...

"Take a look at the news my brother, what's going on with Catholic's Archdiocese it seems like they are settling with some poor sole that was a victim of sexual abuse at the hands and penises of your priests!"

Ouch! He got me good, but he's not the only one who watches CNN in this car. I returned fire...

"Well, look at those nine Muslims that were charged for the gang rape of five girls in Sydney Australia last year. One of the girls was only 14. Reports cite up to nineteen actually participated in the rapes. I'd hate to know the other statistics in predominantly Muslim countries where women are not afforded the opportunity to report their victimization. It seems if Muslims are not raping women they are blowing innocent people up!"

For a minute, we sat in silence.

The Corolla finally came to rest in front of a small, 2-story condominium in North Bay Village. Often our mild discourses ended up into heated arguments like last week's feud about the better tasting knockoff soda, Winn Dixie's Dr. Chek or Publix's brand Mr. Publix. Usually, after all our debates, a peaceful resolution soon followed.

From the back seat, the loud cry of an infant broke the silence inside the cabin. The child's father immediately tended to his crying child's needs.

"Shhhh…Mustafah, Shhhh. Child it's okay. It's okay."Abassi stated as he re-nestled his son into his infant carrier. Mustafah's crying immediately ended after his father placed a pacifier in the child's mouth.

"He was so quiet the whole ride up." I stated.

"Yes he was. He is always a good boy for daddy. Jeremiah can you please pass me my case file my brother."

I handed him his newly-assigned investigation **01-0005091**.

"Okay Jeremiah, if he starts crying just give him his bottle of formula that's in his diaper bag. If he poops, I will change him. I shouldn't be long… 40 to 45-minutes tops. Thanks for keeping an eye on my son my brother."

"No problem Bassi, go handle your business, we'll be fine." I said.

Abassi walked toward the condominium, a couple of seconds later he paused then backtracked to the Corolla and poked his head through the open passenger side window.

"Oh and one more thing Jeremiah my favorite Catholic…"

"What's that Bassi"?

"Please don't molest my son while I'm gone."

I let off a big laugh as CPI Okafor trotted to his case.

"Go fuck yourself Bassi. You fuckin' terrorist." I yelled out the half- cracked window while his son remained asleep.

After a few minutes I checked on Mustafah and smiled. This isn't the first time he has been on a case with us, and I doubt it will be his last. But what do you do when there's nobody else to watch your own children, and you have a new case to investigate? Or what do you do, when your company who specializes in maintaining the welfare of all the children in the state, provides not one provision or concession for the children of its protectors? You make do and you improvise. Babysitters are expensive and you'll be hard-pressed to find one 2am on a Tuesday when the state sends you out on an Immediate/On-call case. For CPIs, Tagalongs allow us to spend a little time with our children even though it might not be under the most ideal circumstances. I always wondered what happened if we got caught— or even better, had to remove someone else's children in front of our own.

At 7:45 pm, approximately 50-minutes from the time we pulled up to the condominium, Abassi walked back to the Corolla with his investigation tucked under his arm.

"That was easy. The home just needs some straightening up and the floors just needed to be mopped. I told them I would be back at an unspecified time and date to see that their house was clean. I just have to finish my notes and complete my CSA and this one seems like an easy close. How was my son while I was away Brother?"

"Pardon the pun…he slept like a baby. Not a peep." I stated as I smiled.

"That's great. Where is your case located?

"It's at the park."

"What do you mean it's at the park"? Abassi asked skeptically.

"Yes man, it's in Tropical Park. This case involves a traveling band of carnies!"

9 HIMALAYA

The millions of lights from Santa's Enchanted Forest mesmerized Bassi, Mustafah, and me as we rode westbound on the 826.   The seasonal carnival came to Miami-Dade's Tropical Park in November right after Halloween and ran until early January of the new year. Touted as 'The World's Largest Christmas Theme Park and FREE Carnival', I knew it was destiny that Ms. Thompson blessed me with this case. Since I was a kid I had an addiction to fair food: smoked turkey legs, foot-long corndogs, Italian sausage sandwiches, and the fresh roasted corn were my favorites. For dessert, I couldn't resist the freshly-dipped candy apples and powdered elephant ears. This Friday, January 5, 2001 marked the Enchanted Forest's last weekend in Miami. Fridays were also some of the busiest days for CPIs in District 11. Mandated reporters like teachers, physicians, and therapists phoned in suspected abuse cases by the hundreds to the Tallahassee registry so they were not in violation of state law. This caused CPIs throughout the state to scurry about making home and field visits hoping to find the victims on their cases. If you didn't see them that Friday, you'd get knocked statistically on your "Victim Seen in 24-hour Percentage", one of the State's seven performance indicators for CPIs. For the ardent, many would venture out that following Saturday to locate their missing victims—with or without compensation. For the rest, Saturday was their day of rest and time to spend with their own children. But in truth, when a CPI received a case of Friday, you never escaped working on the weekend in some shape or form.

"Wow, this is a first for me Jeremiah. I never in my 20-years had a case with carnival workers." Bassi smiled as he turned into Tropical Park.

"I'm surprised the Hotline even accepted this case since the family may reside outside Florida. What do we do if the family resides outside the state? Can we still retain jurisdiction?" I asked.

"The Hotline will take any case even if the family does not reside in Florida. If children are at risk and a removal is inevitable, we remove and place the children in foster care and we take it to Dependency court for a judge to accept or reject. If the children can safely remain with the caregivers, we attain a verifiable address and call an OTI (Out of Town Inquiry) to the family's jurisdiction. We let law enforcement or child welfare services in that state or city take it over from there. What is your case about anyway?" Bassi inquired.

I rifled through my stack of abuse cases and pulled out my most recent acquisition, **01-0005711**. I read it aloud as my co-worker lurched for a parking spot:

16-year old Samson works with his mother, Lola in a traveling carnival outfit. The mother is depriving her child an education by forcing him to work at the carnival against his will. The family travels from town to town, and the lack of stability is harming the young boy. Samson hasn't been in school since he was 13. The child is also forced to sleep in an R/V. Mother is a recovering alcoholic, it's unknown if she is maintaining her sobriety. (24)

"I spoke to the reporter before I left the office this evening. The reporter is the child's paternal aunt who hasn't seen her nephew in four years. Samson's father Tanner is incarcerated in Georgia for drugs. He also has a lengthy history of domestic violence—probably why mom left him. I told the reporter that I cannot force the mother to facilitate a relationship with dad's side of the family; she called DCF because it's the only agency that took the time to listen to her grievances."

After 10-minutes of traversing through the parking lots trying to find a space, Abassi relented and parked footsteps from the main entrance of the Enchanted Forest. He opened his glove compartment and pulled out a makeshift parking placard and placed it on the dashboard.

"I break this out only during emergencies Brother."

I looked at the placard, which was fabricated out of a piece of white cardboard with a battered, photocopied certificate taped in the center. Emblazoned on the certificate was the State of Florida seal with the words, "Department of Children and Families Official State Business". As we exited the Corolla, I stared at the bootleg parking placard sitting on the dashboard of our jalopy and wondered if our car would be here when we returned from my investigation.

"Jeremiah, please carry Mustafah's diaper bag. I will carry the baby in his carrier. Make sure you have your ID."

"No problem Bassi."

The winter air was brisk and refreshing, a cold front passed through earlier today leaving the sky cloudless. The park grounds were packed. Kids and adults across South Florida were trying to get in that last bit of fun before heading back to school and work on Monday. The day also signified the last day of Christmas. When I was growing up my parents always surprised Ronald and me with one last gift—a perk of celebrating twelve days of Christmas. Watching these families enter the amusement park made me want kids all the more. After 5-minutes of walking and an additional 5-minute wait in line, we finally made it to the front of the ticket counter. The ticket attendant, a White lady wearing a floppy Santa Claus hat approaching her 40's looked totally spent and listlessly welcomed us to the Enchanted Forest.

"Welcome to Santa Enchanted forest, the World's Largest Christmas Theme Park and Free Carnival. How may I help you?"

Her monotone voice was barely audible.

"Yes ma'am. I am Child Protective Investigator Jeremiah Abundo and this is my co-worker Child Protective Investigator Abassi Okafor. We are here to investigate a case on a family that works at this carnival." I held up my identification up to the glass for verification.

She surveyed us. Dubious, the ticket attendant asked a viable question, "Do child welfare workers in Florida normally take their children on cases with them"?

Abassi sneered at the comment. I cleverly volleyed back, "This infant does not belong to Investigator Okafor or myself. This child is a product of our previous case…" I leaned into the speak hole of the counter and whispered. "This baby couldn't remain at home if you know what I mean."

The attendant drifted back into her seat and replied, "Only a dimwit, unfit parent would have a young baby out on a chilly night like this! Who are you guys looking for?"

"We're looking for Lola Banks and her son Samson. Do you know where we can find them?" I asked.

"Yes sir, they are on midway. Just go straight past the lighted elf and reindeer display and you'll find them at the Himalaya." The attendant ripped off three tickets from her roll and passed them to me through the window's slot.

"Thank you ma'am for all your help. Have a Happy New Year." I replied as I waved goodbye.

Before we could enter the Forest, we were accosted by a short, Hispanic woman in her early 20's with a digital camera slung around her neck. She wore mock reindeer antlers made of stitched cloth and foam. At the points of the antlers, there were a few embedded LED lights that would blink intermittently drawing your attention. She wore a t-shirt under her denim jacket that read, Santa's Enchanted Images.

"Hey Fellas, would you like a souvenir picture to remember tonight?" She asked.

Bassi proceeded to walk away, but I grabbed him by his forearm and thwarted his escape.

"Sure…we'd love a photo thank you." I replied.

The attendant had us pose at the entrance of the park, under a humongous 15ft wreath with a big red bow tied on to it. There were hundreds of tiny lights wrapped around and through this amazing wreath. The wreath was suspended 20-feet off the ground with wires that were strapped to two tall metal poles flanking the wreath; the poles were painted to look like candy canes. Behind the wreath, dozens of flexible LED light poles were bent into arches to form a colorful tunnel leading you into the amusement park.

I placed my right arm around Bassi as he held Mustafah in his infant carrier in front of us.

"Alright Fellas, on the count of three I want you to say 'Jingle Bells!'.........One!........Two!.......... Three!"

"Jingle Bells!!!!" I exclaimed happily. Bassi didn't say shit and quickly slithered away with his son after the camera flashed.

"Awesome Fellas, you can pick up your prints when you depart the Forest. We have a variety of packages for you to choose from, or if you'd like we can create a mug, a t-shirt or hat also." The attendant politely pitched as she handed me a numbered ticket. We thanked her and walked away. As we traveled through the beautifully lit tunnel, Bassi turned to me and said,

"My Brother, my people at my mosque will never let me live this down."

"Who says they ever have to know?" I smiled while patting his back.

Abassi, Mustafah, and I navigated past the hundreds of people, who stopped, stared and took pictures alongside the numerous Christmas light displays in the Forest. Strings of lights of all colors were wrapped around every palm, banyan and ficus that lined the pathway to the midway, approximately 5-million lights in all. I later found that the ornate light configurations were left up all season: it was just too much work taking them down and putting them back up.

"This is beautiful…the lights, the sight of families having fun, the smell of the carnival food makes me wish I was a kid again. What kid wouldn't have a blast here!?" I proclaimed.

"I took my family here a couple of years ago and it set me back $300. Sad thing is we don't even believe in Christmas." Bassi stated.

"You're a good man Bassi. You have to try things at least one in life that way you never have any regrets." I said.

"I'll try most things, but not all. Are you hungry Jeremiah? I owe you dinner since you sacrificed your evening for me. I can buy you something to eat here since you seem so enamored with fair food?" Bassi stated.

"I'll eat only if you join me Bassi."

"I would love to join you Brother, but everything here is fried in pig oil from the French fries to the elephant ears— But I don't want to discourage you from indulging yourself."

"If I find something that's not deep fried in pork, will you and your son join me for dinner?"

"I will Jeremiah, but my son is still on formula. Didn't they teach you anything about child rearing in PDP?"

"Actually they didn't. I never learned how to change a diaper; I was never schooled on the stages of child development. The PDP class was centered on the casework side of the job. Hell, they never even covered CPR; luckily, I still remember the technique from my college days." I replied.

"When it comes to diaper changing, you'll definitely get your opportunity to hone your skills while you're working here." Bassi stated. His arms were numb from carrying Mustafah, so he wiggled and shook them frantically in hopes regaining blood circulation.

"I'll bet…there's something you can eat over there!" I exclaimed.

I guided us to a vibrant green concession stand, M & M Roasted Corn & Smoked Turkey Legs at the beginning of the midway. The smoke from the large rendering turkey legs and sweet succulent corn appealed to even Abassi's finicky appetite.

"Hi, welcome to M & M's. How can I help you?" The young blonde cashier asked with a heavy Southern drawl.

"Hi, two legs, two ears of corn and two bottles of water please." I requested.

"That'll be $22 please."

I reached into my wallet and paid the lady for our food. Abassi tried to intervene, but before he could stop the transaction, the cashier already shut the register's drawer. The cashier handed us two large turkey legs and ears straight from the grill.

"Why did you do that Jeremiah? I told you I'd pay for it. Here take this money." Abassi tugged on my arm, but was unsuccessful in reimbursing me.

"Abassi, you can take care of the bill next time. The amount of time and knowledge you shared with me—showing me the ins-and-out of child protection, I can never be able to fully pay you back." I said.

My friend was touched by my words. I really enjoyed helping all my co-workers. Supe told me that I displayed a characteristic absent in many new hires employed by the Department—altruism. While other young CPIs came to the agency trying to outshine the veterans. I took the time to help vets perform in a more efficient manner. Like the interactive Excel spreadsheet, I created for the 808. Now my co-workers, Rhonda, Abassi, and even Supe could track their cases and performance indicators effortlessly. Abassi often joked with me, that if I wasn't involved with Tamara, he'd let me date his 22-year old daughter, Abisola; in hopes of making me an official part of the family.

"Let's go sit on that empty bench over there and eat before we hit my case. It's kind of rude to show up at someone's front door brandishing large pieces of poultry and inquiring about the safety of their children." I jested.

"Yes that would be terribly unprofessional, my Brother."

As we feasted on our fair fare, Mustafah slept soundly bundled up in two wool blankets in his carrier. Thousands of fair goers passed us as we sat and talked. I heard joyous screams and laughs from the midway and knew we were close to our destination.

"So how is your family doing Jeremiah"?

"They're doing okay. I've seen Mom once since I came to Miami in July, but I do talk to her on the phone at least once a week. This job can be so overwhelming and demanding at times. I promised Mom and my brother Ronald, I'd come home to visit, but something always comes up—a case that needs to be closed, a home visit that needs to be completed. How did you work here so long and find the time to raise a family? Or better yet how do you remain married?" I asked.

Abassi proceeded to methodically strip both his ear of corn and turkey leg clean. The steam from the hot turkey leg and the cold winter air caused dew to form on Abassi's glasses. He took a swig of water then blotted his mouth with a napkin before he continued to speak.

"You need to make time for things that are important to you. I have to put the happiness of my family paramount before anything. When you promise your kids you'll take them to the movies, you better make it happen. If you promise your wife dinner, you need to hold true to your words. At the end of the day, these are the people who will be in your corner should anything happen to you at this job or otherwise. I see you, Rhonda, Jamie and other DCF employees more than I do my own family, so it's natural to build close friendships with your co-workers. But nothing substitutes the bond that you have with your family. When you leave this agency and you're off working as a social worker in a hospital or better yet…establishing your new non-profit, the people here will forget about you. Even us— our relationship will surely change."

"Out of sight, out of mind." I responded blankly as I stared into my half eaten drumstick. My appetite waned.

"That's correct. Our line of work is so fast paced; you're not afforded the opportunity to memorialize the fallen." Bassi stated.

Around 100ft away, the infectious baseline of Nelly's Country Grammar emanating from the Himalaya's 10,000 watt mega-sound system reminded me of the task at hand. Even from this distance I noticed a substantial line that formed at the entrance of this classic carnival ride. I eyed my wristwatch, *9:50pm*. It was getting late and I didn't want to have Mustafah in this cold air for too long.

"If you want to sit here with Mustafah, I'll be a few minutes."

"No I'll accompany you Jeremiah; I need to work off this food anyway."

"Okay Mr. Okafor? Let's handle of this."

###

After, we worked our way to the beginning of the line, I scanned my surroundings. I saw three carnival workers manning the 59,000 lb ride. An older fellow worked the DJ/control booth, while two other boys with Santa hats and olive, camouflage cargo shorts strapped patrons in the Himalaya's 22-cars. I flagged one of Santa's helpers: the taller of the boys walked towards me. As he came closer, his facial features revealed his young age. Then, I yelled over the sound of the ride's loud motors.

"Hello, I'm looking for Samson Banks. Do you know where I can find him?"

"Yes sir I'm Samson. Can I help you with somethin'?" The pimply faced boy asked.

Before I spoke, I pointed to my ID affixed to a navy-colored lanyard that hung around my neck. Samson squinted and shook his head.

An eardrum-shattering bell rang before the 22-cars began to rotate at a devilish pace. I yelled over the machinery and loud music once again, "Hi Samson, I'm Jeremiah and this is my co-worker Abassi and we work with the State of Florida's Child Protective Investigation division. Is there a way I can speak to you and your mom, Lola?"

"Did we do somethin' wrong? Me and my mom don't even live in Gibsonton anymore. Macon, Georgia is where we call home." Samson replied guardedly. As he talked, he distracted me with his jawbone hinges (TMJ) as they vanished and reappeared in unison with his speech.

"Samson you didn't do anything wrong. Abassi and I are just here to help. Can you take a few minutes from your job to speak with us? We shouldn't keep you that long." I stated.

The lanky boy nodded and yelled to his co-worker, "Hank, I need 15….Can you hold it down for a few minutes?"

After Hank gave him a thumbs up, Samson hurdled over the ride's guard rail onto the midway grounds. The boy was a specimen. From the looks of it he had a BMI of 6%. There was absolutely no fat on this boy whatsoever. *I wondered if his physique was attributed to his years of work here?* He steered us to an area towards the back of the ride which afforded us some privacy. The sound of Journey's 'Don't Stop Believing' blared from loud speakers as the riders on the Himalaya whizzed passed my periphery. Samson reached in his lower pocket of his cargo shorts and lit a Marlboro Red. He took a drag of the cigarette and expelled a cloud of smoke as he spoke.

"What's goin' on sir? What did Lola do this time"?

"We received allegations that you are being forced to work at this carnival against your will. It also states that you and your mother sleep in an R/V and that she may be drinking too much. Any truth to any of these allegations?" I asked.

"Who made this report? Sounds like my aunt Becky made this crap up. I love my life and my job and wouldn't change a thing. I've traveled to over 15-states and met a bunch of people I would never have associated with if we were still locked down in Macon. Lola has a few cans of Natty Ice every now and then, but she doesn't drink every day. She isn't an alcoholic!" Samson responded politely.

"Where is your mother"? I asked.

"She's workin' the gate at the World's Smallest Horse Exhibit, C'mon I'll take you there."

Samson guided us a hundred yards down the midway. As we passed the various rides: the Alpine slide, the carousel, Gravitron, and the bumper cars, he exchanged pleasantries with all the ride attendants. *They were truly one big family.* We finally arrived at the World's Smallest Horse exhibit. I turned to our young guide and asked if the exhibit was a scam and Samson nodded.

"It's a miniature horse Mr. Jeremiah—a baby miniature."

The cashier tending to the exhibit looked bored as she watched spectators pass her booth without a glance. It appeared South Floridians were uninterested in diminutive foals. The cashier smiled as Samson approached; she looked just as young as her son. Lola had ultra-straight strawberry blonde hair and a wrinkleless face. Her voice was raspy, I suspect from her pack-a-day habit. Lola gave Samson a peck on the cheek. After, I asked Samson if he could recuse himself from our conversation, Bassi took Samson aside and proceeded to quiz him on every facet of carnie life, while I worked on his mother.

"Hello Ms. Banks. I'm CPI Abundo of the State of Florida's Department of Children and Families. My Co-worker CPI Abassi will be talking with your son. We received some allegations earlier today regarding your son's welfare."

I read the allegation to Lola Banks, which she denied vehemently.

"Mr. Abundo my child is 16 and in the state of Georgia he is allowed to leave school and make a living. As for the allegations of drinking, I only drink on the weekends, usually during Sunday Night Football and my drinking never… and I repeat never affects my ability to care for Samson. Plus, my boy is almost an adult. As far as our living accommodations, we do live an R/V…. a '96 Coachmen Leprechaun to be exact. Last time I checked living in an R/V wasn't against the law… or has the law changed recently?" Lola proclaimed adamantly.

"The allegations also mention that your child hasn't been enrolled in school since he was 13. Any truth to that?"

"Yes, I pulled him out of school when he was 13 and I home schooled him." Lola responded.

"Oh that's interesting….if I may I ask what is the highest level of education that you've completed?"

"What does that have to do with anything?" She responded irately.

"Frankly, Ms. Banks it means everything. How can you home school your child if you lack the skills to understand the curriculum? How do you teach subject matter you barely understand yourself? It seems that you did a fine job raising a polite, hardworking son. But don't starve him of an education."

"What do you mean"? She asked.

"I'll show you what I mean Ms. Banks."

"Bassi…please bring Samson over here!" I yelled to my co-worker who was around 20-feet away. A few seconds later, Samson and Bassi rejoined Lola and me, while Mustafah remained asleep in his carrier.

"Samson I need you to do something for me before I leave you this evening." I politely requested. A sudden winter wind hit me causing my teeth to chatter. It felt like the temperature dropped another 10-degrees in the past 30-minutes.

"Sure Jeremiah? What do you need from me"? Samson replied.

"I need you to read this for me." I asked as I held up my ID to his eye level.

"D…Dep…Depa…De…Par"

An overwhelming sadness overtook me the second my suspicions were confirmed— the young boy was illiterate. As I looked at Bassi, he slowly rocked back-and-forth in his stance shaking his head. Lola Banks' eyes dropped to the ground.

"I can read Mr. Jeremiah! Really, I can read!" Samson professed. I didn't have the heart to argue. My mind thought otherwise... *No Boy— you can't.*

"Thanks Samson. Just give me a couple of more minutes with your mom alone."

I waited as Bassi, Samson, and Mustafah drifted away from us then I spoke.

"See Ms. Banks, we can play games all night long, but the fact is your 16-year old son cannot read a 4th grade word and this neglect transpired over years. If you love your son you'll address this immediately. Don't allow him to go through the rest of his life living in fear of words." I pleaded.

Lola Banks remained reticent.

"Ms. Banks, I'll need the date you'll be heading back home and I'll need a good address for you in Macon so I can have Georgia's DFCS visit your home. They can assist your family with some services. We also need to take a look at your Coachmen so we can address the allegations about your housing. After that, we'll be out of your hair." I stated.

"Let me just get someone to relieve me at my booth and I'll take you to our R/V. Sorry if I snapped at you earlier." Lola said apologetically.

"No problem Ms. Banks. You lead the way."

10 POO'S LESSON

January 26, 2001
(Liberty City)

I looked down at my Anatomy homework, but couldn't focus on the various diagrams of the lymphatic system. Since my encounter with Lil Boy, I couldn't wait for school to resume, but my plan to immerse myself in my schoolwork was not goin' as planned. Last week, I neglected to turn in my midterm paper to Mrs. Cantor, one of my favorite teachers. The works of Renaissance poets: Langston Hughes, Sterling Brown and Claude McKay weren't enough to peak my interest. Months ago, I was excited about my acceptance into the heralded Miami Northwestern Medical and Allied Health Science Program. My successful completion of the program guaranteed me 30-college credits before I stepped foot on a university's grounds. These days, I didn't lack the ability to excel in school, my desire to do so just wavered. My post-Christmas encounter with Archie weighed heavily on me. My only solace was that Lil Boy took a night job pressure cleanin' gas stations and strip mall parkin' lots, so his presence at our home was kept to a bare minimum. My love life was also in shambles. When Lil Boy disclosed Scrub's side business— regardless of Lil Boy's spiteful motives, I knew it was the truth. On New Year's Day, I confronted Antwon about his drug dealin' and he told me it was a bunch of lies. Scrub demanded to know the identity of his accuser, but I still cared about Scrub enough to spare him the jail time after he killed the old man fo' snitchin'. But I had to break up with Scrub for other reasons. I've seen this type of shit too many times before. Messin' with a drug dealer will always get you hurt. You hurt when you're saying goodbye to him for the last time before he gets sent upstate to do a 10-year bid or you hurt when the detective is askin' you questions about the unfortunate shooting while they're markin' the shell casings on the ground. It's a no win situation. Last time, I felt this way I was watchin' my daddy bein' lowered into the ground, an' to this day I haven't fully recovered. I looked outside my front window to see the decaying

Douglas fir on the swale browning under the hot Florida sun. It was almost 3 ½ weeks since we threw the tree away and packed up the Christmas decorations, but the tree still remained. The fir looked amazing those first few nights, but its allure came and went. I doubt Christmas will ever feel the same way ever again.

"Hi Queen, what'chu doin'? Poo said impishly

"Hey Baby, big sister is just tryin' to get some of her anatomy home work done befo' dinner."

"Is there somethin' I can do to help? I help Ms. Hernandez, my kindergarten teacher all the time. When she needs somethin' passed out she calls on me. When she needs me to take the attendance down to the office and come right back, she calls me. Even when those crazy boys and girls in my class act up, she calls on me to help settle 'em down and I get those kids right. They know of I don't play."

Poo puffed out his bird chest for emphasis and I chuckled at him. As of recent, he was one of the few things that brought joy into my life.

"Poo, I think I'm good right now. But I might need you later to help with my math homework. How does that sound?"

The air quickly deflated out of my little brother's bird chest after he heard my response. His animated demeanor was extinguished. Head down and shoulders slumped he slowly retreated into our bedroom.

"Hey Poo! Hey Baby! Now that I think of it…you can help me with my homework. You can be my model!" I yelled.

He trotted back to my side like a German shepherd bound to their owner.

"There's things in our bodies that keep us healthy and protect us from gettin' sick. The lymphatic system is one of those things." I stated.

172

"The lymp...what"?

"Okay, say it with me *Limb* like off a tree. *Fat* like your Auntie Belinda's dog Roscoe, and *Tic* as in tic-tac-toe. Now let's put it together." I said.

We pronounced the array together in unison. "Limb...fat...tic"

"Now say it faster Poo."

"Limb..fat..tic." Poo responded.

"Good job Poo. The lymphatic system is a drainage system in the human body. All over our bodies there's tiny, tiny tubes that are called vessels. These vessels drain in different parts of your body. Poo, stand in front of me an' open yo' mouth."

Poo opened his mouth, while I pointed to the inside of it with a ballpoint pen.

"In the back of your mouth are our tonsils, these vessels drain lymphatic fluid into our tonsils. Our tonsils protect us from gettin' sick by trapping germs coming in through your mouth and nose. Now give me your arm."

Poo extended his left arm, while I took hold of it.

"Deep inside your bones, there's something inside called marrow or...bone marrow. These vessels are connected to your bone marrow and the bone marrow creates lymphocytes, which protect us from gettin' sick."

"So my bones have things in it to keep me from gettin' sick"? He asked.

"That's correct Poo. Now there's a body part located right here on your left side above your stomach and by your chest called the spleen. Your blood passes through your spleen and those same lymphocytes found in your bones which attack viruses and bacteria to keep you from gettin' sick are also found in your spleen."

"So every second of the day there are things trying to hurt me, but there are things inside of me that that fight these bad things off all day long! Even when I'm not even thinkin' about it, my limbfattic system is keepin' me safe all the time!" Poo stated as he broke down the lymphatic to its rarest form.

I absorbed, then processed Poo's lesson: *(1) There are things in life that are constantly trying to hurt us, but there are forces inside of us that prevent infections from settling in and tumors from forming. (2) If the limbfattic system keeps our physical bodies healthy by unconsciously ridding it of any harmful impurities. (3) There must be similar things inside of us that protect us spiritually and keeps our souls from perishing. This unknown system allowed me to move on after the death of my daddy and will get me through this tough time.*

"Queen are you okay"? Poo asked.

"Yeah, Poo I'm okay…I'm okay."

"Queen if you don't become a big doctor one day, you can always teach little kids science and stuff." Poo stated enthusiastically.

The sound of men yelling outside interrupted our lesson. Poo and I peered outside the front window to see a dump truck block one side of the street while a waste management worker halted traffic at both directions. A humongous metal claw dropped from the heavens and picked up the decaying fir along with a large chunk of earth and released the refuse into the bed of the awaiting dump truck. Two blasts from the grapple truck operator's air horn and the trucks were off to their next pick up.

I smiled after witnessing the sight and quietly whispered to myself… *It's that simple rid ourselves of our impurities.*

Denise Collins stared out the cloudy jitney window as it travelled down Northwest 12th Avenue. The sounds of passengers clamoring and the odd creaks and squeaks of the vehicle itself could not break her train of thought, one minute a gainfully employed associate at Rainbow Staffing Solutions, the next minute jobless. Ms. Denise spent 8-years of her life working for Rainbow, but after a California-based rival company, Total Package Event Services promised to manage and staff South Florida's arena, theater, and stadium events at a fraction of their competition's; Rainbow sent out pink slips the third week of January. Aside from losin' her job, Ms. Denise had other things on her mind: things of a domestic nature. Her Lil Boy-friend came around less and when he did, he was too inebriated to be of any use. Her home became more like rest stop, where he could get a meal and wash up before he vanished for another few days. She promised that there'd be a resolve to this situation before months end; she and her kids deserved better. As the days past, Archie contributed less-and-less to the household expenses, even though he had his pressure cleaning night gig and his hefty disability check. Now with Rainbow Staffing Solutions going bust, she knew times were going to get real tough. Aside from her financial and romantic woes, Ms. Denise noticed a dramatic change in her daughter. Queen appeared so withdrawn lately, and when she approached her daughter to talk; Queen drifted farther away. At first, she thought the news of her boyfriend was the sole reason for her daughter's depression, but realized there were numerous times Queen has fallen in-and-out of relationships, but managed to rebound. She hoped Queen would open up to her soon.

The jitney driver turned on the radio to diffuse the idle conversations. The soulful voice of a familiar artist almost silenced the passengers instantly.

I wish that I could hold you now
I wish that I could touch you now
I wish that I could talk to you
Be with you somehow.

Ms. Denise turned to a teenage girl about Queen's age and asked, "Who sings this song? It's so beautiful."

"It's R Kelly...the song is 'I Wish'." The teenager responded.

I know you're in a better place
Even though I can't see your face
I know you're smilin' down on me
Sayin' everything's okay

Immediately, Ms. Denise thought of her late husband, Songbird. She glanced at the tattoo on her arm and said a little prayer for her family then she requested the driver to pull over at Northwest 12th Avenue and 52nd Street. From her stop to her front door, Ms. Denise hummed the song's infectious melody all the way home.

As Mama opened the front door, Poo rushed her immediately and gave her a big hug.

"Hi Mama! How was work today?" Poo inquired.

"Work was wonderful Baby. Can Mama get some suga?"

Poo hopped on to the arm of the sofa and planted a wet kiss on Mama's cheek then he leaped into the air and landed perfectly on the tile floor.

"Guess what Mama? " Poo stated breathlessly.

"What's that baby?" Mama replied scanning through the day's mail.

"I helped Queen with her homework! She used me as model. She showed me the lim...llimpa...limpastic..."

"Lymphatic System! Hi Mama!" I bellowed from the kitchen.

"Yes, limbfattic system. It helps us from gettin' sick." Poo added.

"Wow, that's such a complicated subject for a 5-year old, you're so smart Poo! Maybe you'll grow up and be a doctor like your big sis?"

"I can do that too Mama, but you know I want to build video games when I grow up. Besides you only need one doctor in the family. Mama, may I be excused so I can get back to playin' my Playstation?" Poo asked.

Mama smiled and then nodded. He ran into the bedroom to finish the next level on his new video game, SSX (Snowboard Super Cross). I emerged out of the kitchen; a cheerful smile blanketed my face, an expression Mama hasn't seen in weeks.

"How you doin' today miss lady"?

"Fine. Fine. Fine." I responded.

Mama continued to scan the mail, placing the junk aside.

"You look much better today…like you won the lotto or like when you got that invitation letter from Spelman for a pre-acceptance tour!" Mama said smiling.

"Spelman Mama? I love that school and their history, but they don't have a medical program there. Maybe Johns Hopkins, University of Pennsylvania or even Harvard." I replied.

"My baby… a Harvard alum, your father would be so proud." Mama replied.

"After I graduate, finish my residency and eventually start my own practice. We're outta here. You will never have to clean houses or work fo' nobody else. Scratch dat, the minute I get my first good payin' job we're outta here."

My last sentiments immediately diverted Mama's attention to her own precarious financial situation.

"That's a beautiful thought baby. How you look after your brother and hold things down here makes me so proud. Yo' father is probably smilin' down on you, sayin' everything's okay." Mama stated.

"Dang Mama, are you borrowin' lyrics from R Kelly?" I said jestingly.

"What made me think I could put one over on you? DJ Queen, the girl who knows probably every lyric to every new song out there. I'm glad to see you in better spirits."

"Yes Mama. After teachin' Poo some anatomy, I realized a couple of things. By the way Mama, I'd like to talk to you about somethin?"'

Mama ripped open a letter marked urgent, which she read to herself and then cursed aloud.

"Damn FPL! Gave us intent to disconnect and this couldn't have come at a worse time!"

"What do you mean Mama? What's goin' on"? The beautiful smile quickly vanished from my face.

"Yes child, the devil is at work again. Rainbow laid me off and my cleanin' jobs have been far and few as of recent. It's goin' to take a minute for me to find supplemental income. Between Songbird's military and social security benefits, we're barely makin' rent."

"Maybe I can get a part time to help with expenses. I'm sure I can handle school and a part time job without any problems." I suggested.

"Baby, I appreciate the offer, but I need you to help with yo' brother. I can find full-time work if I have your support. Besides, you need to concentrate on your schoolwork, the coming year of yo' medical program is goin' to get more difficult. You don't need any distractions from reachin' yo' goal." Mama stated as she refolded the FPL bill.

I knew Mama was right. During next couple of years, the coursework of the Medical and Allied Health Science Program is guaranteed to become more challenging. Also I am required to complete a three month internship at a medical facility prior to graduation.

"Lawd help us child, we'll make it happen. You just concentrate at the task at hand, which is your schoolin' and let Mama take care of the finances."

I looked at my mother and smiled, as an immense pride rushed over me all at once. My parents had an amazing way of comforting others through the most adverse situations even if they had to sacrifice their own comforts. When money is tight and food is scarce, Mama never compromised our health and well-being, even if she had to withstand hours of waiting on lines at DCF to apply for food stamps or wait at the doorsteps of the Camillus House or Miami Rescue Mission for a care package.

"Queen you said had some news for me or you wanted to talk to me about somethin'"? Mama asked.

"Now that I think about it Mama, I'm good for now. I'm sure I can handle it myself, but If I can't, I'll surely come back to you." I said.

"Okay baby, if you do need me I'm always here for you…" Mama stated as she grabbed my hand and clasped it. "…I'm just too lucky to have a daughter like you."

I was unresponsive. Mama sensed something was on my mind, but she knew trying to pry information out of me was a total waste of time. Maybe I'd tell Mama about my situation, but it wouldn't be today. There was too much goin' on for Mama to be burdened with one more piece of bad news. We turned as we heard the sound of clinking keys at the front door, then he entered.

"Hey Y'all, what's happenin'? You havin' a family powwow and I wasn't invited"? Lil Boy exclaimed.

I released Mama's grip and retreated to my room. Mama immediately picked-up on the nuance.

"Boy, I was always told I knew how to clear a room." Lil Boy said attempting to make light of the situation. Then he continued,

"I'm starvin'! What's for dinner?"

"I don't know where are you takin' us out to eat?" Ms. Denise asked sharply.

"Oh...Okay. Okay. You got jokes. You got jokes."

"Why don't you eat this?" Mama stated as she handed Lil Boy the delinquent FPL bill.

###

February 2, 2001

"Alright Class, read Chapter 12 by Monday and I need a 1-page synopsis on what you have read. Now, have a great weekend!"

Mrs. Cantor's 11th grade English students stormed through the classroom door anxious to begin the weekend, while I slowly gathered my belongings. Since the beginning of the school year, I was her ace student and performed amazingly. But for the past few weeks she noticed a definite change in my demeanor, performance, and appearance— nine years of teachin' in one of the toughest schools in Miami-Dade County taught her to identify such things. From my unanimated morale to my haggard appearance to my numerous missed assignments, Peggy Cantor knew immediately there was trouble in the Collins household. The zealous English teacher attempted to contact Mama, but our home phone number was temporarily disconnected. After that, she sent me home with a request for a parent/teacher conference, but the request didn't make it outta my locker. Mama was still jobless and she didn't need to have to deal with my problems to further complicate her life. But today, Ms Cantor had enough. It pained her to watch my self destruction any further.

"Quintavia, are you alright dear"?

"Yes Mrs. Cantor Everything is okay. I just didn't get much sleep last night."

"I can tell you were yawning throughout my whole class. I've been told I can be boring at times, but you look like you were going to fall asleep on me." Mrs. Cantor stated as she attempted to make eye contact.

"Yeah, Mrs. Cantor my brother kept me up all night playin' video games that's why I didn't get much rest. I apologize for dozing off in your class." I stated in half lucid state.

Mrs. Cantor normally accepted a student's' excuses and normally didn't pry into a student's life, but I was different. She liked me because I tried my best to do well in her class, even though English was not my subject of expertise. She always said I had excellent writing skills and was one of the most mannerly students she ever met. She always reminded me there was no doubt I was destined to go far in life if afforded the opportunity.

"I'm sure your brother did keep you up. Actually, my husband is picking up the kids so I'm free all afternoon. Can we grab a cup of coffee, and talk some? I'll give you a ride home of course?"

Normally, I would politely balk at the offer, but I was unbelievably tired and hungry. I didn't pack a lunch or even think about askin' Mama for lunch money. Thankfully, I didn't have to pick up my brother since Mama wasn't working.

"That's sound's great Mrs. Cantor, but I don't do coffee."

"What do you do"? My teacher stated curiously.

"Conch fritters. I can go for some conch fritters."

###

Mrs. Peggy Cantor and I drove less than four blocks away to, 7070 Northwest 15th Avenue; Miracle Fry Conch Fritters aka Miracles. The small building was painted azure and its quoins painted white. The

parking lot was relatively empty with the exception of the Bootleg Man selling CD's out of the trunk of his car.

"Oh my gosh! In almost 10-years of working at the West I never even knew this place existed! You learn something new every day!" Mrs. Cantor attested.

"Oh yeah, if you wanna give your coronary system some extra work just come here, the food is delicious but 90% of the menu is fried."

The plumes of smoke billowing out of the top of the building testified my last statement.

"Have you ever had conch before"? I asked

"No I don't think I have?" Mrs. Cantor replied.

"Mrs. Cantor you lived such a sheltered existence. Conch is a mollusk which is very popular in the Caribbean. It's prepared: breaded and fried; dressed in olive oil, lime juice, salt and pepper; used in stews and mixed in seasoned batter and fried to make conch fritters--sort of like hushpuppies. Unlike the one's they prepare in the Bahamas, Miracles prepares the flat-shaped Hood variety with onions, bell peppers, flour, eggs and seasonings." I advised.

"Wow you sound like a salesman…Is conch the only thing they sell here"?

"No, they sell anything else you possibly think of that can be fried: chicken wings, pork chops, fish and French fries. I suspect if you eat the chicken wings you might taste a hint of fried conch and vice versa."

"Sounds great let's order!" Peggy Cantor exclaimed.

A heavy metal grate with tiny holes painted azure covered the order window. A slot around 8-inches tall by 24-inches wide was left open so money and food could be exchanged. The system protected Miracles' employees from irate customers and potential robbers.

"Hi Ladies, Welcome to Miracles. What can we do fo' you today?" a female voice boomed.

"Ma'am, can you give me a double and a large flop?" I requested.

Mrs. Cantor eyed the menu and turned to me and asked:

"What is flop? Is that some sort of dessert or something?"

"Flop is a mix of homemade lemonade and iced tea…. Do you suffer from diabetes or does your family have history diabetes?" I asked.

"No, thank goodness."

"...then go with the flop Mrs. Cantor"

"Hello. What's the difference between a double and a single fritter?" Mrs. Cantor asked the cashier behind the metal security grate.

"A double is two single fritters fried togetha. We don't cut 'em. When they come out da fryer they the size of a regular envelope". The cashier relayed.

"Okay, may I have one double conch fritter and a large flop." Mrs. Cantor requested with a perky smile.

"Awright, yo' order will be done in a few minutes ladies. That will be $6 please."

Peggy Cantor reached for her credit card and handed it to the cashier."

"I'm sorry ma'am we don't accept cards—cash only."

"That's no problem." Mrs. Cantor replied.

She handed the cashier $6 and placed $2 in her tip jar. Minutes later the cashier produced two doubles fresh out da grease and two large flops in Styrofoam cups. I dowsed my fritter with Crystal's Hot Sauce an' some Lawry's. We walked back to my teacher's black, '99 Ford Explorer not before being accosted by the Bootleg man.

"Hey there beautiful ladies! Got two fo' five. Got dat new Destiny's Child, dat new Jadakiss, dat new Aaliyah and dat new Trick album. You name I got it!" The Bootleg Man bellowed.

I smiled and waved as I said, "No thank you."

"How about you Snowflake? Got two fo' five. Don't like R&B... or Hip Hop, Got somethin' fo' you too! Got dat new Jack Johnson 'Brushfire Fairytales', How about dat New Kids on the Block compilation?"

"Got any Elvis Costello"? Mrs. Cantor asked.

"Got dat new joint right hur Babygirl!" The Bootleg Man bellowed as he magically produced The Very Best of Elvis Costello CD out of his cache of bootlegs.

"Okay, I'll take that one and the new Aaliyah."

"Good choice ma'am."

Mrs. Cantor paid the Bootleg Man a five dollar bill and an extra dollar for a tip. I smiled when I realized how amazingly generous my teacher was. *First the cashier, then the Bootleg Man.* Mrs. Cantor had no problem giving...it was like second nature to her—then again she's a teacher and they always give.

"Awright Ladies. Thanks for yo' business. Come again." The Bootleg Man continued his marketing blitz as we left. "Got two fo' five! Got two fo' five ova here!

###

Elvis Costello's Oliver's Army played softly in the background, as Mrs. Cantor and I sat in her Ford Explorer in Miracles parking lot.

Oliver's army is here to stay
Oliver's army are on their way
And I would rather be anywhere else
But here today

"This is wonderful. I got two CD's— one of them isn't even out yet, two drinks, two conch fritters and was still able to leave our vendors with a small tip. Gotta love small business." Mrs. Cantor said gleefully.

"It's always good to support local businesses. We need more small business owners in our neighborhood." I stated. "Cool music, the piano goes great with that chorus. I like this song...who is it?"

"It's Elvis Costello and the Attractions. He's from England. He came out in the 80's when I was teenager… Damn, I just gave my away age." Peggy Cantor snickered.

Mrs. Cantor took a bite of out of her conch fritter, a plume of steam escaped from the area where she just bit into. "My goodness this is delicious. I taste a hint of onion and the conch…it is not as rubbery as fried clams." She declared.

Then, she took a sip of the flop to wash down her bites of fritter and ceased sippin' almost immediately.

"Quintavia how do you drink this? It tastes like there's 10-cups of sugar in this?"

"Probably is…." I stated giggling then I continued. "…Mrs. Cantor that's how we like it in the Hood. We like everything in excess. If the flop is too sweet, you can take it home and dilute it with a gallon or two of water and then have somethin' to drink for the rest of week!"

My teacher smiled.

There was a Checkpoint Charlie
He didn't crack a smile
But it's no laughing party
When you've been on the murder mile
Only takes one itchy trigger
One more widow, one less white nigger

"Oh my gosh! Did he just drop the 'N' word?" I asked.

"Yes he did. There's various interpretations of this song, but it's all political commentary. Some say that Costello was commenting on the British Army's occupations throughout the world. While others say, it's about Oliver Crowell who helped defeat King Charles I during the England's Civil War. They interviewed Costello and he said he wrote the song after a trip to Belfast, Ireland after he saw that the soldiers were comprised mostly of young, working class men. Hence, the term white niggers. The word refers to socioeconomic class rather than race."

I didn't expect such a detailed explanation from my teacher nor did I really care. Even though the song was before my time, the song still sounded good to me.

"Thanks again Mrs. Cantor for the late lunch—early supper."

An eerie silence crept into the conversation, before Mrs. Cantor intervened.

"How are you doing Quintavia? I mean is everything alright at home? I'm concerned that you have something on your mind that's keeping you from your maximum potential."

I took a bite of my double and sighed. As each day passed, it became more and more difficult to manufacture this façade—inside my spirit was a wreck, while outside I barely held on.

"Mrs. Cantor it's hard to talk about it. My situation is complicated."

"I've got all weekend. My husband got the kids."

Tears welled in my brown eyes, but I still remained in silence.

"History, despite its wrenching pain, cannot be unlived, but if faced with courage, need not be lived again." My teacher stated as she looked out her driver's side window.

I turned to my favorite teacher and she looked at me and smiled.

"That's one of the most poignant quotes I heard in weeks. Did you just come up with that?" I said laconically.

"I wish I could take the credit for that one. All credit should be directed toward poet laureate Maya Angelou."

A sudden rush of emotion overcame me. *The damn burst.* Weeks of concealing my inner anguish released in a matter of seconds. As my tears flowed, I leaned over and hugged Mrs. Cantor.

"Thanks Mrs. Cantor. Thank you for taking time out of your busy life to check on my well-being. I really appreciate it." I replied as Mrs. Cantor used a hard paper napkin to wipe the tears from my eyes.

"Thank you for introducing me to conch fritters, flop, bootleg CDs and for being one of the best students I've had the pleasure of teaching." She said.

Peggy Cantor reclined her driver seat in her Ford Explorer and listened while her ace student shared her entire life with her.

11 COLLISION

"**F**ingerprints, photographs, abuse reports, risk assessment, witness list, homestudy, school records, signed shelter petition, custody release order. The only thing missing is the shelter hearing order; do you have it in your file?"

"No, I'm sorry I don't have it Tiffany. Jeff Swan was swamped with shelter petitions a few days ago. He promised me he'd get me that document signed by Judge Lauder before my staffing with services, I guess he forgot. Do you have an Attorneys List, I'll call him right now and remind him that we need that document." I said

Tiffany Blankenship was a gatekeeper—she was the shit. She was in charge of accepting new court cases entering the services component. The services component would then monitor the family's service progress throughout their dependency case. In my brief tenure, I've dealt with Tiffany approximately eleven times. Hopefully she'd let me slide and allow for this transfer to go through—even if I didn't have the shelter hearing order. A shelter hearing order is a document that is signed by the judge authorizing the removal of a child from their caregiver(s). A veteran foster care worker and former CPI, Tiffany knew the system well. She also knew our system had issues. Like DCF attorneys juggling 8-10 cases in a session. Between TPR (Termination of Parental Rights) trials, adjudicatory hearings, status hearings, dependency filings, and shelter hearings, the amount of legal documents a DCF attorney was responsible for was insurmountable. It's not a surprise that the recidivism percentage for DCF attorneys was almost that of CPIs.

"Don't worry about it, I'll drop Jeff a Lotus Note to remind him about the shelter hearing order, but if I don't have it in my hands in three days, you're ultimately responsible for attaining the document. You may have to go down to Court Records, request the court file and pull the original document yourself or you may have to camp out in front of Jeff's door down at DJJ and mug him for it." Tiffany stated.

"Thanks Tiffany. That will work. I know getting on a gatekeeper's bad side isn't the brightest thing to do if you want to work here. I'll make sure you have that document in your hands within 72-hours." I stated appreciatively.

"Jeremiah, I've been here for 13-years and this place works better when we work together. Continue to be a man of your word and you'll be fine."

"Ms. Blankenship as always it's a pleasure doing business with you. Do you know where I can find Unit 413? My friend, Tamara Norvil, is detailed in 413." I politely asked.

"Denim's unit... 413 is down this corridor and to the left. Tell Tamara that she still owes me my griot and crab legume, she promised to make for our office Christmas party."

"Will do Tiffany. Take care."

I walked down a sterile corridor in District 11's South Hub. The cubicles were similar to those of the Rohde. Usually, a cube consisted of a desk, two chairs (one for you and one for the client) and a filing cabinet. I've only been here a handful of times and I could see the benefits. Primarily, you weren't under Administration's ass every waking moment of the day because the South Hub was over 25-miles away from the Rohde. At the Rohde, Administration just traveled five floors down, and they could easily check in on us. If you fucked up they didn't come down to visit you, you brought your ass up to them.

After rounding a corner and making a left. I proceeded to knock on a wood door that was cracked-half open, but I peeped inside prior to knocking. Then I saw silver plated name plate which sat on a desk—Pierce Denim. Behind the desk was a broad shouldered, Caucasian man. He wore several pieces of gold jewelry— two or three bracelets, a couple of rings and a thick rope chain with a pendant of St. Michael hanging from the end of it. He also sported a thick bushy mustache and dark, thick slicked backed hair. Tamara's description was dead on when she described the Denim's unabashed exhibitionism of his chest hair, which would make Tom Selleck blush. Regardless of the horror stories I heard about him— the ex-Air Force guy…turned ex-cop…turned child protective investigative supervisor, I would give him the benefit of the doubt. I gently rapped on CPIS Denim's door two times.

"Yes can I help you son." Denim replied. His soft spoken voice did not match his imposing physique.

"Hello, I am CPI Jeremiah Abundo of Central unit 808; I came to visit one of your CPIs, Tamara Norvil. Do you know if she's in?

"So you're the magnanimous CPI Abundo. Come on in son…come in. I wanted talk to you and your supervisor for the past few weeks, but we've been so busy here. Take a seat over there." Denim ordered.

I didn't know what to make of the invitation, but I decided to let it play out.

"Yes, Abundo you may not know anything about me, but I know a helluva a lot about you and that's not necessarily a good thing."

Denim rummaged through his rolling filing cabinet and pulled out a case file, **00-2514211** and dropped it in my lap. *Ouch.*

"Open it Abundo. Open it and I'll tell you why I'm so perturbed at your behavior and Norvil's"

I opened up the case file, but didn't find anything wrong or any documents missing.

"Mr. Denim, I beg your pardon, but I don't see anything wrong with this case file." I responded.

"Look at the notes section on the left hand side."

"Yes, I see them. All the notes appear to be in order and they have Tamara's or my signature under each entry."

"That's exactly the damn problem! Why are your notes in this case file? You didn't ask my permission to accompany Norvil on this case. If you claimed OT on this investigation, you and your supervisor will have to answer to this." Denim yelled emphatically.

"What are you talking about? Where does it say in Chapter 39 that a CPI is obligated to venture on an abuse investigation alone? Going out on cases can be a dangerous affair, but I'm not sure you'd know anything about that. By the way I didn't charge the State for any of my services on this case; consider it my Christmas gift to the State." I retorted.

"Dangerous? You don't know what dangerous is son. For your information, I used to be in the Air Force and I flew combat missions in Nam…And I used to get shot at for a living as a cop…So you'll never know what the definition of dangerous truly means." Denim stated loudly as he hovered over me as I sat.

"Optimal words are *used to* Mr. Denim. You're no longer in the Air Force and you're no longer in law enforcement. You're here in this office dealing with me…" I stated as I stood up and confronted the CPIS. He didn't flinch as I continued, "…and frankly, your scare tactics do not antagonize me one bit. If you have an issue with me— take it up with my direct supervisor, Jamie Watkins. If you need her number I'll gladly provide you her number…then again you should have her information already because you've dealt with my Supe firsthand. If you don't have anything else of importance you'd like to discuss with me, I'd like to speak with CPI Norvil."

A small crowd gathered at the door CPIS Denim's office. Both of us treaded lightly as they watched. I walked out of CPIS Denim's office without looking back. Chances are I'd hear something about this encounter from my supervisor before I made back to the Rohde building. If Denim didn't blast a slanted email to the entire Department of what transpired, I'm sure one of the spectators outside Denim's office would spread the word. Gossip is a common practice at the Department. From who's sleeping together (DCF'n) to who's up next for a rare promotion to chatter of important changes in District protocol— most gossip was trivial, but often vital bits of information were also exchanged as word spread. Gossip essentially became a necessary evil. After minutes of walking around aimlessly, I finally located Tamara's office. The office was barren and devoid of any character just a few important numbers thumb-tacked to the wall and piles of abuse cases which covered Tamara's desk. Many CPIs chose to sparsely decorate their cubes in this manner because it saved time and energy packing up, when they resigned and moved on to their next career or endeavor. I pealed a slice of pink post-it-note and jotted some information down and then stuck the note on Tamara's computer monitor. I made my way to the building's exit, and pulled a Filter-King out of my shirt pocket and lit it as soon as I exited the building. I stared at the ground and spied a few dozen old butts littered about. Then I remembered what Tamara told me— CPIS Denim also smoked. *How awkward would it be if he decided to come out and spark up one of his Camel lights right about now?* After I took a second puff on my cigarette, a familiar voice interrupted my smoke session.

"Jeremiah, I got your note Babe, I'm glad I caught you before you headed back north." Tamara stated.

I turned to find CPI Norvil looking every bit ravishing. She wore a snug size 6 Anne Klein One Button Skirt Suit and a pair of black pumps. Her long permed hair was pinned in a French braid. Tamara even donned a pair of glasses even though she had no issues with her vision. I loved the sultry librarian look.

"You look amazing T. You've been keeping yourself up these days." I stated as I flicked my cigarette away.

"You'd be surprised what a good man will do for you." Tamara replied as she edged closer to me.

"Oh you got a man, who's the lucky guy?"

Tamara leaned over and gave me a quick peck on my lips. The slightest incidental contact from her excited me beyond belief.

"Okay, Tamara let's not start this here. Your boss already has it in for me. I'm sure his cock-blockin' ass will find some archaic state law or district policy which prohibits employees from sleeping with one another." I jested.

Tamara laughed.

"I heard what happened in his office. You're such a rebel Jeremiah. You got this whole place buzzing."

"Oh yeah? I figured as much. He cornered me and grilled me about a case that we went out on together. I'm sure by the time I get back to the Rohde Jamie will find out, but I'm not worried about it. Jamie had a run in with him over a transfer case. I believe it involved one of your co-workers, his name was Preston…Preston Hall I think?"

"Wow! Preston graduated the PDP class before us and he tendered his resignation a week ago. Anyway, don't worry about Denim. Rumor has it that he has one foot out the door. He applied for a manager position at Xenyx Security— it's just a matter of time before I get a new supervisor." Tamara stated.

"Wonderful, we must celebrate over a late lunch—my treat. Did you get a case yet?" I stated jubilantly.

"Yes, I got a case first thing this morning and I met with the children at school. But I have to visit the home this evening and meet with the parents after they come home from work. I'm sure they'll slap me with another case before day's end." Tamara stated without worry.

"I haven't gotten a case yet T, but I know I will. I had to come down to your building to transfer a case to services. By the way, does anyone in your building have anything that needs to go up north? Flex fund requests, daycare referrals, mileage, case transfers. I can save someone a trip."

"I'll check Jeremiah and we'll meet up at your car."

###

"What a week! I'm glad Friday is here." Tamara stated as she rubbed the bottoms of her feet with her hands.

I quickly glanced at Tamara and smiled as I navigated my Ford Taurus northbound on US 1.

"I know the feeling. I don't know how long my body can take this punishment. I'm barely getting four hours of sleep and some nights I wake up at 3am or 4am so none of my cases fall out of compliance. I don't want to keel over one day like Eleanor Santoro due to a heart attack." I said.

"For real? A CPI was hospitalized? Where did she work"? Tamara inquired.

"She was in North unit 446. My unit paid her a visit at Palmetto General. The Central Area took up a modest collection along with a Hallmark and gave it to her husband Juan. He was heartbroken. But I can see how the job got to her, between the running around and the worrying it takes its toll. It didn't help that Eleanor was 5'4" and almost 225lbs."

"225 lbs?"

"If she was a boxer she'd be in the same weight class as Lennox Lewis and Vitali Klitschko. Too many #3-combos and 2-piece dinners if you ask me." I replied.

"I guess a burger is out of the question for lunch?" Tamara chimed.

"No. You can eat whatever you like—burgers, chicken, tacos or anything you wish. Or if you prefer Filipino food I have a thick *lumpia* marinating in my pants for you?" I offered semi-jokingly.

Tamara didn't say anything, so I wasn't sure if she heard me; was contemplating my proposal; or was just ignoring my crass comment all together. I redirected my conversation immediately.

"But seriously T., when you work at the Department, you're always on the go and eat the quickest and cheapest things possible. When you get home the last thing you want to do is slave in a hot kitchen for a couple of hours. If you have kids, you're transferring your bad eating habits to them. Or better yet, how do you maintain a consistent exercise regiment with our unpredictable schedules? By the way, you owe Tiffany Blankenship her griot and crab legume."

"Shit, I forgot about that." Tamara exclaimed.

"Where are we going to eat by the way? We're in your part of town." I asked.

"Go down a couple of blocks. At Southwest 152nd Street, there's a strip mall with a little restaurant that has the best Chinese food, **Gold China**. I know you're Filipino, but you do eat Chinese food?

"What doesn't a Filipino eat?" I replied.

She gave me a wry smile and shook her head.

I glanced at my Dickies wristwatch and couldn't believe my eyes. It was almost *4:51pm* on a Friday and I was yet to receive my first case. I enjoyed my lunch and relished any time I spent with Tamara especially when it was in the daytime. Even though Gold China wasn't Filipino food, I welcomed the change from my daily fare. Since I came to Miami, my diet consisted mostly of Cuban cuisine: ropa vieja (shredded flank steak in a tomato sauce), arroz con pollo (chicken and rice) and pan con bistec (Cuban Steak Sandwiches). In Palm Beach, I never tasted Cuban cuisine in my life, but in the past few months I definitely made up for lost time. Tamara had the #5 lunch combo: pepper steak, pork fried rice and wonton soup while I feasted on the blue crab with ginger and scallions.

"Great choice for lunch T. My mom used to make a variation of this crab dish when I was a kid. She used to pick the meat out of the crabs and toss it onto my plate. I'd mix the lump meat with my white rice and I was in heaven." I said before taking a big bite full of crab and rice.

"Sounds great. If you like crabs I need to make you some of my legume for you. I'll even pick the meat out the crabs and toss it on your plate." Tamara stated as she sopped up some pepper steak gravy with her egg roll.

"Maybe you can whip some up for my family. We're meeting at my Uncle Bayani's house on Sunday, February 18th. They originally wanted to make it a weekend— an out-of-town retreat to the Keys, but I told them that state employees don't get Presidents' Day off. Besides, we have our mandatory district meeting with Chet Parker on the 19th."

"I'm flattered. I finally get to meet the famous Bayani and the matriarch Cynthia Abundo. I'll make your family function if you promise to come to Naples to meet my sister, Karen and my niece and nephew."

"Deal." I affirmed.

"I'm not going to lie to you Jeremiah because you're such a good friend, but I've been looking around."

Around? I ceased my efforts extracting a stubborn piece of claw meat from its shell. "Oh yeah? What are you looking for?" I asked curiously.

"Looking for other jobs. I'm still young and I'm not sure if investigating child abuse case is what I want to do for the next 20-years, especially here. Who knows if it's humanly possible to work at this place for 20-years? I looked into becoming a foster care worker, but word is they're going to privatize the foster care component in the next year or so. Plus, seeing the foster care workers around my office and talking to vets like Tiffany Blankenship makes me have second thoughts. The job seems more demanding than CPI. When a child in care needs to travel or has a court hearing or even a dental appointment, you're at his disposal. If a child runs away from placement, they'll call you 4 o'clock in the morning to retrieve that child and find alternative placement. I'm thinking of getting out of the child welfare field altogether. Maybe I'll apply at the State Attorney's Office or with Border Patrol—they're always looking for multi-linguists."

"The thought has crossed my mind too. I wanted to try to complete a year then explore my options. My uncle Bayani offered me a job at his mortgage brokerage firm. You'd cry if I told you how much he makes on a house." I stated.

"Give him my resume and ask if he has a place for someone that speaks four langu…"

The piano hook of 2Pac's 'I Ain't Mad at Cha' blared out of my Nokia 5110. I was elated when I learned how to convert MIDI computer files into actual ringtones. I looked at caller ID and shrugged my shoulders. *A Friday without a case? Never in a million years!* I pressed the **'Send'** button and accepted the call:

"DCF. CPI Abundo speaking. How can I help you?

….Hi Supe, what's going on?

….I have an Immediate in Liberty City?

…I'm in the South and I can pull the case here,

…I will call you later if I have any issues.

…Okay Supe, you have a great weekend as well."

I pressed the **'End'** button and terminated the call.

"Gotta case?" Tamara stated gingerly.

"Yup."

"Need some company"? Tamara inquired.

"No T. I'll hit this one solo. I still have to talk to Jamie about my altercation with your supervisor. I don't want to cause any more issues for you or me—we're still on probation. But if you could help me pull my Immediate, I'd really appreciate it."

"You got it Babe."

###

I cruised down Northwest 62nd Street in route to my Immediate case, **01-0009008**. I was pleased when I picked up my manila investigation folder and it was feather light: no prior abuse reports and no criminal records. When I caught the light at Northwest 12th Avenue and Northwest 62nd Street, I cracked open the case file and read the allegations:

Initial Abuse Report 01-0009008 (Imm)

On December 26, 2000, Quintavia was in her kitchen cooking her family Christmas breakfast. Mother's paramour, Archie Bedford cornered Quintavia in the kitchen and rubbed his penis on Quintavia, then groped her breast. He was under the influence of alcohol at the time. Quintavia's mother, Denise, was at work at the time and was unaware of the incident. This case is being coded as an Immediate since there is a 5-year old child also in the home, Marcus Collins. It is unknown if this is the first incident of sexual abuse and if the A/P continues to have access to the children. The reporter would like to be contacted by the CPI.

I looked across the street at Da Beans and remembered my Christmas night from hell—12/25/2000. It was just a few weeks ago, but it seemed like forever. I smiled when I realized that Coretta Jenkins and her siblings didn't have to endure a single night of abuse after my visit to their home. *Good Job CPI Abundo! Good Job!* And even though my job was arduous: the gratification of helping others was unparalleled. I reached over to the passenger seat and grabbed my cell phone and dialed the reporter on my new case:

"Hello, may I please speak to Peggy Cantor?"

"Yes this is she. Who may I ask is calling?"

"My name is CPI Jeremiah Abundo of the Department of Children Families. I am calling because you phoned in a report to Florida's Abuse Registry regarding the suspected sexual abuse of a child."

"Wow, I didn't know you guys work after hours? I expected a call back on Monday."

"Yes ma'am. Kids don't stop getting abused when the clock hits 5 o'clock. We work 24/7, 365 days a year." I replied somewhat irritated.

"I see...thanks for calling me back. I called this case in because I noticed a drastic change in one of my student's scholastic performance as well as her demeanor." Peggy Cantor stated.

"...please expound ma'am."

I pulled my car over at a Citgo station on Northwest 54th Street and Northwest 12th Avenue. I rolled down my driver's side window and pulled a Kool from my shirt pocket. I lit it with my new, purple Zippo, a Secret Santa Christmas gift from Rhonda. I carefully scanned and surveyed my surroundings; ironically, my Taurus was the same model as those issued by the Miami-Dade PD.

"Yes Mr. Abundo. If you're familiar with Miami Northwestern Senior High; it's located in one of the roughest neighborhoods in Miami. I've been at this school for nine years, and Quintavia Collins is probably one of my most talented and most-gifted students I've encountered—hands down. Crazy thing is English isn't her strongest subject. "

"Did the child disclose to you personally"? I asked.

"Yes, she disclosed to me earlier today."

"Well on behalf of the Department, I would like to thank you for calling this report in. You may have saved these children any further injury and anguish."

"May I ask you a question Mr. Abundo before we hang up"?

"Sure, what is it?"

"Do you disclose the reporter information on these cases? I don't know how Quintavia will react when she finds out I called the case in. After all, I will still remain her teacher for the next few months and we still have to maintain our classroom relationship." Mrs. Cantor asked.

"Well Mrs. Cantor, you're bound by state law to phone the Hotline if you suspect any abuse. As for your anonymity, we will never disclose your identity. However, when I read the allegations to the subjects usually they ascertain the reporter's identity through the context of the allegations. I'm sure Quintavia didn't disclose the details of her abuse to anyone else."

"I see your point Mr. Abundo. I think I can live with Quintavia being mad at me, if some intervention takes place. Please give me a call if you need anything. I'll be available to you this entire weekend."

"Will do. Thank you for all the information."

An unusual serenity enveloped our house, a peace the family hasn't seen since Archie 'Lil Boy' Bedford moved in. Since Mama suffered her layoff, his presence was scant. He successfully distanced himself from any of the Collins' financial obligations, while maintaining his infrequent mealtime privileges. This evenin' Mama was making her famous fried fish. However, the smell of fried tilapia dipped in buttermilk and seasoned flour wasn't alluring enough to entice Lil Boy. On Fridays, our family refrained from eating white or red meat, it was a tradition that dated back when Songbird worked for the cruise lines. He'd come home with a sack of fresh fish usually jack, snapper, or grunt. The catch was compliments of local fisherman at the port. As Mama sweated in the kitchen preparing dinner, Poo and I sat in the living room.

"Poo some words sound alike and are spelled alike, but have different meanings. These are called homonyms. Like train…train can mean like a choo-choo or train can mean to teach somebody how to do somethin'. "

"I still don't get it Queen."

"That's okay Poo. You'll get it in time." I said consolingly.

"Mama that fish smells sooooo good. I can't wait to eat." Poo stated.

"Dang, boy if you keep eatin' like you do, I'm gonna start callin' you Pooch." I stated jokingly as I grabbed at my little brother's excess stomach meat.

Poo gave me a big hug. As siblings, we jabbed at one another, but our verbal attacks were of a benign nature. Two raps on our front screen door detached us from our embrace. I walked to the door to answer the caller. Before openin' the door I glanced through the door's peep hole then took a second glance for confirmation. *We didn't order Chinese…Mama cookin' fish tonight?* The only Asian faces I saw in this neighborhood belonged to those doin' nails or selling synthetic hair at the flea market. Intrigued, I opened the door.

"Hi, I'm CPI Jeremiah Abundo of the Department of Children Families and I'd like to speak to Denise Collins." CPI Abundo stated as he flashed his identification behind the screen door. He stood a shy under 6ft tall. He had a pitch black Caesar that was lined up perfectly. He lacked any facial hair and he seemed young—no older than 25. He wore a plaid, blue Phat Farm button down that was tucked into his navy Dickies work pants. He rocked a pair of brown Natureveldt Clarks. He was a cutie pie.

"Yes sir, that's my mom she's in the kitchen right now, I'll get her for you." I smiled and retreated into the kitchen.

Seconds later, Mama emerged out of the kitchen wearing a red bandana head wrap and a gingham apron.

"Yes, I am Denise Collins. How can I help you?" Mama stated through the closed screen door.

"Hello Ms. Collins. I'm CPI Jeremiah Abundo of the Department of Children Families and I received an abuse report involving your children about two hours ago. Can I come in so we can discuss the report? He stated as he flashed his identification a second time and slid one of his business cards under the door.

"Of course please Mr. Abundo please c'mon in....of course." Mama replied.

Mama guided the investigator to the living room sofa.

"Poo can you please excuse us. Can you go to your room or help your sister with the fish?" Mama requested as Poo headed to the kitchen.

"Your dinner smells delicious. I smelled it as soon as I got out of my car." Mr. Abundo stated. He said the smell conjured memories of his own mama's cooking.

"Thank you, you're free to stay for dinner on the grounds you don't take my kids." Mama joked.

After the statement, I thought of any wild shit Ms. Denise may have done recently that would prompt a call to DCF. *Did someone see her wack Poo the other day at the Popular Supermarket for actin' up? Or did one these spiteful-ass neighbors call in a report on Mama when she uncharacteristically took a couple puffs on a roach that Lil Boy left in our ashtray— just a couple of hits to calm her nerves?*

"Thanks for the offer Ms. Collins. Are both of your children here?"

"Yes they are."

"And how about Archie Bedford? Is he around?"

Mama looked at the CPI's business card.

"No Jeremiah. He comes to the house every now and then— mostly then. You don't mind if I call you by your first name?" Mama replied.

"You may, as long as I have the pleasure of doing the same?" The young investigator replied.

She nodded.

"Denise, the allegations I have are of a very sensitive nature. Please let me read the entire narrative to you and I'll be happy to answer any of your questions after."

Jeremiah read the allegations to Mama. A range of emotions swept over Mama, from sadness to guilt to pure anger. Mama was a hot mess.

"What happens now? What can I do"? Mama said despondently.

"This report will be forwarded to Miami Dade Sexual Battery Department as well the State Attorney's Office; they're responsible for making an arrest and pursuing further criminal action. I will send a referral to Kristi House so your daughter can receive counseling. Kristi

House can also provide you counseling as well. You will be responsible for taking your child to the Kristi House's intake. In the event, she says she doesn't need counseling, convince her otherwise. She will thank you for your insistence when she gets older. I am here for your family if you need anything at all, I'm here for you." Jeremiah stated tenderly.

Jeremiah took his business card from Mama and jotted his cell number down on the back of the card and gave it back to my grief-stricken mother.

"Denise, I normally don't give this to my clients. You can use it to call me anytime…anytime at all but if you call me at 3am and I don't answer you…it's not that I don't like you, it's probably 'cause I'm asleep."

Mama surrendered a brief chuckle.

"Seriously ma'am, I really want your family to get past this. How's your financial situation?"

"It's seen better days Jeremiah."

"The Department can help you with your overdue bills, rent, furniture, and aftercare expenses. You just tell me what my agency can do to assist your family and I'll get it processed in a week or two."

"Thank you Jeremiah. I always tried to do the best for my chil'ren. And if you'd ask me, I'd tell you the DCF would neva show up to my house in a million years. But I'm glad you came and knocked at my door. Where's yo' family from?" Mama inquired.

"My people are from the Philippines. There's not too many Filipino social workers out here, so definitely there must have been some divine intervention that we meet." Jeremiah replied.

"Amen to that. What else do you need from me?"

"I'm going to briefly interview your children, and when I am done with them, I'm going to have to sit down with you again and go over some forms and get some signatures. While I'm interviewing your children you can get your bills together, so I can submit my flex funds application— first thing Monday. One other thing Denise, what is your safety plan as it relates to Archie Bedford." Jeremiah asked

"Safety Plan? I might kill his ass if he steps foot in here again. I intend on packin' his shit up tonight. He ain't welcome here no mo' and that's my word!" Mama stated confidently.

"I'm glad you're putting Quintavia's and Marcus' well-being first."

"Should it be any other way Mr. Abundo"?

"You'd be surprised Ms. Collins."

From the kitchen, I listened in while I scraped a cast iron skillet with a Brillo pad. I was emotionless.

Poo's interview with Jeremiah lasted no more than ten minutes. The 5-year old, didn't have a lot to say about the incident because nothing happened to him. He had no special encounters with Lil Boy, just the routine every day things you encounter when you deal with a loser like Lil Boy like "…he drinks beer everyday" and was "…angry all the time". Jeremiah did congratulate Poo on his ability to scarf down countless fillets of tilapia effortlessly. The highlight of their interview came when Poo asked Jeremiah if he knew Kung Fu like in the movie Crouchin' Tiger, Hidden Dragon. The CPI responded "Of course I do!" and affirmed his ability to skip atop bamboo trees. His next interview with me would prove a more challenging and difficult one. Jeremiah mentioned that he wouldn't ask specific questions regarding the abuse, since the County's Sexual Battery detectives and forensic interviewers from the State Attorney's Office would handle this line of questioning. In addition, his interview with me was my first, real interaction with an adult male since the incident. This was a pivotal moment. *Would I and I could open up? Or would I continue to bury my hurt deep inside?* Ms. Denise retreated back into the kitchen and Poo lay down in bed, dizzy with all the fish he ingested. I remained with Jeremiah in the living room. Like her daughter before her, Mama eavesdropped on CPI Abundo's entire interview from the confines of the kitchen. As I waited to be interviewed, I sat on the sofa and stared up at the ceiling fan with my mouth buried in the palm of my hand.

"Hello Queen, my name is CPI Jeremiah Abundo of the Department of Children Families. Do you mind if we talk a little?" Jeremiah stated gingerly.

My lips remained pursed. I was still in disbelief Mrs. Cantor beguiled me with a $2 conch fritter into revealin' my entire business. Jeremiah was relentless.

"I hope you don't mind if I call you Queen? Your little brother insisted I call you by your nickname like I addressed him by his. Poo— that's such a cute nickname. When I was interviewing him he couldn't stop eating your mom's fish! Each time he laughed the hem of his t-shirt would drift above his belly button like Winnie-the-Pooh. Is that where his name derives from?"

Like Mama, I succumbed to Jeremiah's corniness.

"No Mr. Abundo he got his name from our daddy. When he used to place Marcus in his bath water, Marcus couldn't help from doing a number two." I retorted.

"Jeremiah is fine with me. No need for formalities. I'm old enough to be you older brother."

"Okay Jeremiah. I'll answer any of your questions, but I don't feel like talkin' about that experience with you."

"Queen I don't expect you too. When you feel the time is right and the person is right, you can let it all out. But tonight isn't that time. Can we talk about some other things though?" Jeremiah asked.

"Sure. No problem."

In the distance, **R. Kelly's I Wish** played over a small radio somewhere in the house. South Florida radio stations never understood the concept of overkill even though Ms. Denise and I couldn't get enough of this song.

"Man, Robert Sylvester really out did himself with this one. I love this song. It reminds me of my old man. He used love to sing himself." Jeremiah stated as he put his pen and pad down.

"Oh yeah? My daddy used to love to sing when he was alive. Kells wrote this song about his own mother that passed." I added.

"I knew he was talking about his mother. My friend, Tamara, swears he wrote this song about 2pac, but he can't be. There's a part at the end of the song where he sings 'Come on and braid my hair'. Could you imagine 2pac sitting on a stoop braiding R Kelly's hair? That's not happening! But you see we got more in common than you think. We have fathers that have passed on, fathers that loved to sing, and we like the same type of music." Jeremiah professed.

"Jeremiah, you're definitely not the typical DCF worker."

"Is it because I'm Asian? I've been getting that a lot of from this house lately." Jeremiah chuckled.

"No. 'Cause you're not an asshole. You guys to come to my school all the time and I've seen the way your people handle their business." I said expressionless.

"Wow! Thanks for the compliment. I'm glad you don't consider me an asshole. A shithead maybe…but never an asshole."

I laughed again at this corny boy's jokes.

"Seriously Queen, If someone were to come to my house and question me about my kids, I would want to be treated with a certain level of respect. You may be my client today, but I may be on the other end of the interview tomorrow."

"So you got kids Jeremiah"?

"No. Unfortunately, this job doesn't afford me the spare time for any practice. Any hopes of reproduction on my part will have to be of an asexual nature."

I let out a humongous guffaw this time, loud enough for Mama to come and check on my well-being. When I signaled everything was okay, Mama retreated back into the kitchen.

"I thought the biology/pre-med student in you would appreciate that comment." Jeremiah added.

"I do. I really do…so where do we go from here Chong? And you can spare me the formalities; I heard the whole process you explained to my mother."

"Chong?" Jeremiah intrigued.

"I hope you don't mind the nickname. It's a Black thing…a term of endearment. We all got nicknames. You have a choice between Chong, Bruce Lee or J— your choice?"

"I'll take Chong. It means dude in Tagalog, my parent's native language."

I smiled.

Chong reached into his shirt pocket and pulled out a business card. He wrote his cell number down and gave it to me.

"Do me a favor Queen, help your mom gather up those documents and call me on Monday so I can pick them up, I really want to help your family."

"We'll get it together this weekend and I will call you before Monday." I replied with a smile on my face.

"Queen, can I do anything else for you"?

"No, Chong you were just perfect."

"Can you get your mom for me so we can wrap this up? The young CPI eyed his Dickies wristwatch cursing at the time.

Two hours after knocking on our screen door at *7:45pm*, CPI Jeremiah "Chong" Abundo was finally on his way home. Mama literally begged the DCF worker to take a plate of fish home, but the CPI refused her most adamant attempts. Mama and I remained at the front door and watched as the CPI drive off. Although Chong was polite and unobtrusive, Mama desperately wanted some alone time with me, so she could tend to my needs. The night sky was clear and not one cloud covered the twinkling stars. The humidity was almost nonexistent. Even though it was such a perfect night for a talk on the front stoop, we decide to remain inside—away from the ears of nosy neighbors. While Poo was fast asleep in our room, Mama and I sat upright on the living room sofa. We remained motionless for a minute trying to figure out the best way to begin this. I held Chong's business card in my hands and fiddled with it.

"Chong…he's real cool, and real polite Mama. I'm glad we got to meet him. He wants us to get our paperwork and bills together this weekend, so he can help us attain some funding. He even said he can help subsidize Poo's aftercare expenses." I said.

"Yes he is a real gentleman; I didn't even know DCF could help families like that. All I thought they do when they come to yo' home is snatch yo' chil'ren." Mama replied.

"We need to make sure we…"

Mama quickly interjected.

"Baby, I am so sorry that you've been livin' with this pain for the past month, but I'm not sure why you didn't come to me earlier?" Mama said as she ran her fingers through my short doo.

"Mama, I kept it buried inside of me 'cause I could never find the right time to tell you. The night before it happened I said some real horrible things to you, so I was afraid you wouldn't believe that it actually happened. Then a week or so ago, I worked up enough courage to tell you and then you lost your job with Rainbow. With all the things we goin' through— our messed up financial situation an' all…I didn't want to burden with you with my situation." I stated.

"Let's get somethin' straight Queen. You should never have to protect me from anythin'. I'm yo' parent and I am responsible for protectin' you from anythin' an' anyone. You my child—not the other way around. I feel horrible I even brought Lil Boy into our lives."

"But Ma…", I began to retort, but suddenly stopped mid-sentence

"Queen, please speak yo' peace, I wanna hear everythin' on yo' mind. You've earned my undivided attention an' you kept things bottled up long enough." Mama stated

"Mama, money's been so tight around here: there's time we needed Lil Boy's grip. He did help keep the lights on and our water flowin'." I said.

"Where's he now baby? He ain't here! We are and even if he could pay our bills for the rest of our lives, the money and the convenience just ain't worth it. I'd rather live with you and Poo under the Julia Tuttle in a box than have my chil'ren endure what you did. Things might get tight, but we'll get through it. Don't we always?" Mama stated while rubbing my hand.

"Yes ma'am we'll make it through."

I gave Mama a kiss on her cheek and a hug, the rare display of affection from her eldest took her by surprise. But Ms. Denise's words tonight proved to me why she is my hero and will always be. For many of my friends, who have been victims and continue to remain prisoners, you'd cry if I told you how many of their parents don't believe 'em when they've disclosed. Actually, I think they do believe 'em deep inside, but sometimes lights, water, an' rent are just too much a sacrifice, then to own up to the truth that someone is hurtin' their babies.

"You feel like a little spring cleanin'?" Mama asked.

"Spring doesn't start until March Mama—that's a few weeks away."

"It's finna start tonight. Go fetch some garbage bags out tha kitchen. We packin' this nigga's shit up tonight and callin' Goodwill in tha mornin'!"

12 RHONDA

February 9, 2001

Rhonda lifted her thin-framed glasses and nestled them just above her hairline. She rubbed her eyes and then her forehead. She didn't know what was worse, having to discuss important matters with Perry Washington, the father of her children or having to beg him to spend time with his two boys, Theo and Jovan. Even on her 29th birthday, Perry did not concede. At the office, everyone knew of Rhonda's personal turmoil and suggested that she move on, but she couldn't. Advice did little to help pay the bills and it definitely didn't help with her boys when she had an investigation to tend to. As the father of her children bantered on over the phone, the CPI scanned the numerous personal keepsakes that adorned her office. She picked up a spongy mock orange that sat on the top of her filing cabinet. She smiled as she read the black silkscreened lettering:

FLORIDA CLASSIC MCMXCIV

The memento reminded her of better days with Perry, the man who she still loved. In 1994, Perry Washington and Rhonda Jackson met while attending The Classic held at Tampa Stadium. The annual football game pit the Bethune-Cookman University's Wildcats against the Florida Agricultural and Mechanical University's Rattlers. It was by sheer luck that, Perry and Rhonda met, as they begrudgingly left their seats for a hotdog, just as the Battle of the Bands halftime segment began. Some argue the choreography and fanfare produced by Cookman's Marching Wildcats and FAMU's Marching 100 is more exciting than the game itself. Regardless who won, no one could doubt the choreography and musicianship displayed by both bands was a sight to see. While they were in line waiting to buy their hotdogs, Rhonda thought it was so caviler that Perry offered to pay for her order, when she was fifty-cents short for her hotdog and soda. The two ended up watching the remainder of the game together; Perry in FAM orange and green and Rhonda in Cookman maroon and gold. By game's end, Cookman edged FAMU by a field goal, 27 to 24, but a beautiful union was spawned as the two instate rivals exchanged hugs and phone numbers and parted ways. Both were seniors at their respective schools, Perry was enrolled at the College of Pharmacy & Pharmaceutical Sciences at FAMU while Rhonda studied Social Work at Cookman. Even though they still had months to go before they officially graduated; the two made it work. Through sacrifice and sheer will, their relationship flourished. At onset, their relationship was rooted in compromise as they took turns driving over 240-miles to see each other on weekends. Now Rhonda found it impossible to get Perry to drive less than 2-miles for his own children.

"Rhonda, it's just not happenin' this weekend. I need to fly out tonight and Needleman expects me present in front of the board on Monday." Perry stated adamantly.

"Well, how about yo' mama? Can she pick up the kids from school?" Rhonda stated exasperatingly.

"That's not gonna' fly either Rho. My mama's on the road. She's probably half way to Atlanta by now." Perry stated.

"Well we gotta problem don't we? It's yo' week with the chil'ren, and like always you blowin' them off. I have plans this evenin'; now my life is in a holdin' pattern, while you do you? This is craziness!" Rhonda stated shaking her head.

"Rho I don't know why you fussin' fo'; this trip is for my job and this pharmaceutical company job allows me to pay all that child support which keeps you and my boys in a life of opulence. What do you have on your agenda that is so important anyways?" Perry inquired.

"My unit is taking me out for my birthday. They've planned this for weeks."

Perry laughed before he commented.

"So you wanna' hang out with your co-workers after hours, have a few shots of 'Trón, an' scarf down some chicken wings, while I go on a business trip. I fail to see the immediacy." Perry offered snidely.

"I guess it doesn't matter that it is my birthday and that I don't go out often? There are plenty of times I had to go out on cases and you left me high and dry. I guess it shouldn't be a surprise that you'd bail out on me once again." Rhonda stated as she squeezed the mock orange in her hand. When she released her grip, it took a few seconds for the orange to regain its natural shape and form.

"Rho, listen to what you're sayin'. You gettin' mad at me 'cause I'm goin' out of town to make money for our children, while you go out to dinner. On top of that, you goin' to dinner with people you see more hours of the day than you do your own immediate family. Your job got you bent!"

The statement echoed in Rhonda's head. The truth frustrated her beyond belief.

"Perry go on your trip...me an' the boys will be fine. Just understand that these boys need their father. Me and you are ancient history, and you may have moved on with your new life an' your new family, but don't deprive your boys of things that money can't buy...you have a safe trip Boo."

"Rho, Happy Birthday. Tell the boys I love 'em and I'll swing by the house and get 'em next week."

Rhonda ended the call on her cellphone.

After listening to Rhonda's conversation I couldn't help but feel sorry for my friend. I could have intervened minutes ago but I didn't. When Rhonda goes through these motions with the father of her children, there's no talking to her. I've known her for over five years and supervised her for just as long, and she's one of my favorite people working at the department. She's loyal, loving, passionate, and selfless, this is what makes her one of the best CPIs is the District— possibly the State. To me, Rhonda is an all-or-nothing chick. This is why I admire her so. If you're fortunate enough to penetrate her tough, no-

nonsense exterior and pierce her very soul: she'll love you forever. When she loves you, she loves you with all her heart. When you strip your love away, she's a shell of a woman like the one standing before me. I guess I love Rhonda Jackson because she reminds me of myself a long time ago.

"Hey girl, are you alright?" I inquired

"Yes girl, I'm awright. I'm sure you heard…I guess the boys will have to join us for dinner." Rhonda replied.

"No problem, the more the merrier. Besides, your boys are angels. Did you know where you want to go for dinner?"

"Since you guys are payin', I'm thinking Benihana's or seafood?

"Your choice Rho, sky's the limit!" I exclaimed.

"Where are the Fellas"?

"Bassi and Jeremiah are out on cases. They got two a pop…actually Bassi got three. The Fellas flipped a coin to see who would go out on your case." I said.

"Jamie I could've went out on my own cases. Everybody is so busy, I feel horrible that they had to go out of their way for me." Rhonda stated.

"Rho, you've been in this unit long enough to know that on birthdays CPIs in the 808 don't go out on new cases. Why should it be so different for you? Last year you went out on a case for Daniel and that guy only lasted 2-months." I stated as I hovered over my good friend.

"Thank goodness for my Fellas—I owe both of 'em big hugs and kisses. I have some cases that are approaching 45-days old, that I will send your way for review and closure. Are you going to have your computer on this weekend?" Rhonda asked.

"Rho, since you've been in this unit when has my computer ever been off?" I countered as I admired the numerous keepsakes and pictures of Rhonda and her boys. Then, I looked at my watch and asked, "When are you picking up your boys"?

"Actually, I'm leaving right now, but I'm comin' back to the office. I have to fax some service referrals and input some of my notes in the system. Did you need anything while I'm out?"

"No, I'm perfect, Rho. Be safe."

I adjusted my rearview mirror to make eye contact with my two boys, Theo and Jovan who sat quietly in the backseat of my '98 Honda Accord. Theo stared out of the passenger car window as we sped southbound on Northwest 27th Avenue. I flicked on the radio to break the monotony.

"Theo that's your song baby!" I exclaimed. I proceeded to sing the hook to Missy Elliot's Get Ur Freak On:

Go, get ur freak on
Go, get ur freak on
Go, get ur freak on
Go, get ur freak on
Go, get ur freak on
Go, get ur freak on
Go, get ur, get ur, get ur, get ur, get ur freak on

Theo, a bright skinned facsimile of his father was unfazed. My 7-year old smiled, but was unmoved at my attempt for interaction, while Javon, Theo's 3-year old brother, bobbed his head and kicked his legs and feet to the song's repetitive beat. When the song finished, I turned down the radio's volume.

"Theo did you get to finish any of your homework in aftercare?"

Theo remained quiet.

"Theo, you heard me boy! Don't make me repeat myself a second time!" I said excitedly.

"Yes Mama, I did some sentences in aftercare and I have a math worksheet due on Monday."

"If we can knock out yo' homework tomorrow mornin', we can go to the park have lunch and you and your brother can play on the playground— you can even bring your football and we can get some trainin' in before the season starts!" I offered hoping to divert some attention off their absent father.

Theo's smiled widened as he acquiesced at my proposition.

"Mama the park sounds good, but we can leave out football."

"Why's that Theo"?

"'Cause you ain't got no arm!"

I chuckled...

"Excuse me? " I retorted.

"Yeah when we play catch we have to stand like 8-feet apart from one another. I wanna play catch—not practice shovel passes!" Theo stated.

I laughed once more.

"I know yo' daddy has an arm like a cannon and I know you wanted to spend the weekend wit' him, but he had some important business and had to go outta town on. He told me to tell you that he loves you and yo' brother and he'll see guys next week." I stated as I peered through the rearview mirror awaiting a response.

"Mama, isn't yo' job busy an' important too? You always find time to take me and J to the park or the pool. Even when you got to work an' you can't find anyone to take care of us, you never leave us behind." Theo stated.

Now, it was my time to remain silent. To draw a comparison between my occupation and Perry's would cast their father in a negative light. However angry I was with that man, I never made him look deficient or weak when I spoke of him to his boys. The statement also touched me. The fact that my son recognized my efforts as parent pleased me beyond belief. I always put my kids foremost. Like how, I had to ask my friend Sheeda to use her mailing address so Theo could attend Lakeview Elementary, an "A" rated school across town, rather than Bentwood Elementary, a "C" school only two blocks away from my home. During the holiday season, I even took a second job working at a local Walmart, so that my boys could have a little something extra under the tree.

"Mama, Daddy is goin' to teach me football." Javon declared as he entered the conversation.

"Yes Javon. Daddy is goin' to teach you football." I said.

"Are we goin' to yo' job Mama?" Theo asked.

"Yes, we are. I have to finish up some paperwork and do a few things on the computer. Then my unit is takin' us out for my birthday dinner." I stated.

My boys celebrated when they heard the news.

"Oh yeah? Why do you like goin' to my job?" I asked

"I like goin' to your job 'cause Mr. Jeremiah played catch with me in front of the building last time we went and Mr. Bassi showed me how to make cool paper airplanes— then we went to the top of the parking garage and we threw them over the side." Theo said gleefully.

Those are my Fellas. A smile washed over my face when I thought of them.

"Worky...worky" Javon added.

"I remember the last time we went out for dinner, Mr. Jeremiah and Mr. Bassi were drinkin' green bottles of beers and actin' crazy. Mr. Jeremiah was blowin' smoke rings out of his nose and Mr. Bassi was doin' the Bankhead Bounce. I can't wait to see them." Theo said as he laughed hysterically.

I applied some extra pressure to the Honda's accelerator and turned up the radio.

THE DEPARTMENT

"Theo...Javon you can play in Mr. Jeremiah's office, but don't touch any of his things and please keep it down. We should be outta here in less than an hour. Theo, I'll be in the next cube. Watch yo' brother and holla if you need me."

I gave Theo a backpack filled with toys, crayons, colored paper, a few books and snacks. I kept the kidpack in the trunk of my car specifically for situations like this. The kidpack also worked perfectly for my removals. My boys knew the routine: play quietly, clean up if you make a mess, and ask Mama or one of your relatives (Auntie Jessica, Auntie Jamie, Uncle Jeremiah, or Uncle Bassi) if you need to go to the bathroom. As I walked out of Jeremiah's cubicle, Theo grabbed a coloring book, while Javon haggled with some knockoff Lego blocks. The floor was relatively empty with exception of a unit 443 who worked the 3pm to 11pm shift. Ms. Thompson, the unit secretary, left early for a dental appointment and my Fellas, Bassi and Jeremiah were still on their cases for the day. I walked back to my office and nudged my mouse to deactivate the screensaver. I logged into my computer and began entering my notes for **Abuse Report 01-0007065**:

January 13, 2001, 5 pm
Richard Beasley (DOB: 01/02/99)

CPI had face to face contact with the said child, who was doing much better than when CPI initially observed at Mount Sinai Hospital on 1/10/01. The child's hematoma has subsided. The child will be set for discharge between 2/13/01 and 2/15/01. Child will need to have medical follow ups after his discharge. CPI requested medical discharge summary from Dr. Proctor, JMH. CPI has also notified law enforcement (Detective Harris, City of Miami PD) and CPT (Dr. Ruth Ellington)

Signature:_____(Rhonda M. Jackson)

January 13, 2001, 5:30 pm
Samantha Beasley (DOB: 12/07/84)

CPI had face to face contact with mother who was informed that a petition will be filed against her on 01/15/01 for medical neglect. Mom informed CPI that the child sustained his injury on 12/29/00 around 2pm in the afternoon. Mother stated said child Richard fell off the bed as previously mentioned, but mom did not seek medical attention because she was scared she would get in trouble. Mother informed CPI of the children's fathers (who are not listed on the birth displays.) Said child Richard's father is Steven Butler (DOB: 07/14/78). The father of Sebastian Beasley is Nicholas Reardon (DOB: 10/06/80). Currently Nicholas Reardon is incarcerated for L&L assault/child....

I abruptly stopped typing as I heard a familiar voice coming from Jeremiah's office. Before I could intervene, I balked when I realized the voice belonged to District Administrator Chet Parker.

"Where is your mother guys? Is your mother here getting interviewed? Or is she here for picking up something?"

Javon kept playing with his blocks, while his older brother Theo remained quiet staring at administrator Chet Parker.

"Oh my gosh, I am so sorry you guys have to be here. But you have to work with me, I'm your friend my name is Chet. What are your names?" Chet Parker inquired as he knelt down.

But nuthin'. Chet Parker attempted to communicate with the little brown faces, the best way he could. He conducted a mental scan his ethnic memory bank— of TV shows, movies, and pop culture that involved people of color.

"Hey little guy, slap me five!" On bent knee, he extended his soft, pale palm to Theo.

Theo looked at the White hand and blurted, "Diff'rent Strokes".

"Yes! Yes! Diff'rent Strokes. Diff'rent Strokes." Parker repeated exuberantly.

I covered my mouth to suppress my laughter. Uncannily, Parker had a striking resemblance to the actor Conrad Bain who played Mr. Drummond. Through the magic of first-run syndication and cable TV, Diff'rent Strokes, a TV sitcom involving two boys from the ghetto, Willis and Arnold, who are adopted by a wealthy, White millionaire, lives on for generations. At our house, my boys and I watched, Diff'rent Strokes dutifully at 9pm on Nick-At-Night before my boys went to sleep.

"Sing…sing. Diff'rent Strokes for Theo."

"Okay so your name is Theo. That's great. My name is Chet." The district administrator smiled when he realized that he made some headway.

"Chet. Sing. Sing. Diff'rent Strokes." This time Theo requested with more animation and giddiness. In my adjacent cubicle, I was in tears. At that moment, my only wish in the world was that my state-issued cell phone had the technological capability to capture live video. This was going to be a moment to remember.

In his deepest baritone Chet Parker belted out his best rendition of the show's opening theme song:

> **Now, the world don't move to the beat of just one drum,**
> **What might be right for you, may not be right for some.**
> **A man is born, he's a man of means.**
> **Then along come two, they got nothing but their genes.**
>
> **But they got, Diff'rent Strokes.**
> **It takes, Diff'rent Strokes.**
> **It takes, Diff'rent Strokes to move the world.**

I almost pulled an abdomen muscle from laughin' so hard. Theo and Jovan couldn't suppress their laughter any further. The administrator's face reddened instantly. I finally rushed in.

"Bravo. Bravo. Bravo. Mr. Drummond…oh I mean Mr. Parker." I stated applauding as I entered Jeremiah's office. "That was the best version I've heard of the Diff'rent Strokes anthem I heard in a long time. I'm shocked you know the lyrics by heart!"

"Jackson, are these boys participants on one of your cases?"

"No Mr. Parker they are actually my children. Boys introduce yourselves to Mr. Chet."

"Hi Mr. Chet, Hope you don't mind me clownin' you like dat? But last time I heard 'slap me five' was on that show. Plus, you really look like Mr. D.—Mr. Drummond." Theo smiled.

"Mama. Mama. Mr. Chet funny. Mr. Chet sing song!" Jovan said as he jumped in to my arms.

"Jackson, your kids are not supposed to be on the floor, I'm sure you know it's against district policy! On top of it, your comedic children were left alone for a substantial period of time! Where is Jamie? I need to talk to her about this situation!" Parker blared as he stormed off in search of my supervisor.

Parker's indictments hit me like a freight train. His words cycled in my mind:

Against district policy?...
Left alone? ...
Situation? ...
What'chu talkin' 'bout Mr. Parker!

I was hoping my administrator countered with a joke of his own. But he was serious and seriously embarrassed. The encounter was unsettling: my appetite instantaneously vanished and I felt disorientated.

"Mama, did I get you in trouble? Theo asked.

"No baby. If it didn't happen today it was bound to happen in the future. I'm glad it did go down though; it's nice to see how people really feel around here."

Unit 808 was finally seated at **Shuckers Bar & Grill, 1819 79th Street Causeway, North Bay Village, FL 33141** around 8:25pm, two hours after the dinner's scheduled start time. But late meetings, lunches and dinners were common in the unit. Those first to the restaurant would secure a table, while stragglers filed in from their various investigations and commitments. The practice cultivated patience in the unit members because everyone assumed the role of straggler from time to time. Tonight's stragglers were unit secretary Mrs. Jessica Thompson and CPI Abassi Okafor. Abassi's third investigation required him to visit a mother at the Pre-Trial Detention Center, 1321 Northwest 13th Street Miami, FL, 33125 to determine the whereabouts of her three children. Mrs. Thompson was late because she simply couldn't catch a ride to the restaurant. Much to Rhonda's dismay their late arrival caused them to miss Shuckers spectacular Happy Hour Specials— namely their $5 frozen drink special. After the day's events, she'd gladly pay double the price for any of restaurant's famous mixed drinks: rum runners, piña coladas, daiquiris or margaritas. The unit sat around two square wooden tables that were pushed together. Shuckers offered delicious, budget-minded fare, but their outdoor seating overlooking Biscayne Bay was the reason why this was an 808 favorite. One of the Winter's last cool front's past through the night before eradicated any humidity in the air. A subtle bay breeze blew orange flames unpredictably contained in dockside tiki torches.

"Oooooh Mama look at those people over there!" Theo stated excitedly as he pointed at a 17-foot Boston Whaler Montauk pulling alongside an empty slip.

Rhonda ignored the request and took the last sip of her peach daiquiri and signaled the waitress for a refill.

"Theo have you ever been on a boat before"? I asked.

Theo shook his head to indicate no.

"Maybe I can borrow my uncle's boat and we can go out one weekend? We can do some fishing? His boat is a little bigger than that one. We'd take your mom and Javon of course." I stated watching Rhonda for a reaction. *But nuthin'.*

"Mr. Jeremiah I'd like that." Theo said as he sat on his knees on a wooden chair.

For someone devoid of children, I got along with them very well maybe because I didn't have any little brothers or sisters of my own. At the office, kids gravitated to my cube in hopes of scoring a few pieces of candy from a mason jar I kept atop my desk. Amazing what a 5-cent, sour-apple Jolly Rancher will do to unleash a child's most-deepest, hidden secrets. Suddenly, I felt something brush against my right thigh.

Then, Rhonda gave me seductive smile as she stated loudly, "Jeremiah, you're gonna be some woman's lucky catch someday! You work hard! You love chil'ren! You're responsible! And you so damn cute!"

"Who said that he's wants to be ensnared by a woman!" Bassi stated with a tinge jealousy.

The table chuckled at the jab.

I felt Rhonda's stroke once again, but way further up my leg this time. Then, again and again and again. I stiffened up immediately. I turned to look at her, but her gaze was fixated somewhere off in Biscayne Bay. Everyone at the table maintained their idle conversations, even Theo and Javon, oblivious that Rhonda, a mother of two, was using my penis as a stress ball under the table. I was in heaven.

"Attention people…attention it's getting late and I'd like to make a birthday toast to my favorite female CPI in the district. To Ms. Jackson may you find happiness and prosperity in the coming year. Thank you for your friendship and camaraderie, we all love you!" Supe exclaimed.

The unit members raised their glasses and bottles. The Fellas clutched unscathed Heinekens, while Jamie and Ms. Thompson raised diminutive glasses of Moscato. The birthday girl who switched from daiquiris to piña coladas lifted her cocktail glass wildly, while her other hand remained on me. Even Rhonda's boys held up their sweet iced teas contained in coconut-shaped sippy cups.

"To Rhonda!" We all chimed.

Mrs. Thompson reached into her purse and pulled out a small box wrapped in red gift wrapping paper— its size was no bigger than a box of checks. Our unit secretary then gave it to Rhonda along with hug and a kiss on the forehead. Rhonda arose from her seat, finally letting me go. Everyone's eyes were glued on Rhonda as she removed the gift wrapping paper. Bassi and I looked more eager than the celebrant to discover its contents. When Mrs. Thompson asked us for fifty-bucks each, she made no mention what she intended to buy Rhonda for her birthday.

"Rhonda, a little something from your second family to you." Jamie stated.

Then, Bassi gave me a wink, which reminded me of our earlier discourse at the Enchanted Forest regarding co-workers and family. *Out of sight, out of mind….The people here will forget about you.* The thoughts sobered me up immediately, so I took a long swig of my Heineken and decided to live for the day. Tonight, the 808 was my family.

"Oh my gosh y'all, thank you so much for this wonderful gift! I know it must have cost you a lick!" Rhonda stated as she held up her brand new Ipaq as her perfectly manicured, pink-glittered acrylic nails, which glistened in the moonlight.

"Mama what is that"? Theo asked.

"It's a PDA. You can put all your phone contact and addresses in here. Store your music and pictures an' you can even play solitaire and bunch of other games on it. This will definitely come in handy." Rhonda stated.

On a 42"-plasma screen TV which hovered over the bar, a breaking news story from Oahu, Hawaii interrupted a special on Miami Heat's Center Alonzo Mourning slated to start in 50th NBA All Star game. The USS Greeneville, a US nuclear submarine collided with a Japanese fishing trawler, the Ehime Maru during an emergency surfacing maneuver. Nine of the Ehime Maru's crew perished as the Ehime Maru sunk into the depths of the Pacific in minutes. Rhonda's exuberant spirit, sunk equally as fast. I excused myself from the table to smoke a cigarette while my supervisor followed close behind. We posted up just a few feet away from the others— at the end of the dock.

"What's going on with my girl? She seems like she having such a shitty day"? I asked.

"She is Jeremiah. She really is." Supe replied.

I offered my supervisor a cigarette which she politely declined.

"I came for a talk not a toke. You know I don't smoke Jeremiah." Supe said.

I smiled.

"I've definitely noticed a change in Rhonda. I didn't know she could pound 'em down like that. She's makes Bassi and me look like amateurs." I stated as I took a drag of my Kool. I was careful not to disclose my most recent under-the-table encounter with my inebriated co-worker.

"Don't worry about her binge drinking. I drove her and the boys from the Rohde building and they are welcome to spend the night with me. Last thing Rhonda needs is a DUI to add to her awful day. Before dinner, she got into again with her boys' father, Perry. She couldn't find a sitter, and had no other option, so she brought the kids to the office around 4pm. Chet Parker found them in your cube playing unsupervised and he went ballistic. He stormed into my office and strongly advised that I write Rhonda up for violating district policy. I think it's uncalled for, but you know how Administration is. I'm going to talk to Parker next week—try to let things blow over and see where he stands on the issue."

"District policy? Where does it say you can't bring you children to work?...especially at 4pm on a Friday? It must have been a ghost town at the office." I chimed.

"It was a ghost town Jeremiah. You know when Rhonda tells her boys to stay put, they never disobey her. You'll never hear her kids running around the office. Honestly, they play so quietly sometimes I don't even know they are in the office most of the time." Supe stated trying to evade the noxious smoke from my cigarette. "There's something a little more to Parker's story which he left out. He just didn't care to share it with me."

I nodded in affirmation.

"I also wanted to personally thank you for helping Bassi and Rho. From going on new cases to picking up their children from school when they're in a jam, you never let us down, we're lucky to have you in the unit." Supe stated.

"No problem Supe. If it wasn't for them I'd be like my other PDP counterparts—hired today out tomorrow." I stated as I admired my unit from afar. Bassi switched seats with mine and was now sitting beside Rhonda. *I wondered if he'd get the treatment?*

"I did get a call from Pierce Denim the other day. He told me that you came in to his office and almost attacked him when he confronted you about going on cases with one of his CPIs...a Tamara Norvil, I believe her name was?" Jamie stated. Her forearms were draped over the wooden dockside rail facing the bay.

"That fuckin' liar I didn't attack him!"

"But you did go out on cases with CPI Norvil without my knowledge?" Jamie asked calmly. The tone and volume in her voice remained constant.

I reached into my shirt pocket for another cigarette but she quickly grabbed my wrist.

"No need to tear up your lungs on my account or hide things from me Jeremiah. I know if you went to help Tamara it was for a good reason. I do ask that you tell me where you are going and who you are going with as it relates to this job. If you go to a client's home and they stick you up— and blow your brains out that's going to be on you. If you happen to get into an altercation and survive, Administration is going to be all over you and me...and if that happen you'll really wish you were dead." Supe stated wryly.

"Supe, I am truly sorry...I didn't think about it that way. I definitely do not want to compromise your livelihood." I said apologetically.

"Water under the bridge Rookie. Let's get back to the table. They look antsy without us." Jamie said as she grabbed my wrist like a toddler and led me back to the table.

13 MIA

February 14, 2001
(Carol City)

I looked at my wristwatch and contemplated walking away, but knocked on the aluminum door one more time. I heard the pitter patter of little feet, then the sound of larger ones converge on the front door.

"Yes ma'am, I'm looking for Archie Bedford, my name is CPI of Jeremiah Abundo of Department of Children and Families."

"Archie ain't here right now. I haven't seen him in the past week. Is there something I can help you with?" Gwendolyn Meriwether asked.

Gwendolyn's son Archie Meriwether held on to her mother's denim shorts for balance. In my quest to find the elusive Archie "Lil Boy" Bedford, I visited five different residences in Miami Dade County and even attempted to locate Lil Boy in Broward County just two miles away from Bayani's home in Miramar. The more research I did on this man, the more I wanted to meet him. I learned Archie Lawrence Bedford was born on August 6, 1945 in Palatka, Florida. Ironically that was the same day the United States stunned the world with its first Atomic bombing on Hiroshima, Japan. The bomb's name was "Little Boy". Archie's ignorant parents adopted the nefarious moniker and it stuck with him throughout the years. True to his name, Lil Boy left a path of destruction wherever he went. Archie's herculean ability to reproduce offspring amazed me. His children aged from 37-years old to 10-months old— 15-children from 6 different women. Crazily, 3 of his children were given the name "Archie". Supe ordered that I locate him and at the very least document my attempts to address the allegations with this alleged perpetrator. At the Department, you'll always need the help of others to complete your job; I learned that no man is an island. My first step in trying to find Lil Boy was to fill out a diligent search request and have our Analytic Unit find any useful contact information (addresses, phone numbers, and names of relatives). The Analytical Unit used a slew of restricted databases to find clients from the Department of Motor Vehicles to LexisNexis®. On this case, they furnished me six known addresses where Lil Boy lived or used as a mailing address; and I ventured to each of them. After my third address, I could've ended my search, but I wanted to meet the man myself.

"No ma'am. I just have a few questions to ask him. If possible, I'd like to leave you with my business card, just in case you do bump into him?" I stated as I handed Ms. Meriwether a card.

"If I do see him I will tell him that you're looking for him." She said.

As the front door shut and I walked to my car, I thought of the complex web created from the Collins investigation. Ten of Archie's children were under the age of 17, so based on a directive from Supe; a new abuse case would have to be generated if Archie had any contact with any of his minor children residing in any other household. Based on this rationale, I had to phone in four additional/separate abuse reports to the Hotline to address Lil Boy's other minor children: they too may have been victims to Lil Boy's sexual aggression one time or another. If you failed to make the call, and God forbid one of his other children disclosed they were abused...you're a goner. Some call it CYA (Cover Your Ass) even overkill or paranoia, but for child welfare workers throughout the state, this was a common practice. Nothing is ever simple at the Department. As I sat in my Taurus, I caught a glimpse of myself in my sun visor's vanity mirror. *I looked like straight shit.* My eyes were red from insufficient hours of sleep and small dark bags started to form under my eyes. I even saw a few gray hairs emerge. The numerous, empty packs of Kool Filter Kings that littered the floor of my vehicle proved my addiction to nicotine only escalated since beginning my tenure. Let's not mention the internal things that are going on inside your body that you are oblivious to like Stress, the silent assassin. The more cases that piled up on my office desk, the more I could feel that killer stripping the life from me little-by-little. Undoubtedly, the rigors of the job were taking its toll. I asked my partner, Bassi Okafor his secret on remaining positive and productive in such a chaotic, fast-paced environment. Bassi told me that every now-and-then a case comes along, which invigorates your spirit and reminds you of your importance. For me, the Collins case did just that; I took a heartfelt interest in this family's future. I reached into my back pocket and retrieved an email that Queen sent to me a few days ago. When I got around to it, I planned on getting a frame for it like Supe Watkins did with her keepsakes then I'd hang it in my cube. I unfolded the email and read it to aloud:

February 10, 2001

Dear Chong,

I hope all is well with you and your job. When you first showed up at my door, I resented my teacher, Mrs. Cantor for tricking me, and then calling your agency. But as I take a retrospective of everything that's happened to Mama, Poo and me, I'm glad you entered our lives. As we speak, Paramount Furniture is assembling the twin beds you helped acquire for us and Mama was elated when she opened our February electric bill from FPL and discovered our past due balance was taken care of. Chong, I'm not just writing you this letter to thank you for all the tangible items you've offered my family, but to thank you for rescuing me from the horrible place I was in. After I was violated by A.B., my life was pretty much in shambles. I didn't know where to turn or have anyone to discuss my pain with. You came into my life and allowed me to open up to others at my own pace. And even though I did not air out my hurt with you personally, you sent me to some great people at Kristi House, who knew exactly how I was feeling. When we called you— about 10-times regarding the status of our case you called us back almost immediately and that means the world to us. You're not the stereotypical child welfare worker you see on TV and in the movies who comes off as indifferent. You care and it shows. It shows in the words you choose and how you say them. For this, I'm forever grateful. You've even made me want to consider changing my major from medicine to social work—not! Seriously, I'll leave social work to the pros like you. Thank you for doing what you do.

Yours Truly,

Miss. Quintavia "Queen" Collins

P.S. –Mama gotta new job as a customer service rep at Paxco Insurance! Woot! Woot!

I folded the letter up and smiled. Bassi was right, one case does make it all worth it. Seconds later, my cell phone chimed to the ringtone of the week—'Big Pimpin' by Jay-Z. I refolded the letter and I answered my phone:

"Hi Ms. Thompson? What's going on?"

"I got an Immediate for you Honey…."

Still riding on the euphoria of the moment, I gladly accepted the case without complaint.

Initial Abuse Report 01-0011115 (Imm)

Mother Patricia Rosen had her two of children removed when she was 17-years old. Patricia was in foster care at the time and failed to complete her case plan and her two children were never returned to her care. Mother is now 24 and has given birth to two other children. Mother also smokes marijuana and is addicted to Xanax. The reporter is anonymous.

I always read my preliminary abuse reports thoroughly before attempting to meet with the family. Addressing subjects by their first names and knowing their ages proved a good way to engage new clients. This particular case proved especially challenging since none of the children's names or ages were provided to the Hotline. I tried using a number of databases accessible to investigators in District 11: birth displays, local criminal records and economic assistance records, but I was unable to find anything regarding Patricia Rosen's children. Frustrated, I never understood why child protective investigators in Miami Dade County had such limited access to Dade County Public Schools' (DCPS) database. **01-0011115** and cases like it are the ones I disliked the most—ones with little to no information and ones with anonymous reporters. As an added migraine, **01-0011115** had no home address provided. The only information provided was mother's name and her work address, Publix Supermarket, 19585 Northeast 2nd

Avenue, Miami, FL 33156. I had a strong urge to drive to Patricia Rosen's job and walk directly to the store manager's office; flash my ID and have Ms. Rosen summoned to me at her place of employment. *Why not?* Most CPIs would take this route; it was fast, efficient, but terribly embarrassing if you were the subject in question. An unexpected visit from a nosy DCF investigator to your job, never sat well with any employers. I reclined in my car seat and flicked on the A/C in my Taurus and pondered my next move. Then, I pulled out my trusty Zippo from my pants pocket, flicked the lighter's silver hinged top open with my right thumb while spinning its flint-wheel all in one motion; I then flicked the top closed with a quick flick of my wrist. I did it over and over again…

FLICK…ZZZZ…CLACK!
FLICK…ZZZZ…CLACK!
FLICK…ZZZZ…CLACK!
………………..

By the 10th or 11th repetition, I reached for my pack of cigarettes in the passenger's seat and pulled out the last one in the pack. As I placed it in my mouth, I laughed when I discovered a solution to my dilemma.

I smiled as I stepped off the green Toledo scale at the store's front entrance: the combination of nicotine and sporadic meals, kept my weight, a-lean-mean 177lbs, relatively the same since I started working for the Department. I was tempted to remain on the scale's platform because the extra inches gave me a good vantage point of the entire store. I looked around, then reached into my pocket and dialed the store's phone number on my cell phone. I pressed the number "4" and was directed to the Customer Service desk.

"Hello, I would like to speak to Patricia Rosen."

"Sure, who may I ask is speaking?"

"My name is Pablo Jones."

"One minute Mr. Jones..."

Such fine manners for a customer services rep! The moment of truth…I kept an eye/ear out for any movement in the store. I didn't know if Ms. Rosen worked in Meats, Produce, the Bakery or even handled stock. Then it happened, I watched as a middle-aged rep walk towards lane 5 and exchanged places with a cashier that appeared in her mid 20's. The cashier wore her dirty blonde hair up and had a tight, well-trimmed body. She gave her replacement a magnificent pearly smile as she walked to the customer service desk. *Could this be somebody's mother? And the mother of four at that?* I quickly mashed "End" on my Nokia. From a distance I watched as the cashier's mouth form the words "Hello?" "Who is this?" "Are you there?" before hanging up the phone. Full of myself, I couldn't wait to tell Bassi, Rhonda and Tamara about this one. I felt like Wile E. Coyote perched high atop a canyon a millisecond before dropping a humongous boulder on the annoyingly-lucky Road Runner. I waited a few minutes for my alleged perpetrator to regain her position in lane 5 before I made my move.

From an aisle cooler, I grabbed a lemon-lime Gatorade and positioned myself in lane 5.

"Hello, welcome to Publix." The cashier stated.

"Hi can I please get a pack of Kool Filter Kings?"

"Sure no problem, can I see your ID sir?"

I showed the cashier my driver's license. As she leaned in to confirm my date of birth, I spied the cashier's green name tag and confirmed her identity.

"One minute sir let me get your cigarettes from the service desk."

A minute later, Patricia handed me my green and white pack of cigarettes.

"That will be $4.75 please."

With no other customers in line, I flashed my state ID and introduced myself.

"Hi Patricia, my name is CPI Jeremiah Abundo of the Department and Children and Families. I need to talk to you about your children."

Patricia appeared annoyed, but in control of her emotions.

"Hey Mr...can you give me 10-minutes? My shift ends in 10-minutes and I can talk to you then." Patricia stated while scanning for her co-workers.

"No problem Ms. Rosen. I'll be outside." I said giggling. My plan went perfectly. Thoughts of Wile E. Coyote pranced around in my big head.

"Brilliance. That's all I can say. Sheer, unadulterated brilliance!"

I really disliked coming to a client's place of employment to initiate an investigation. The stigma of being associated with an open child abuse case could never be advantageous to an employee's standing. As Patricia Rosen exited the store's automatic doors with her green work vest tucked under her arm, I could tell she wasn't happy. She walked towards me, as I sat on a bench at the north end of the store.

"What the hell is going on? Is it DCF's protocol to come to people's jobs to harass them? I need your supervisor's phone number!" Patricia stated infuriatingly.

"Ms. Rosen we received an abuse case involving your children and there was no home address listed. Based on the limited information provided, I had no other option but to visit you at your job. If this matter wasn't important, I wouldn't be sitting here in front of you...would I?!" I snapped back.

Lately, my temper has been shorter with my clients and my tolerance for their insubordination was all but gone. In the past, when clients wanted to vent I let them. I acquiesced and gave them the latitude to yell, curse, and snarl all they wanted. Now, if a client barks **"Who gives you the right to question me as a parent?"** or yells **"DCF needs to mind their own business—they got problems of their own!"** I took personal offense to these criticisms— real personal. Then a number of random thoughts would infiltrate my mind...here's a few of 'em: *Listen, Lady...like I like coming to your fuckin' house 2am morning and dealing with your dysfunctional-ass family! or Sorry, sir...even though you were hit with a spiked mace ball when you were a kid, you can't do the same thing with your own child— how about I whack you in the ass with it a few times for old times sake? or There's nothing in the world I'd rather be doing than to have to deal with a shitty-ass parent such as yourself who should never have been blessed with having a child—or even worse children."*

"What's this shit about anyway?" She retorted.

I read the allegations to the irate parent who rolled her eyes in disgust, immediately my random thoughts consumed me once again.

"This is bullshit. Who called this in?" Patricia demanded.

"I couldn't tell you Ms. Rosen. The reporter of this case called it in anonymously. I do need to meet with your children and check out your house."

"Do I have a choice"? Patricia stated rhetorically.

"What's your address ma'am"?

###

I slowly closed the door on the Rosen's stainless steel refrigerator; and I was completely satisfied after I saw the unit fully stocked with food.

"I guess it helps that you work at Publix." I said jokingly.

"Yeah, you rarely find someone who works at a supermarket with empty cupboards." The mother of two stated.

For the past hour, I spent interviewing Patricia Rosen and her two children, Anthony and Rosa María Ellen Rosen. After our shaky, initial meeting, Patricia opened her home to me without any contingencies. The two bedroom apartment appeared to be almost faultless—even immaculate. All the beds were made and the birch, laminate flooring throughout spotless. The home was free from clutter. The home actually looked like a showroom you'd find at IKEA. Even the children were perfect. Every sentence was punctuated with a "Thank you" and "You're welcome" and their cordiality extended when they conversed with one another. Andy, 6 and Rosie, 5 attended Virginia A. Boone Highland Oaks Elementary School and appeared to be excelling according to the numerous citizenship and attendance awards that plastered the family's living room wall. According to Patricia, the family migrated from New York City three months ago after her husband, Ryan, landed a job at a South Beach web design firm. One year after Patricia and Ryan married; Andy was born—named after New York Yankees' left-handed pitching ace, Andrew Eugene Pettitte. When the couple had their daughter, Patricia named her after her favorite actress at the time, Rosa María Pérez famous Brooklynite, actor, director, and choreographer. It's no surprise both Andy and Rosie were born in the Big Apple.

"Okay Jeremiah, We'll be at your office on Monday. I assure you my husband and I do not use drugs." Patricia stated firmly.

"I appreciate your cooperation Mrs. Rosen and allowing me into your home freely, but it seems so odd someone would concoct allegations which are so specific?" I replied.

"Who knows? Some people just don't want to see you get ahead", Patricia stated.

The sound of fumbling keys and the turn of a deadbolt interrupted our conversation. Ryan Rosen entered his home plopping his Apple Ibook on a console table flanking the front door. He gave his wife a peck on the cheek and extended a pink, sun-baked hand toward me.

"Ryan Rosen, pleasure to meet you."

"CPI Jeremiah Abundo, Department of Children and Families. I spoke with your wife Mr. Rosen and she told me that both you and her are willing to take a drug test at my office on Monday. She also told me that these are your only children."

"That's right. Andy and Rosie are our only kids and they're more than a handful." Ryan advised.

"They seem like they're really good kids—very well mannered." I added.

"Do you need anything else Jeremiah? I have to get dinner ready if you don't mind?" Patricia stated.

"No ma'am. I just will need to see your children's birth certificates from New York City. My supervisor is going to look for those in my file." I requested.

"I believe they're in a file folder in our bedroom, I'll get them for you. " Patricia stated as she drifted away into her master bedroom.

Ryan and I gravitated to the living room wall which showcased all the family's accomplishments. From the kid's handwritten school awards for Citizenship to Ryan's web design certification from DeVry, each accolade was pinned, taped, stuck or fastened alongside one another. There was no deference placed on any single award, everything was just stuck up there randomly."

"This is real nice. No frames. No frills just thumbtacks and tape." I stated smiling. "This is really different."

"Oh yeah, The Wall of Fame! We want Andy and Rosie to know their accomplishments are just as great as ours. The kids really get a real kick hanging their certificates up!" Ryan stated.

From the master bedroom Patricia beckoned, "Ryan! Ryan! Can you come in here and help me look for these things!"

"Excuse me Jeremiah. You know women…they never have difficulties finding our wallets! We'll be a second."

My eyes scanned the Rosen's Wall of Fame. A yellowish document caught my eye; its weathered appearance distinguished it from any other document on the wall. I peered closer to read its inscription:

Excelsior High School
This Certifies that
Patricia Gloria Sotolongo
has fulfilled the requirements for graduation as prescribed by the…

Patricia Gloria Sotolongo? I reached into my pocket, checked the time on my Nokia, *6:47pm,* and held the 3-button down. The phone rang three times before Rhonda picked up the phone:

"What's up J? Are you still on your case"?

"Sure am. How about you Rho? Are you still in the field?"

"No I just got home, but I still have to enter my notes and submit my assessment. Oh… about the other night at the Shuckers I'm so sorry if I got a little bit carried away." Rhonda stated.

I smiled when I remembered that beautiful night. Lately, Rhonda and I have been even closer since the incident. We even planned on going on a date in the near future. Rhonda knew about Tamara and me and she was still down. I know I must be crazy to even think about cheating on Tamara since she's the total package—but I must be out of my mind to think that word would not get around to her the way people talk around here. Even though I knew I was playing a dangerous game, I didn't care. I was getting lazy and cheap…lazy for not wanting to drive over 35-miles for a piece of tail and cheap for not wanting to fork out the extra money for gas and Sunpass tolls for it.

"Rhonda, I have no issues with a beautiful woman rubbing on me, but as penance, can you run a check for me?" I said.

"No Problem J. Who's the individual?"

Several minutes later the Rosens emerged from their bedroom. Ryan folded up the sleeves of his button down dress shirt; a trail of perspiration ran down his back.

"Jeremiah, here are the kid's birth certificates from NY. They were tucked away in an unopened box. If you'd like I can a copy them for you right now if you let me boot up my computer—or would you rather I email them to you?" Ryan asked politely.

"Folks, you have been extremely nice but something came up." I replied.

"Up? What's up"? Ryan stated as his pleasant demeanor quickly fleeted.

I looked at Patricia, who shut her eyelids and cocked her head to the ceiling. She then shook her head hoping to awaken herself from this nightmare, but the patter of Rosy chasing Andy in a game of Tag confirmed this was definitely reality. I waited for the two children to retreat into the bedroom before I continued.

"Ryan what came up was your wife's past. When she was a teenager, she had a couple of her children removed from her care. She never finished her case plan or completed services, so she was never reunified with her children. I'm afraid this current situation will have to be addressed in dependency court, if your wife is to remain in this home with Andy and Rosy."

"This shit is crazy. She is a great mother and she has never lifted a finger at our children. What does her past have to do with anything? She was a kid...a teenager who knew nothing of life." Ryan stated adamantly.

"I agree with you. Your wife appears to have changed her life around— a total 180. She is working; she does a great job caring for your children. She's responsible. She's definitely not the same person as she was when she was 16." I stated.

"Then what the hell is the problem! Why do we have to go to court? Why do we have to revisit the past? Why doesn't DCF just leave us alone?!" Patricia erupted finally breaking her silence.

I felt it...my temper rising.

"Because there's a document somewhere in your thick court case file sitting on a shelf at the Juvenile Justice Center with your name on it that says you are not to have contact with your children until you present yourself before the courts. Right now you're in violation of that order and technically, these kids can come with me right now—
But I ran it by my supervisor and she gave me the okay to leave your children in the home as long as their father is present. I can also ask you to leave your home, but Andy and Rosie would be the victims."

Patricia thought about responding, but hugged me instead.

"What do we do Jeremiah"? Ryan asked.

"You will need to go to court tomorrow at 1:30pm at 3300 Northwest 27 Ave. I will draft a straight file petition advising the courts that Patricia has given birth to a new set of children in the State of New York, and we'll request for a case plan. You will have to complete all the tasks that are requested of you by the courts and the Department—parenting skills, therapy, and drug counseling if the judge feels you need it. At that hearing Ryan will be awarded the sole custody of the children, until Patricia finishes her case plan. Then, a new custody release order will be drafted giving you both custody of Andy and Rosy. The whole process can take anywhere from three to twelve months."

The Rosens agreed to the Department's offer and I'm glad they understood and accepted the situation. People do change, and when they are our past clients, we pray that the change is for the best. I jotted down the court information and gave it to the couple. Just before I left, Andy and Rosy rejoined there parents in the living room, they were winded from all the running around. I smiled when I saw their family together. As I passed through the Rosen's front door, I spied a mezuzah affixed to its frame. In my tenure, I've investigated so many people from so many walks of life— no one is excluded in this line of work. From affluent to poor, Black, White and in between I found out we're all the same.

"Oh by the way Jeremiah, will we need a lawyer for tomorrow?" Ryan blurted.

"No folks, I think you should be fine, but you have the right to bring one if you think the State's deal is inequitable....oh and one more thing folks...please don't be late. First impressions are everything. I will see you in court 1:30pm tomorrow...Bye now."

February 15, 2001

I emptied my pockets into a red plastic deli serving basket and walked through the metal detector. I expected a buzz to follow—which occurs every time I pass through one of these things, but I passed through with ease. An afternoon at the Juvenile Justice Center (JJC) was always a blast. JJC is one of the nine courthouses that comprises the Eleventh Judicial Circuit of Florida, which serves Miami Dade County. For a CPI, a trip to the courthouse could last anywhere from 15-minutes to 5-hours. I always brought a few cases to work on during the wait time and my laptop in the event I had to bolt to a new investigation right after my court hearing. Having a court date never provided you immunity from receiving new cases— Immediates included. I currently had 36-live cases under my name and this number kept swelling. This was probably the busiest time of the year in our business. I couldn't wait for the Summer to come fast enough. I caught a reflection of myself in a piece of office glass and adjusted my navy blue tie which matched my navy dress pants. I chose to sport a regular white long sleeve shirt. I completed my ensemble with some cheap black leather oxfords from Kmart. My jet black fade was in desperate need of a trim from a barber's hand I tried my best to come to court looking my best out of respect to the courts and my clients; unfortunately my dapper attire could never shield me from the emotional tirades from select judges.

I walked upstairs to the second floor where all the juvenile detention and dependency hearings are held. The North Wing held all the delinquency hearings. However, one courtroom in the North Wing, 2-7 was reserved for dependency cases. The Wing's waiting area, consisted of a 200+ seat waiting area for parents/guardians and their children who committed non-capital offences. From batteries to burglaries, agitated parents/guardians waited to hear their child's case to be called. At the back of the waiting area, law enforcement officers from throughout the County, hobnobbed and waited to testify. Their location also allowed them to survey the waiting area and the court rooms just in case something popped off. It never did though. These youngsters knew better: you'd have to be crazy to fuck with South Florida's most powerful and organized gang. As you entered the North Wing, 10-announcement boards displayed the juvenile judges AM/PM calendars. In dependency court, the cases are listed: in alphabetical order by the child's last name first, by hearing time, followed by the type of hearing (shelter, status, filing, adjudicatory trial, judicial review, TPR trial, pickup order). A Shelter/Detention hearing, the first hearing of a dependency case, always occurs on the PM calendar around 1:30pm. I never knew why they chose this time in particular, but I guess it allowed parents throughout the County ample time to attend. In this proceeding, CPIs and DCF attorneys submit legal documents explaining why we: removed a child from his parent/guardian (Shelter/Detention Petition) or left a child in the custody of his parent/guardian and are requesting court-ordered supervision. (Straight File Petition). In straight file petitions, custodianship is never severed, but the family is expected to participate in a services case plan. It is possible to request the courts to sever custodianship of one parent, while allowing the non-offending caregiver to remain in the home with the child (ren) as in the Rosen's case. In their case, Ryan Rosen, a non-offending caregiver, will be awarded sole custody of his children, until the courts are satisfied that Patricia Rosen is no longer a danger to any of her children. I scanned the boards for the Rosen's case and cursed when I saw their case was to be heard in front of the Honorable Isabel Baxter, 2-2. Last month, I was castigated in court for not serving a father for a hearing, even though his whereabouts could not be ascertained. On record—in front of everybody, Judge Baxter called me a nincompoop. Sometimes the subtlest insults are worst, this one had me scrambling for a dictionary after the hearing; by the time I realized that I was called an idiot in open court it was too late to rebut. I took a brief scan for my clients in the North Wing before walking to the South Wing.

As I entered the glass doors of the South Wing, and I saw the Rosen's sitting in front of courtroom 2-2. The seating area in the South Wing was a fraction of the North's—about one-quarter the seats. This afternoon it was a packed house, almost each of the waiting area 50-or-so seats was taken.

"Hi folks, thank you for coming on time." I stated while extending my hand to Ryan Rosen and his wife Patricia.

"Do you know when they will be starting? I told my boss that it would be an hour or so." Ryan asked.

"I really don't know sir it all depends how deep the calendar is and your judge." I replied.

I knew the real answer. Based on the volume of the waiting area and Judge Baxter's long-windedness the Rosens were going to be here for awhile. This is why some parents purposely default on cases. Imagine telling your boss you're going to take an extended lunch break to handle some personal business. You tell her you'll be back by 3pm but don't come back until 6pm. Then, tell your boss you'll require some more leave time the following week and possibly a few weeks after that. It's a matter of time before your boss says, "Sure, you can take as much leave time as you want, just don't bother coming back to work." Some parents know that without a job and suitable finances, they feel they won't get their kids back anyway, so they give up.

"Thank you Jeremiah for allowing me to stay in my home with my kids. Ryan's mom is picking them up from school for us. They don't even know what's going on." Patricia stated.

"That's great folks. When they get a little older maybe you can explain everything to them. Oh, I almost forgot, the judge will need to know that you're drug-free before she can okay the placement. Please come with me so I can show you where to sign in for a drug test." I advised.

I led the couple to a small glass booth by the entrance of the Wing. A man and woman sat behind this booth, which reminded me of a dunk tank. The gangly white gentleman and heavyset black woman laughed as they discussed last night's episode of WHO WANTS TO BE A MILLIONAIRE.

"J. Abundo! What's going on?" The gangly man exclaimed.

"Hanging in there Ricky. How are you guys doing? Busy I see."

"It's a mad house Jeremiah, this mornin' we tested around 20 adults. Your two will make 5-more for the PM calendar so far!" Evelyn Dickerson professed.

Ricky Esposito and Evelyn Dickerson worked for the court's drug intake unit and were in charge of testing parents before every hearing. Evelyn supervised the women as they provided a supervised, urine sample; Ricky did the same for the men. It was almost impossible to falsify or taint a test, since Ricky and Evelyn new every trick in the book—because both were recovering addicts themselves.

I felt my cell phone vibrate in my pocket. I looked at the number and accepted the call:

"Hold on a second Supe..." I covered the phone's microphone as I addressed the Rosens.

"Folks please sign your names on that clipboard...the courtroom number is 2-2 and the judge is Baxter. Just listen for your name when the bailiff calls it and I'll meet you in the courtroom." I said.

I retreated outside of the South Wing for some additional privacy.

###

"Go ahead Jamie."

"Jeremiah I know you're at court but I need your initial review on the Figueroa case sent to me before 4pm and we also have a 24 for you."

"Shit! I fuckin' forgot about that review. I'm still in court, but I have my laptop. I'll get that review to you before 4pm Supe. But damn Jamie another case though? I haven't even been out on the 24 you gave me this morning!" I replied as I felt my temper rising.

"Do your best."

"Really Jamie? My best? I'm trying not to get an ulcer over here. Do the higher ups know how dire the situation is down here? Catching a case a day—sometimes two is brutal. This shit is for the birds!" I blared as some passersby paused to gawk at the crazy DCF man.

"Do your best Jeremiah, I'll see what I can do to authorize the OT hours." Supe stated.

"Jamie I don't need friggin' overtime...I need time itself. The amount of work you're giving us is way too much! I have two 24s and I'm still stuck in court. I'm totally spent and I know at this pace I'm bound to fuck up on one of my cases. This is a bunch of bullshit! Straight bullshit!! Are you talking to Administration about what's going on down here?" I questioned skeptically knowing I just crossed the line with my CPIS.

"Well, Jeremiah there are a lot of people out there who need a job, if you feel you're incapable of handling this one, maybe you should reconsider your place here. This job has been this way before you got here and it will remain the same after you leave!" My unit supervisor snapped back.

I heard the annoyance in my supervisor's voice; a tone which she never comported herself when dealing with her co-workers. Supe shocked me into silence.

"Jeremiah?....Jeremiah?...Are you there?....Let's talk about this Monday. It's never a good idea to argue over the phone, these types of things should be discussed face-to-face. Do your best today and call me later if you need me. I have to go up and talk to Parker about Rhonda's mandatory write up. I think I'm getting written up as well." Jamie stated more calmly.

"I'm so sorry to hear that Supe. Bye and good Luck."

She hung up...and I felt awful.

I plopped down in one of the waiting area chairs and cracked open my laptop and began my risk assessment on the Figueroa case. It took me 15-minutes to complete the assessment. The assessment consisted of 30-or-so questions dealing with risk and safety factors surrounding the child and his caregiver i.e. *"Does the caregiver suffer from any mental health issues?"*, *"Does the caregiver have a history of being abused as a child?"*, *"Does the child have a history of abusing small animals?"*, *"Do people who have no familial relationship frequent the home?"* I added a few brief notes to my case regarding the condition of the Figueroa children and the date and time I saw them, but I lacked the focus and concentration to fully develop my notes because I still felt guilty about my encounter with Jamie.

"Hey young buck how are you doin'?"

The familiar voice jogged me from my work.

"Hey Mr. Tolliver how are you doing sir? Nice to see you." I stated as I rose from my seat to give Ely Tolliver a bro hug.

"I'm back with the Department right now, Early Services Intervention. I'm in ESI unit 112 I left PDP since I heard they might be privatizing certain components. I have another few years and I can put in for my pension and maybe enter the DROP" Ely said as he clutched a gargantuan, brown file folder.

"Congratulations Mr. Tolliver, you have my utmost respect and admiration to work at this place for as long as you have. I haven't been here a year and I'm up to my neck with cases. I just got another one a few minutes ago…my second of the day and now I'm stuck in court on this straight file petition from yesterday. We're just waiting of Judge Baxter to be seated" I stated.

"Well young brother, I hate to break this to you, but you're gonna be here a for a minute. Judge Baxter is covering Van Buren's calendar as well. I'm here on a JR that was scheduled at ten o'clock this morning, Baxter is handling Van Buren's cases first then she will handle her own calendar. She probably ran through 30-cases this morning." Ely said as he took a seat beside me.

"Shit, so basically I'm going to be here 'till around 6 o'clock or so?" I stated listlessly.

"Yes sir, you're goin' to be here for a while, so cop-a-squat an' get comfy!" Ely responded gleefully.

"Well damn, Mr. Tolliver... what's so funny? Do you like being stuck in court? I'm sure you have other things to do after you leave here! This shit is crazy!" I replied. *I could feel my temper boil over once more...*

"Yes sir, this shit is crazy young man." Ely volleyed back with even less care.

"Well fuck this job and fuck this whole scene! It seems like everyone's life is much more important than mine or anyone who's crazy enough to work in this madhouse!" I barked. ...*Meltdown.*

My diatribe caught the attention of some clients talking with their attorney a few seats away. Ely noticed and attempted to rein me back in— at least emotionally.

"C'mon young buck let's go have a smoke outside. This one is on me this time."

###

I unloosened the Windsor knot of my tie and unbuttoned the top two buttons on my dress shirt and followed Ely for a smoke. We situated ourselves right outside the glass doors of the South Wing where we could still have a line of sight at 2-2. As we leaned over a thick stone guard rail which overlooked the first floor's courtyard, Ely lit a cheap generic cigarette for himself and then offered one to me.

"Listen young brother, you're going to have to watch your temper, especially around these clients. If you lose it in front of them, they'll never respect you." Ely flicked the ash of his cigarette and continued.

"The reason I was fuckin' with you in there is because you reminded me of myself 20-years ago—hotheaded, hardworking and passionate. You couldn't tell me nuthin' because I thought I knew it all. I'd go out on case after case, workin' on a few hours of sleep. Shit, there were times I was so deep into my cases, I wouldn't bother to change clothes or even wash my ass. I'd just go on…one day to the next. Everything was a blur."

I listened attentively. I took one puff of Ely's generic cigarette and decided just to hold it between my fingers for effect.

"Do you remember what I told you months ago when we first met"? Ely asked.

I thought to myself for a few seconds then responded…

"You told me I'm a cog in this big machine and when they are done with me they will replace me with a newer part."

"That's correct Jeremiah. You're the new replacement part and they hired you to replace old farts like me! Unfortunately, the pace you're workin' I bet you don't make it to your third year workin' for the Department." Ely stated.

I listened to Ely's wisdom and knew he was right. Recently, I have been forgetting simple tasks and have been intolerable to everyone around me. Ely nailed it on the head when he described life as a blur.

"So where do I go from here bossman? How do I survive working here"? I asked.

"First of all you need to learn to play the game young buck, and not preoccupy yourself with all its fuckery. Take me for example. I'm old. I'm slow. But I know how to play the game. I never stay too long in one position at the Department. I work a year max then move to the next thing. I've worked in foster care, CPI, economic services, Adult CPI, diligent search and even did a stint in transportation after Shorty Diamond stuck a gun in my face. I don't give these people the time to get rid of me. Second thing you need to realize is that there's certain things you can't change such as when court hearings start and how many cases they want to give your brown ass!" Ely punctuated his lesson by blowing gray smoke out of his nose.

I immediately thought of my heart to heart with Uncle Bayani on the Intercostal, who reminded me of just these facts:

Kung di ukol, di bubukol …If it is not relevant, it makes no difference.

"Just be cool young brother. The Department needs smart, talented young investigators like you to handle these cases."

I smiled after hearing Ely's affirmation.

"Speaking of cases Mr. Tolliver, what's that mammoth one under your arm? Looks like your carrying a phone book."

"Oh this case? It's the judicial review that's being heard—or should I say will eventually be heard. I think the case came out of your unit. Rhonda Jackson removed on this one initially. The mother's name is Deidre Jones and she has two sons, DeAndre and Devon."

"The name doesn't ring a bell Ely."

"Look over there…the lil thing sittin' by the entrance of 2-1, that's Deidre Jones that's the 18-year old mother on this case."

I peered through cloudy glass doors at the mother. Deidre's dark mocha skin glistened from the court room lights; the glow was surely accentuated by her excessive use of Keri Lotion. She wore a cheap sand colored short set which looked fresh off a Flea Market USA rack. Deidre wore a pair of plastic purple flip-flops that exposed her ashy feet. Here edges that bordered her temples wore thin from excessively tight ponytails or one-too-many poorly done sew-ins.

"Yeah, now I remember her! She tried to abscond with her newborn, Devon from Jackson Memorial Hospital, after Rhonda placed a hold on the child. At first she had us all fooled when she gave the hospital a bogus name, but Rhonda immediately recognized her from her priors. Deidre was in the system as a child, and she had a few priors with her son DeAndre who suffers from Sickle Cell—all involving medical neglect." I said.

"Yes sir, it's a sad situation. Deidre grew up in foster care and there's a good chance her kids will as well. Van Buren wants mother to: follow up with the child's hematologist weekly, wants her and the children to have therapeutic supervised visitations, wants mother to keep a job or prove she is enrolled in school, and then she wants her to complete a six-week parenting class. Oh, I almost forgot…she has to prove she has somewhere for her and the children to live and it can't be with the maternal grandmother Silvia who had her rights terminated as to Deidre." Ely explained frustratingly.

"Seems like a lot for one person to handle." I added.

"It sure is. The sad thing is that Van Buren is big on permanency and achievin' this in a year. He made it was no secret that he wants Deidre on a concurrent case plan and highly emphasized this request at the dependency filing."

"You lost me Ely. All I've done since working at the department is CPI work. What is a concurrent case plan?"

"Jeremiah, a concurrent case plan is an alternative plan that is made to run alongside the reunification plan. The alternative plan can be long term placement with a relative, adoption, or SIL…Subsidized Independent Living if the is child old enough. My whole issue with this is the Judge's insistence on a concurrent case plan for my client. Deidre hasn't been an afforded an opportunity to fail; we are assuming that she will. To strip her children away from her after a few failed tasks is unfair. Just because Deidre's mother had her right's terminated as a parent doesn't mean Deidre is destined for the same path. Besides, Deidre's mother Silvia has gotten her life on track— now she works for the County, driving school buses for Dade County Public Schools."

I walked up to the glass entry way and stuck my face closer to the glass this time. I stared at the Deidre Jones who was a very pretty girl. She reminded me of a younger version of Tamara. The single mother was fiddling with the buttons on her cell phone, while twirling it in her hands. The two seats that flanked her were unoccupied. I then looked across to 2-2 at the Rosens. Ryan clutched his wife's hand as they waited for their shelter hearing to begin. The couple looked impeccable in their matching business suits. I spent a couple of minutes surveying these two images…and then drawing similarities and differences:

Deidre and Patricia had their children removed from their care when they were teens. Both mothers made bad mistakes, Deidre missed a few of her son's medical appointments, while Patricia gave birth to cocaine-exposed infant. Both came to court today for the love of their children. *Then why do their paths differ?* Maybe it's Deidre's lack of family support or the fact that Patricia left her children behind in Miami to start a fresh, new life in New York. Then, why would the courts allow Patricia a new life with her children, Andy and Rosy, while disallowing Deidre's mother, Silvia, any guardianship or cohabitation with her grandchildren? Both women had their rights terminated as to their children. The longer I analyzed the situation, the more things became unclear. *Does it even matter that Deidre had the courage to attempt a case plan, while Patricia never even stepped foot in a courtroom after her children were removed?*

"Yes young buck, if you've been here a while you see this foolishness happen day in and day out." Ely stated as he approached from behind. I could smell his smoky breath as he leaned in closer. But my eyes remained transfixed at these two women.

"I can imagine Ely…sometimes we're so busy, we fail to see the obvious, especially when it's right in front of us." I murmured.

"If you ask me, it starts with the judges. Judges are just like you and me. They breathe the same air and walk the same earth and they will be judged by the same God come judgment day. They also make the same mistakes and they go through the same motions with their own children—namely their teenagers. Look at Judge Brown, his kid just got out of residential for addiction to prescription pain killers. Judges are definitely not immune to racist thoughts or class bias just because they've donned a black robe and a gavel—if anything it's just amplified." Ely stated as I remained motionless.

Ely hovered alongside of me as we peered through the same cloudy glass, "This shit has been goin' on for years—generations.

Deidre's fate was sealed before she stepped foot in this place. No supports. No chances. The worst kind of racism or classism there is, is the one you cannot put your finger on, but it has you scratchin' your head years later askin' what just happened?"

Our eyes simultaneously focused on Judge Baxter as she finally emerged from her chambers. Her bald, portly bailiff provided escort as they entered courtroom 2-2 at 2:45pm—an hour and fifteen minutes past schedule. The waiting area was abuzz.

14 WELCOME HOME

(Little Havana)

Sweat poured down from his forehead to his brow as he waited at the door of the communal bathroom in Ms. Regina Suarez's rooming house. In a day, Lil Boy Bedford's life was flipped upside down since his association with Denise Johnson and her trifling-ass children ended. He continued to wait, but with each second that passed his blood began to boil and his stomach raucously churned. Regardless how strong he appeared, he was in agony.

"C'mon man it's been 10-goddamn' minutes! Yo' time is up Chico!" Lil Boy demanded as he pounded on the bathroom door.

If he had to piss, he'd just go on the side of the house of Ms. Regina's 3/2 like he normally does, but he had to take a massive number two. If he listened to his first instincts and left Denise Collins alone he wouldn't be in this mess. Now, his stomach was bubbling from a-half dozen cans of Natural Ice and some ridiculously hot Jerk chicken from Irie Isles. Suddenly, the bathroom door cracked open allowing a wall of steam to rush out at one time, the steam overtook Lil Boy all at once causing him to wince then sneeze. A millisecond later, Lil Boy felt the ooze of piping, hot shit cascading down his pant leg. Unfortunately, he only had two good pair of pants after The Collins family altruistically decided to give 95% of his worldly goods to Goodwill.

"Hey Archie she all yours bro. Make sure you scrub your dirt ring after you take a bath hermano!"

Lil Boy stood frozen until 5-foot, 1-inch Efren Lugo passed before he made a move into the bathroom. He didn't want to draw attention to his recent mishap. A few seconds later, he slinked into the bathroom, cursing the little spick all the way.

Lil Boy felt a little better after he cleaned himself. He soaked in warm water and mineral spirits. Nowadays, his rage fluctuated like the South Florida weather in December. One minute it's 90-degrees the next day an Arctic cold front sweeps across the state causing a hard rain followed by a chilliness that can dip down into 30's in some parts of Miami. The warmth of the bath water caused him to slowly doze off. He mumbled as he succumbed to the drowsy affects of the warm bath water. Visions of recent events danced through his head. Like the night, a cigar chompin' Cuban detective named Nunez arrested him right on his job site as he pressure cleaned the grounds of Zeledon's Gas and Go on Northwest 79th Street and Northwest 7th Avenue. When the police took him in, the cops refused to allow one of his buddies to move his Econoline van from the gas station. Hector Zeledon, the owner of the gas station immediately had the vehicle towed; it's a mystery what happened to Archie's cleaning equipment after the vehicle was hauled off. He blamed his situation on that, "Damn Denise and her hooker-ass daughter!" Then, he saw himself sleeping on a frigid bunk in Dade County Lockup. While in Lockup, Lil Boy had to avoid Quintavia's ex-boyfriend, Antwon "Scrub" Bennett for two weeks. Lil Boy knew the two weren't together, but he wasn't sure if Queen shared their kitchen rendezvous with the muscle-bound jit. After a few more incoherent mumblings, Lil Boy was out cold.

He felt the first can which felt piss hot, then reached to the back of the True TSD-47G Sliding Glass Door Refrigerator and grabbed the coldest can of Steel Reserve 211 he could find. He walked down the various aisles filling his basket with essentials: bread, peanut butter, potato chips, and prepackaged luncheon meat. Lil Boy had a compact refrigerator in his boarding room to keep his perishables. When the blue hand basket was full he approached the cashier. Freedom Market was like most local convenient stores in the ghetto— the prices were higher than larger grocery store chains and the shelf life of most products were doubly dubious. But these small stores were accessible to most who had no transportation to travel and shop at the larger stores, so they proved themselves invaluable.

"A what's up Archie? How are you doing my friend? Long time no see!" The Middle Eastern cashier said while ringing up his groceries.

"I've been out of town on business Ray, but now I'm back." Archie replied.

"Speaking of business are we doing any today? Do you need to make a withdrawal"? Ray asked covertly as he scanned his store.

"Not today. I need all these groceries to last me till next month. We'll do some business next month Ray, I promise." Lil Boy answered as he gazed at the Sig Sauer P220 which graced Ray's hip—Freedom Market's official loss prevention measure.

"You sure my friend? Right now I'm offering fifty-five cents on the dollar. I don't know what the rate will be next month"?

"Damn that is a good rate Ray. Now that I think of it give me a fifty dollar withdrawal and give me a pack of Backwoods." Archie said.

Ray rang up Archie's basket of groceries and then keyed in two dozen-or-so phantom items. He rang the beer and cigars separately.

"Mr. Archie. You groceries come up to $127.45 and your can of beer and Backwoods comes up to $3.25. You can go ahead and swipe your card my friend." Ray stated.

Archie paid for his beer and Backwoods with cash then he fished out his red, white and blue EBT card from his tattered wallet. Then, he swiped his card and keyed in his pin.

"A…Archie can you try to swipe it again. It says 'Sale Denied: See ESS".

Once more, Archie swiped his card again and inputted his pin…

"Sorry Archie. Same error code. Your shit is fucked up. You need to talk to the people with the State. I can't process your withdrawal but since you're a preferred customer I can credit you the groceries." Ray advised.

"Thanks Ray. I'll pay you back. You have my word."

The following day Lil Boy woke up early and ventured to Florida Department of Children and Families Access Office in Opa Locka to reconcile his account. He usually frequented the Caleb Service Center off Northwest 54th Street and Northwest 22nd Avenue which was closer, but his cousin Alyssa Bundy, a former administrator had some pull over in the Opa Locka office. Even before Archie could take a seat in the waiting area, an Economic Support Specialist was tending to him by 9:05am.

"Hi Mr. Bedford, I'm Hal Johnson, Ms. Bundy asked that I assist you today. If you could just follow me I'll pull your case on my system."

"I have no idea why they'd put a sanction on me. I'm a disabled vet living on a fixed income. I can't be without my benefits." Archie stated adamantly while following the burly ESS worker down a maze of cubicles.

"What branch did you serve under"? Hal Johnson asked.

"Army."

"Oh yeah? Army man? I served as a Marine for two tours, Semper Fi." Hal Johnson said proudly.

A few more twists and turns and the two vets finally made it to Hal Johnson's cube.

"Here we are Mr. Bedford, please take a seat."

"Damn Brother, they need to give you two of these offices. This setup is way too small for you!" Archie stated as he surveyed the 8ft by 6ft cubicle.

Hal Johnson smiled and handed Archie a Post-It-Note, pad and a pen.

"Mr. Bedford, please write your name, DOB, and your Social Security number. I will also need a photo ID as proof of identification."

Within seconds, Archie jotted down his information and handed Hal Johnson his driver's license. Hal inputted Archie's information in the system. Hal Johnson rolled a pen between his fingers as he read the information on his monitor. Archie tried to read the notes himself, but due to his failing eyesight it was almost impossible to decipher the muddled, green monochromatic text.

"So what's up Brother? What's goin' on with my money"? Archie asked.

"Says here:

that AB does not reside at current address and his contact information is unverifiable. Says Quintavia Collins and Marcus Collins are not provided benefit from FS disbursement. AB is subject of an open child abuse investigation, 01-0009008; AB may be deliberately avoiding contact with CPI Jeremiah Abundo. AB must provide proof of residency prior to reinstitution of benefits. If AB is located please contact CPI Abundo (305) 377-1000."

Instantly, Archie's body language and demeanor morphed. With furrowed brow and clinched teeth and fists, Lil Boy banged on Hal Johnson's flimsy desk causing Hal's kinetic motion balance mobile to separate from its base. The act of aggression severed the bond of the two vets immediately.

"Hey man, what the fuck is this? I came hur for yo' help and you finna cut my benefits. I fought for this county and this is the thanks I get?" Lil Boy erupted banging on the desk once more causing the mobile's base to crash to the floor this time. Heads popped up from their cubes after hearing the commotion.

Hal Johnson leaned down and picked up the base and carefully

reassembled the mobile on his desk. He then picked up his office phone and began dialing CPI Abundo's number.

"What the hell are you doin'? Don't believe all that bullshit on the 'puter. Shit ain't true!" Lil Boy blared.

"All I'm doin' is my job Mr. Bedford. If you didn't do anythin' wrong then you'll be alright." Hal Johnson stated.

Lil Boy attempted to snatch the phone from the former marine causing the headset to crack Hal Johnson on his chin. Although no blood was drawn, all deference to pleasantries and cordialities immediately ceased. Hal Johnson's co-workers started gravitating to his cubicle in droves.

"Out of respect to your service, I'm goin' to allow you to leave peacefully. But if I have to lay hands on you Mr. Bedford, you'll wish you never met this marine." The hulking Hal Johnson calmly stated.

Archie watched in awe as veins magically popped from Hal Johnson's biceps, hands and neck, Archie arose from his seat and moved towards the exit.

As Lil Boy waited for the 27 bus or one of the various jitneys to take him back to the Little Havana, he was visibly shaken. He stopped off at a gas station and bought a fifth of Wild Irish Rose. Aside from his food stamps woes, he found out that someone notified the Department of Health (DOH) that he was working under the table. The DOH's Division of Disability Determinations (DDD) scheduled a redetermination hearing to address the matter on March 9, 2001—just three weeks away. The wind picked up indicating a storm was brewing – one of the last cold fronts of the year was passing. Lil Boy removed the plastic wrapper from the top of his bottle of Rose, and tossed it onto the sidewalk. He watched as the wind lifted the wrapper menacingly and haphazardly down Northwest 27th Avenue. From a distance, Lil Boy saw the 27 trudging down the street. He chugged down his bottle of Rose in a single gulp. He felt a droplet of rain on hit his forearm, then another hit his cheek. His money was officially fucked up—$1200 in disability benefits and almost $350 in food stamps. His work van was at the pound and his equipment was gone. Lil Boy was convinced The Collins Family was to blame. As the 27 approached it began to rain harder, he scoured through his pockets for his EASY Card bus pass. *But Nuthin'.*

He cursed aloud, *"Damn this fuckin' life! Damn the Collins Family! They made a mess of my money and my good name!"*

Lil Boy flagged the 27 down and its doors opened. He tried futilely to mask the frustration in his voice.

"I'm a disabled vet sir, and I lost my bus pass could you let me on?" Lil Boy begged.

The bus driver smelled the alcohol immediately and answered Lil Boy's request by shutting the doors in his face. As the 27 pulled away, Lil Boy hurled the empty bottle of Rose at the bus and missed—badly. As the sky opened up, Lil Boy began his one hundred block hike down the Avenue soaking wet and defeated.

February 18, 2001

Queen's attention alternated from the dresser mirror to the television. The breaking news of racing legend Dale Earnhardt's death shocked the world—even to people foreign to his sport. Everyone knew Dale Earnhardt was the pinnacle of success when it came to NASCAR. The Intimidator, nicknamed after his aggressive racing style, perished after he collided with car 86 driven by Ken Schrader at the Dayton 500. Queen's eyes watered when she heard the racing legend's accident was caused by him trying to stave off other drivers tryin' to take the 1st and 2nd place spots from his fellow team riders. My sister broke into tears when she learned that one of the team riders was his own son Dale Earnhardt Jr. The news story made both of us miss our father a little more. If Songbird was alive I think he'd be proud of the children that he helped create. The young lady that stood before me never failed to amaze me and always made me thankful to have a big sister such as her. As Queen, looked into the mirror preparing herself for her big night out, she tucked her white t-shirt into her form fitting jeans, then turned to see how she looked from the side—she winked at me and I winked back giving her my seal of approval. Since Mama landed steady work, she set aside some extra money for her daughter. Mama knew how hard Queen was studying in school and how much time she spent helpin' with me. When payday arrived, both the Collins women got paid. Queen eyed her Hello Kitty watch *4:35pm,* she blew me a kiss and waved goodbye as she bolted out of our room.

"Mama I'm out tha door, Simone, me and the girls are goin' to Aventura Mall to catch a movie, then we're grabbin' somethin' to eat... if you need me hit me on the hip!" Queen stated

"Hit you on the what"? Mama asked.

"My cell phone mommy. My cell phone."

"Awright baby be careful and have a good, good time. Tell Simone not to drive too fast baby!" Mama advised my sister as she gathered her belongings.

"Okay Mama. We'll be safe."

Mama held the door open as her eldest child pranced to her friend's car. Half way down the walk way Queen doubled back. With all the talk of deaths and accidents today, she ran up the two step stoop, and gave Mama a kiss on the cheek.

"I love you Mama, thanks for everythin'."

Then she ran to Simone Andrew's 1988 Toyota Tercel where her trio of friends clowned her for her overt show of affection. Mama smiled and rubbed her tattooed forearm as she watched Simone's Tercel zip off down the street. Mama closed the front door to find me standing in front of her.

"Mama, Queen told me I couldn't go with her to see her movie because she said it was too scary for me and it would give me bad dreams." I stated.

"Oh yeah? What movie is yo' sista goin' to see"? Mama asked.

"They went to see **Hannibal**. Queen told me this guy eats his own brain! Yuck!" I said as my face cringed with disgust.

"How about we do somethin'…just you and me?"

"Can we go to Chuck E. Cheese's"?

"You got it Poo…just you and me."

I jumped in the air and clicked my feet. The sight amazed my Mama beyond belief.

###

Mama always enjoyed taking her children to Chuck E. Cheese (CEC). When Songbird was alive they'd take Queen here usually on birthdays or anytime she made her school's honor roll, which was frequently. Mama watched as I climbed up a neon orange rope ladder to the top of a mammoth soft play structure then vanish into large plastic tubes of various colors: blue, yellow and green. Every other tube section had a Plexiglas cut out to assure protective parents that their children were safe. I made sure Mama saw me as I popped my big head through one of the sections, while banging hard on the Plexiglas. Overall the amusement center was a good value. The food and drinks were affordable enough for Mama's budget. However, the games always left her pocketbook a little lighter. The ticket exchange rate in CEC was comparable to that of the Zimbabwean dollar. Mama eyed the Chuck E. Cheese Hoops game, her husband's favorite game. When the family needed a quick 100-tickets, Songbird would obliterate the high score on Hoops by making bank shot after bank shot with the midget-sized basketballs. Suddenly, Mama's feelings of nostalgia were interrupted by a baby's cries. She turned to the booth behind her to find a very young mother slightly older than Queen holding an infant so young she had no business bein' out in public. The cries continued.

"Hey little one. Hey little itty bitty, What's wrong with the baby?" Mama purred trying to pacify the infant.

"I don't know what's wrong with her. I tried to feed her, but she won't stop crying." The teenage mother replied.

"I'm a baby vet—I gots two beautiful one's under my belt. Mind if I try holdin' her?" Mama asked.

The young mother smiled affirming her response. Mama rose from her seat as the young mother passed Mama her child. She looked down at the tiny bundle and felt trembling.

"What's your daughter's name?"

"Her name is Cheyenne...she was born in Wyoming."

"She's beautiful. Is this yo' first child?" Mama asked knowing the answer already.

"Yes. She's my first."

"At this age you have to keep your child bundled and warm. Socks, cap, and even mitts. She just came out of yo' belly weeks ago and you can imagine how warm it was in there!" Mama smiled at the young mother.

"Thanks for the advise my name is Elizabeth."

"My name is Denise, pleasure to meet you."

Mama handed Baby Cheyenne back to her mother and waved goodbye. In that brief moment, Mama asked herself, *I wonder how it would be to hear the sound of lil feet around the house again?* But the notion was quickly dismissed, as she answered her own question in the same breath. *Nope, there'll be no grands runnin' around at the Collins residence anytime soon!* She smiled and refocused her attention on me, who was now heaving hard plastic balls down a skee-ball lane.

The amber Miami street lights lulled me as we drove home; the closer we got to our destination, the heavier my eyes got. There was a hole in the Astro's muffler, which created a low, audible moan as Mama mashed the accelerator. Due to this inescapable noise, you really had to speak up— almost yell, when you rode in the Collins' new whip. The day Mama picked up our new vehicle from the lot Queen and I already had a name for her, 'Mona' short for 'Mona Lisa'. With her new position at Paxco Insurance and her rapid refund check from her 2000 Tax Return, Mama bought the used, but solid 1994 white Chevy Astro Van. She chose the 6-cylinder vehicle since the van was big enough to transport her two children and all of her cleaning equipment, should she need to make some extra money on the weekends cleanin' houses. Queen and I loved Mama's new car because of the convenience, but we really loved "Mona Lisa" 'cause it was Mama' own.

"So did you have fun Poo"?

"Yeah Mama, that was too much fun!"

"It's like old times. Back when yo' daddy was alive and workin' at the Port and Queen was in elementary school: it was just you and me.

We'd go to the park, run errands, and go do laundry at the washhouse. We used to have so much fun and you would never cry or give me any problems." Mama said nostalgically as she kept her eyes on the road.

Mama was tempted to look directly at me who was safely buckled into the backseat, but her driving skills were rusty after years of relying on public transportation and bummin' rides.

"Mama can I ask you a question"? I asked as I stared out the Astro's window."

"Sure, baby you can ask me anythin'." Mama acknowledged.

"Mr. Archie doesn't come around the house no mo'...an' even though I didn't care for him much, it was nice to have a man around to teach me things like how to throw a spiral wit' a football an' explain how they setup those big ol' buildin' cranes so quickly...will I ever get a daddy again Mama?"

"Poo, when a man and a woman meet, they got to get to know one another before settlin' down and gettin' married. Songbird is always gonna be yo' daddy, but one day another man might come along and if he treats you and yo' sister halfway as decent as Songbird did that guy might have a chance. I trust a man on how well he treats my chil'ren and how well he treats his own." Mama stated with her eyes fixated on the road.

"So Mr. Archie is outta tha picture"?

Mama burst out laughin' after hearing the metaphor.

"Yes, Mr. Archie is definitely 'outta tha picture'. I don't know when we're gonna hea…"

Before Mama could finish her sentence, she peered at the rearview mirror once more to find me fast asleep. Of the Collins kinfolk, I was told I had the kindest, sweetest demeanor: I could find enriching qualities in the most barren things and people—even is a wretch like Archie Bedford.

As Mama drove she felt immense pride thinking of her topsy-turvy, but wonderful life. Her family endured plenty and they are still thriving. She thanked God for blessing her with two of the most amazing children. She felt a nip in the air and rolled up the van's windows. She took the scenic route since she was in no rush. Too scared to turn on the radio 'cause it racked her nerves, Mama hummed a tune to herself. Minutes later, she found herself in front of our home. Mama threw the Astro's shift lever in Park and noticed I was still fast asleep. She walked around to the other side of the vehicle and slid the van's door open; she unbuckled me from my seat and carried me into the house. I felt her knees buckle as she joyfully exclaimed, *"My baby's growin' up to be a young man!"* The thought made her smile. When she made it up the stoop, she unlocked the front door and proceeded to lay me down in my bed. Suddenly, she heard the front door slam shut, she looked at the wall clock *7:25pm* and knew it couldn't be Queen— her curfew wasn't until midnight and she knew my sister wouldn't be back until then. She shook me and awoke me from my slumber.

"Poo. Poo. Wake up baby! Wake up baby!

"Yes Mama, are we home yet"? I responded groggily.

"Wake up! I need you run to Mrs. Pam's house and have her call the police." Mama whispered forcefully.

The sound of glass breaking and loud guttural yells fully awakened me from my semi-conscious state.

"Yes Mama, I'll run over thur right now." I responded.

As I attempted to bolt out the bedroom door, Mama snatched me by the collar.

"Poo I need you to go out the window Baby!"

I looked at Mama and I knew there was something terribly wrong. From being homelessness to wonderin' where our next meal would come from, Mama was never scarred, in fact she was fearless. Mama gave me an enormous hug and whispered a few words into my ear. Tears began trickling down my face. Then she popped the thin, 14kt

273

gold Figaro chain an' her wedding ring which hung from it and tucked it in my pants pocket.

"When you see yo' sista tonight, give her this. Tell her that I love you both with all my heart!—I will see you soon!"

She then helped me climb through the half-cracked single hung window. If she was small enough to climb through, she'd be right behind me. Since moving in, Mama always complained about the broken window, but our cheap, apathetic landlord always gave a number of excuses when it came down to fixing it. When I was on the other side of the window, I wiped the tears streamin' down my face and for a brief moment I stared at my mother, tryin' to memorize every curve and detail of her beautiful face. When Mama smiled at me then nodded, I bolted into the dark alleyway to locate Mrs. Pam.

Mama moved to the bedroom door— just steps from confronting the interloper. She attempted to locate anything that could be used as a weapon, but she was unsuccessful. She closed her eyes and took a few deep breaths before the door swung opened. Mama was almost floored by Archie's putrid smell, a mix of strong grain alcohol and burnt plastic.

"Archie what the fuck are you doin' in my house! You know I got a restrainin' order out on yo' dusty, ol' ass!" Mama belted to the best of her ability. But Archie too sensed the fear in his ex-girlfriend's voice.

"Fuck a restrainin' order and fuck you." Lil Boy replied as his nostrils flared and his fists clinched.

He slowly edged closer to my Mama, but she had no where to go. She rubbed her tattooed forearm and readied herself...

But her last bit of courage vaporized as Lil Boy rushed Denise Collins.

15 WELCOME BACK

We sat outside Bayani's 2-story, 4000-square foot home. The cabin of my Taurus smelled of fried pork and crabs. As promised, my girl, Tamara Norvil whipped up some of her famous fried griot and crab legume for my family's gathering on this February 18th, 2001— the day before Presidents Day. Tamara marveled at Bayani's house as she waited for me to finish my cigarette.

"Damn Jeremiah, your uncle made his fortune in real estate? I definitely think we're in the wrong occupation!"

"Yeah, I don't know how he does it. He brokers two or three houses a day. He tells me the banks are just giving loans away with little questions asked. Are you interested in buying something here in South Florida...I'm sure he can get you a great rate?" I stated curiously waiting her response.

"Not sure yet Babe that all depends on my job status. Things have gotten better since Denim left. Less stress. Less micromanaging. But there are other elements of the job that will never change." Tamara stated leaving me still in limbo.

Since learning of Tamara's intentions of moving on from the Department— and me, I tried not to get too emotionally attached. *What's the point?* Since getting a new supervisor, she called me less. Strangely, as weeks passed, I saw this new sense of confidence emerge in my girl. When I offered my help on her cases, she balked immediately. During an On-call case she received at 2am last week, she removed six children right out of Chocolate City aka Arthur Mays Villas Housing Projects in Goulds by herself— no police backup or departmental assistance. She crammed all of the children in her '99 Nissan Maxima and took them straight to the South Hub. To see Tamara emerge into a stronger person actually made me want her more. But as she drifted away I found it hard to share my high and low moments with her. She made it clear that she had one foot out the door. *So why burden her with stories and memories of a job she'd rather leave in the past?* Things happen and things change so quickly around here. You just have to accept it. I took my last drag out of my Filter King before I extinguished it in the car's ashtray, the last trial of smoke traveled up-and-out of the open car window Tamara was hanging out of. She turned to me and she never looked so beautiful. With her hair in a flip and the contrast of her bright white smile against her rich chocolaty skin, she looked like the girl of my dreams…but like any dream I knew sooner or later I'd wake up and she'd be gone from my life forever.

"Do you know they are starting to make cars without cigarette lighters and ashtrays"? I stated trivially.

"Yes sir, times are changing and people are changing. You can't remain the same person forever; we must constantly evolve and be better."

"Yeah I know. I was really thinking about giving up smoking. It's just not the same. In college everyone smoked. At school and at parties you lit up everywhere you could. Here no one smokes—scratch that, there are a few people that smoke from the various agencies at the Rohde. We all come down at certain times of the day and light up together. It was a group of eight of us when I first started. Now it's down to four. I'm hoping the four that split from our group kicked the habit voluntarily."

"Jeremiah you'll eventually have to make that decision to kick the habit on your own. Like all addicts the first step in recovery is realizing you have a problem. Have you ever wondered why I never bugged you about your smoking?" She paused knowing I didn't have an answer to her question. "It's because I wanted you to come to grips with your own addiction…and see you did."

"We'll thank you for that." I responded.

"I also wanted to thank you for being there for me these past few months. Your friendship has been amazing. I don't know how I'd make it this far without your support." She said.

276

Tamara reached over and gave me a long kiss. I had thoughts about taking her—right here in front of Bayani's house in the backseat of my Taurus, but I caught myself.

"Thank you again for that." I stated with satisfied grin.

"I hope your folks like me."

"Why wouldn't they? You're smart. You have a job. You're beautiful. Shall I continue?"

"No, I mean I'm Black and you're Asian. I'm Haitian and your people are from the Philippines." She said.

I reached over and touched Tamara on her chin.

"There's a lot my people and your people have in common!" I exclaimed

"Name one..."

I took a few seconds before answering.

"Well first of all, Haiti is an island and the Philippines are a cluster of islands!"

"Good try but geography doesn't count. Shit...New York City is an island, but what do our countries have in common with that?" She asked.

"Okay, I got one for you T. There is a stereotype that Filipinos eat dogs. In fact in some Northern parts of the Philippines they do eat dogs. There is also a stereotype that Haitians eat cats. I don't know if that's true? But if it is true then our peoples-- Haitians and Filipinos have something inherently common, namely their use of domesticated pets as culinary delicacies."

We burst into laughter.

"Jeremiah you're an idiot. Let's go meet your folks so they can get a taste my cat legume!"

###

Over The Vocopro Champion Karaoke system, an instrumental of Jimmy Buffet's 'Margaritaville' filled Bayani's spacious living room. The sound was just loud enough so that the partygoers could converse without having to scream over the music. It was always an Abundo family tradition to have a massive feast, and then partake in an off-key karaoke session enhanced by the unpredictable effects of alcohol. It's not a coincidence that Karaoke is one of the most popular pastimes for Filipinos: a Filipino named Roberto del Rosario held the first patent for the first karaoke machine called the Minus-One. So far, the evening went perfectly. All the Abundos were in attendance: Mom, Bayani and his wife Ingrid, kuya Ronald, and me, Tamara was the only non-family member in attendance. At dinner, everyone loved Tamara's fried griot and crab legume. But she told me, she felt a little uneasy, being the only Black person at the function. When Mom or Bayani made a comment in Tagalog, she wasn't sure if they were talking about her so she stayed close to me throughout the early part of the evening and just smiled—carefully censoring each word she uttered. Tamara finally let down her guard during dessert, when Ingrid was cutting rectangular pieces of leche flan and plating them of Styrofoam plates. Leche flan was Ingrid's specialty. She made this popular Filipino custard dessert with: eggs, condensed milk, fresh milk, sugar and vanilla. Bayani, who was downing shots of Pinch Scotch Whisky and chasing it down with authentic bottles of San Miguel the whole night, blurted out the unimaginable right at the dinner table:

"So Tamara, when are you and Pamangkin going to have children? It would be great to have a Tiger Woods in the family? ...we need some athleticism in our blood line!"

Ingrid was so embarrassed at her husband's statement she almost hurled the 10" pairing knife that she was cutting the Filipino custard with at his forehead. The females abstained from drinking and the men couldn't stop.

Kuya Ronald belted the chorus of the famous Keys anthem while hugging Tamara:

Wastin' away again in Margaritaville
Searching for my lost shaker of salt
Some people claim that there's a woman to blame
But I know it's nobody's fault

"Pamangkin, may sigarilyo ka ba?" Bayani asked.

"Definitely Uncle, let's step outside" I replied.

We walked outside to the patio where we took baby swigs of our bottles of San Miguel while taking puffs of our cigarettes. I smiled as I watched kuya Ronald and Tamara through the single-lite French doors now attempting their version of **Endless Love**. The song popularized by **Diana Ross and Lionel Richie**.

"So how do you like her?

"Who Tamara? She has a pretty good voice." Bayani replied.

"No I don't mean her voice, I mean what do you think about her?"

"Oh, you mean that way. She's seems like she has a good head on her shoulders, she seems like a nice girl—cute face and shape and a *Malaking pwet*. A little quiet at first, but I think I got her attention." Bayani replied.

"You mean you don't have a problem with her not being Filipino"? I stated combing for words.

"Cut to the chase. Do you mean if I have a problem with her being Black? Itim? I don't. Do you Pamangkin?"

I didn't know what to make of the comment. Bayani was notorious for his saying things he didn't mean while he was drunk, but then again Bayani never withheld his true feelings about anything.

"I concur with my brother-in-law. Tamara seems like a great girl Anak." Mom chimed in as she wrapped her arms around my waist, while dodging the trail of smoke emanating from my cigarette.

"You have to appreciate a girl who can cook Anak. Tamara gave me the recipe for her crab legume without hesitation. I told her I didn't need the recipe for her fried pork since Filipinos prepare very similar dishes—*crispy pata* and *pritong baboy*. Right now she's in the house writing the recipe down for Ingrid."

"I'm happy you guys like her, but I'm not sure she's sticking around. She's kinda fed up with the Department. She might be moving on soon." I stated as I extinguished my cigarette by dropping it in my empty bottle of San Miguel.

"How do you feel about that"? Bayani asked.

"I'll be ok with it. She put in her work and deserves her happiness. Working at the Department is equivalent to the aging of dogs. Dogs age relatively quickly in the first few years. Whereas investigators and case managers are expected be seasoned experts of their field within months of signing on. Not to mention the physiological effects of the job—I feel like I have been working at this place for seventeen years." I stated as I held my mother's hand.

"I see it in your face Anak and on your head. You didn't have that many gray hairs when you first started. As your mother, I think you need a well-deserved break. I spoke with Tamara and she's willing to call out sick tomorrow. You guys need to come with us to the Keys. Rent a couple of scooters, have a few mixed drinks and enjoy your lives because life is way too short to worry all the time. Don't worry about the bill…the tab is on me. " Mom stated

"I don't know Ma… Our big district meeting is tomorrow."

"Jeremiah how many times have you been out since you started last August"? Bayani asked.

"Zero"

"You see Jeremiah. Your job might not be the stressor. You might be putting way too much into it. The Department functioned without you before they hired you. I'm sure they can do without two of its investigators for a day." Mom added.

I listened to Mom and Bayani as they made their convincing arguments. *Maybe I was putting too much into my job?* Other investigators would call-out sick during the busiest days of the week, Mondays and Fridays, just to catch up on their outstanding work. It seemed the more responsible you were and opted to come to work; the more the Department would punish you with more and more cases. The more I thought about the situation, I couldn't help but remember the immortal words Ely Tolliver used to explain his longevity at the Department:

"…you need to learn to play the game young buck, and preoccupy yourself less with all its fuckery."

Tamara has one foot out the door; maybe it was time to for me to follow her lead. My head swirled. I haven't skipped school since high school. I glanced through the French doors once again and watched as Tamara hugged Ronald after their rendition of the 80s love ballad. My decision was made.

"Alright I'll call out tomorrow." I boldly stated.

Mom and Bayani applauded my decision.

"Well let's wrap up this karaoke session Pamangkin. We have a 4½ hour drive to the Keys in the morning. We still have to pack and get some rest. We can take my Excursion since…I'm sure it will fit us all without us being too *sikip!* We'll let Ronald do most of the driving, since he drank the least." Bayani stated.

"Sounds like a plan." Mom added.

###

As the women, cleaned the table and washed the dishes. Bayani sat on the sofa nursing a headache, while Ronald and I carefully packed up the Karaoke machine. Another Abundo family tradition was to leave the karaoke machine with the family member who hosted the party. Hence, The Vocopro Champion would remain with Bayani and Ingrid this evening. While completing our respective tasks, we watched attentively to the local news, WKLR, to hear tomorrow's weather forecast.

...Dale Earnhardt is survived by his sons Dale Jr. and Kerry, both of whom are also NASCAR drivers, his daughter, Kelly and his wife, Teresa...

WKLR ran a brief montage of the fallen driver's life. Ronald and I looked at each without saying a word. When our own father passed away due to pancreatic cancer six years ago, the family was never the same. Ronald became more distant and the family got together less-and-less for these type of functions.

"God bless the dead." I uttered under my breath.

"You can say that again kuya. It seems that all the legends are leaving us— Tom Landry, Charles Schulz, Owen Hart, Biggie, Tupac...and now The Intimidator." Ronald replied.

And In Breaking News, a woman was killed today by her estranged lover in Liberty City...

The anchor cut to a live feed in front of the Collins residence off of Northwest 11th Avenue & Northwest 52nd Street. Police tape blocked entry into the apartment while the coroner's white, late model GMC Savana Cargo Van was parked just outside the doorway. There was no mention or sign of Queen or Poo.

The news hit me like a 10lb sledgehammer to my chest. I felt lifeless for a second…then I felt a surge of energy consume me all at once, fueled by a mixture of rage and despair.

"MOTHERFUCKER!—FUCKIN' MOTHERFUCKER" I yelled causing the women to rush out the kitchen and Bayani to awaken out his semi-conscious state. Ronald remained silent placing his hand on my shoulder.

"What's wrong Anak? What's wrong?" Mom asked worriedly.

I said nothing.

My entire family was glued to the 42-inch Samsung Plasma in the living room and remained silent as the reporter provided details of the incident:

Denise Collins. a mother of two was brutally murdered today by her ex-boyfriend Archie Bedford, Police suspect in a botched home invasion. Neighbors alerted the police of a domestic dispute at the Collins' residence, when the authorities arrived; Bedford barricaded himself in the home. Negotiators managed to convince Bedford to surrender, but when law enforcement entered the home they found the mother deceased. Law enforcement is not commenting on the cause of death. Collins' two surviving children will be turned over to the Department of Children and Families services. This is a truly a sad story in every sense. Back to you Bob…

As I hopelessly stood there watching, footage of Archie Bedford being ushered into the back of a patrol car, thoughts of the Collins family haunted me. Like the response Denise furnished after learning someone was hurting her child *"Safety Plan? I might kill his ass if he steps foot in here again…"* Unfortunately, Ms. Collins sentiments did not come to fruition. I remembered the family members' faces after I told them of the services I could help them attain. I remembered the feeling after reading the thank you email Queen penned to me. The same email I tuck in my back pocket wherever I go: the same email that provides me a little added strength to keep working this tough-ass job. I thought of how the future pre-med student would fair, now that her biggest cheerleader and supporter was gone. Bassi was right when he said one family will inspire you to stay, and make your tenure at the Department worth it. For me, the Collins Family provided me this strength. When I realized this family would never be the same, tears streamed down my face uncontrollably: it was the first time I shed a tear since my father passed away. I excused myself from my family members to collect my emotions. They said nothing as I retreated outside to the patio.

When the patio door shut as I passed through, Bayani looked over to Tamara and asked, "What happened"?

She murmured, "Those are his clients... those are Jeremiah's clients."

Any thoughts of kicking my nicotine habit would have to wait a little longer. As I took a long drag of my Filter King while reading the wrinkled email authored by Quintavia "Queen" Collins...tear droplets bled through the paper and smeared some of the lettering on the note. I was interrupted by the sight of my mother and Tamara walking towards me.

"Hey Babe, How are you feeling? Tamara asked

I remained quiet and kept staring at Queen's thank you email.

"Anak, what could you have done to prevent this? This just goes with the territory, I see this all the time as a nurse. I know you did your best for this family." Mom added.

"Jeremiah, c'mon now baby, what could you have done?" Tamara asked.

A wave of guilt washed over me. *Maybe this wouldn't have happened if I could have talked to Lil Boy Bedford? Maybe I could have done a little more to find him?* But they were right, what else could I have done to prevent such evil from happening?

I finally broke my silence.

"Maybe I couldn't have stopped Archie Bedford from killing that poor woman and destroying the lives of those children. But I can try to do my best to help Denise's children deal with this bullshit… Mom, I don't think I'll be going with you and the family to the Keys because I'll be working tonight…. Tamara, who is working the On-call for the Central area?" I asked

"I believe Patricia James is working tonight." She replied.

"Can you call her and tell her to call me when Tallahassee dispatches her on the #02 Additional? I'll call Jamie so she can okay me going out on this case tonight." I stated.

With eyes filled, Mom looked at me and gave me a peck on the forehead. She now knew the reason why she's only seen her youngest child once since I left the fold seven months ago. She swelled with pride as I prepared to go on my investigation.

I rode shotgun as Tamara drove my car to the Miami Police Department's North Station at 1000 Northwest 62nd Street. I eyed the time on the Taurus' dashboard clock, *12:15pm*. The weather was unusually cool for February and the blustery east winds pushed the Ford Taurus to its right as we drove down I-95. I told Tamara that she didn't have to accompany me, but she didn't take no for an answer. After a quick shower, I threw on a black DCF polo shirt and a pair of Khaki pants. Three shots of Café Cubano and a blast of Listerine and I was ready for work. I remembered the advice the middle-aged sage Ely Tolliver told me – *If you lose it in front of them, they'll never respect you.* I knew I had to compose myself for the benefit of the children, but I also had to make myself emotionally available if they needed me. As Tamara jetted south, I glanced at my pseudo-girlfriend who appeared more livid than sorrowful. If they could strap Archie Bedford into Old Sparky up in Starke Prison today, Tamara looked like she wouldn't hesitate to flick the switch on the murderer. We rode together quietly into the night until we reached our destination.

"Detective Salinger please, CPI Jeremiah Abundo of the Department of Child and Families and this is my partner CPI Tamara Norvil." I requested as I flashed my identification.

The officer at the reception window paged Detective Zach Salinger who worked Homicide.

"One minute Mr. Abundo, he'll be right out." The officer replied.

It was common practice that children who were abandoned or suffered the loss of a parent due to death were brought directly to the precinct—away from the hoopla of media, cameras, and voyeurs. If the case came during a weekday, the children were often brought directly to the Rohde building. Miami Dade Police precincts lacked the facilities to handle recently abused, abandoned and neglected children, so I wanted to get Queen and Poo out this environment as quickly as possible. Unfortunately, in my experience, the Department afforded fewer accommodations for children entering foster care than the precincts. Immediately, I remembered my baptism into Florida's Child Welfare system, my first day on the job when I had to care for the twins, Marco and Ronny Beltran for almost eight hours before placement was secured. I wisely called placement for Queen and Poo as we drove to the precinct. Suddenly, a thick steel door adjacent to the receptionist's window swung open.

"Is someone looking for Detective Salinger"? A bald, cleanly shaven man announced. Zach Salinger had a thin, tall build and his red paisley tie was unloosened and his white shirtsleeve dress shirt was unbuttoned at the top.

"Yes, Detective Salinger, I am CPI Jeremiah Abundo of the Department of Child and Families. I'm here on the Collins case. This is my partner CPI Tamara Norvil."

"Well…I am totally impressed with your outfit. I didn't even phone this one in to the Hotline and you guys are here already?" The detective stated cheerfully.

"We aim to please." Tamara blurted annoyed at the detective's glib comment.

I looked at Tamara and shook my head disapprovingly then continued, "Well Detective I'm here because I have an open case with the family and we knew the case would be called in. Since I've had dealings with the children, I wanted to make sure the kids knew the State was here for them."

"That's mighty fine of you Jeremiah. Quintavia doesn't want to speak to anyone— even the female officers and detectives. Marcus was distant at first, but he opened up after we him fed a few slices of pizza. Quintavia is going to need a lot of help…lots of it. Thanks for coming out. Please follow me."

Detective Salinger led us to a control room which held several monitors. Salinger pointed to monitor 1A, which provided a live feed into an interviewing room; Quintavia sat at a rectangular desk with her head down across from her Marcus sat coloring in a coloring book.

"Is there a way I can get a copy of the A-form for my file? I'll give you a copy of the abuse report after you phone it in to the Hotline…and please include your business card" I stated.

"I still have to call it in even though you're here"? Detective Salinger asked.

"I'm afraid so. An abuse case number still has to be generated and a narrative based on your account needs to be provided to the Hotline." Tamara interjected.

"Okay no problem…will do." Detective Salinger stated.

"Detective, the news report states that Bedford killed Ms. Collins in a botched home invasion. Any truth to that?" I asked.

"To tell you the truth Jeremiah, we're not sure yet. We have crime scene at the residence collecting evidence as we speak. Bedford refused to speak to us without a lawyer." The detective said

I handed the Detective a copy of **Abuse Report 01-0009008**. Detective Salinger scanned through the document as he rubbed his cleanly shave chin.

"…So that recent Lewd and Lascivious charge was as a result of this abuse case"? Detective Salinger asked.

"Yes Detective. You're looking at revenge as more likely the motive than robbery." Tamara stated.

"Detective, were the children brought to the precinct with anything other than the clothes on their backs"? I asked.

"I'm afraid so Jeremiah, since the home is an active crime scene their personal affects were not allowed to be removed." The detective responded.

"So there is no way I can get into that house to get a few belongings for the children." I asked futilely.

"Not until the technicians are done collecting evidence."

"Can you tell us how Bedford killed Ms. Collins"? Tamara inquired

"Blunt head trauma. The son-of-a bitch pounded her head in with a frying pan. It all makes sense now in light of the new information you provided." The detective stated as he handed me back my abuse report.

"Can I go in and see the kids? It's going to be a long night and I want to take the kids somewhere where they can get rested up." I stated as I shook my head while watching monitor 1A.

Detective Salinger led us to another steal door just outside the control room. The Detective swiped his ID badge through a card reader to the right of the door and a second later a click indicated the door's latch was freed.

"Just pass through that door and they'll be in the room on the second door to your left." Detective Salinger advised.

I balked to allow Tamara to pass through the doorway, but she didn't move.

"Jeremiah I think you should hit this one solo. I'm sure the kids will be relieved to see you and not another investigator whose only purpose is to throw them in foster care and be on her way." Tamara stated.

I nodded and proceeded to interview room 1A.

Tamara glanced at the wall clock *1:20am*. From the control room Tamara and Detective Salinger watched the reunion unfold on monitor 1A minus the audio. As the metal door swung open, Marcus "Poo" Collins jumped to his feet and ran towards me and clutched my right leg. I squatted down and hugged the child: my arms could barely reach around the circumference of his midsection. Startled by the commotion, Queen slowly raised her head leaving a watery puddle on the wooden tabletop. When she saw me, she arose from the table and staggered towards Poo and myself and crashed into us. She buried her face in my chest. The three of us latched on together for what seemed like an eternity. By this time, Tamara was in tears and Salinger, a 20-year veteran with Miami Police Department's Homicide Unit was bit misty-eyed himself.

16 DECISIONS

I headed south toward downtown Miami. Tamara rode shotgun while Poo and Queen occupied the backseat. Poo slept soundly as he rested his head on his sister's left bicep. Queen stared out the window with her fist balled up covering her mouth. Early morning removals proved the most challenging, mostly because everything was closed. In Miami Dade County, this included one of the few places to take children during the course of removal episode, the Rohde Building. Due to budget cuts, security at the building was nonexistent. In the early 90's, an 8-foot high steel fence with sharp pickets was erected around the perimeter of the Rohde's 87,000-square foot lot. Amongst other things, the fence prevented the Miami's homeless from sleeping on the stone benches located in the Rohde's courtyard and discouraged the night denizens from defecating and urinating on the common grounds. The only way to gain access into the building was through an adjacent freestanding parking garage or an electronically controlled gate in front of the building. Entry into the garage was prohibited after 11pm The State's frugalness peeved its investigators and foster care workers alike since they had to leave their personal vehicles outside the complex by parking meters. Literally, a worker removing a child had to constantly be on the lookout as she hustled newly displaced children into the unsecured building. If the removal was conducted on the weekend, the newly displaced children were wrangled into a stifling, hot unsecured building—the result of more budget cuts. In fairness, this wasn't always the case. In the first few months of my tenure, the State flipped the bill for a paid overnight security guard. But as the fiscal year approached-- and the district's budget dwindled down, come May such luxuries like security and A/C were usually sacrificed.

I was resourceful; on most of my midnight removals I bypassed the hassle and uncertainty of the Rohde building and went to a Denny's, IHOP, Walmart or any other 24-hour establishment. This evening I had to stop off at the Rohde for few bits of paperwork—an IPR, some fingerprinting cards and a copy of the shelter petition. I coasted into a line of empty parking spaces adjacent to the Rohde Building, outside of the 8-foot high steel fence which lined the perimeter of the building. I parked the Taurus at a parking meter right next to the entry gate. I looked at the watch on my car radio, *2:10am.*

"Ladies, I'm just going to run upstairs to pick up a few things. I don't want to wake Marcus up. I should only be a few minutes. T, please hop into the driver's side. If some weirdo approaches the car flush it. The Miami Police station is just next door. I'll just walk over to you when I'm done if I don't see the car here." I stated.

"Hey don't you want us to go up there with you? Where are we going? Where are we going to wait for placement"? Tamara asked in succession.

"This place isn't safe. Don't worry about it…I got it covered. Just keep the kids company when I'm gone." I stated as I brushed Tamara's face with the back of my hand.

I knew it would take awhile before placement was secured for the siblings since I begged the new placement coordinator, Frankie Paz to locate a single placement for both of the children. Tamara and Queen watched as I walked to the steel gate door, gain entry with a quick swipe of my ID and then sprint to the entrance of the Rohde where I swiped my ID once again to gain entry into the building.

"Hey Mama? You doin' awright? My name is Tamara by the way."

Tamara watched Quintavia through the car's rearview mirror and was relieved as she saw Quintavia remove her hand from her mouth to speak. With her left hand, Quintavia continued to stroke her brother's head, which now rested in her lap.

"Thank you Tamara. It's nice to meet you. They call me Queen. I appreciate you and Chong coming out tonight." Queen said softly.

Chong? Tamara chuckled to herself. "Chong and I are happy to be of service. You know he keeps the letter you wrote him in his back pocket wherever he goes and he makes sure he shows it off to everyone whenever he is given the opportunity to do so." Tamara stated

Tamara caught a rare smile radiate from the teenager's face.

"Well, my family definitely appreciates what he did. When we needed him he was there. No question was too petty or too trivial for him to pick up his phone. Mama always tried to do her best for us, but sometimes came up short. That little assistance…the beds, the help with the light bill, the aftercare assistance for my brother Poo helped our situation immensely. It helped Mama land that job she was so proud of. An' I could never forget that lil bit of counselin' I received too." Queen stated unsuccessfully holding back tears.

Tamara identified that the child's feeling were still too raw to discuss the night's events. She steered the conversation another course almost immediately.

"Chong? That's an interesting nickname for Jeremiah, but you know he's Filipino not Chinese?"

"Yeah I know. It was a toss-up between Chong, Bruce Lee or J? He told me that in his people's language Chong meant dude. You Haitian? Right? Americans are notorious for stereotyping. In my neighborhood, we call people who work at convenience stores A-rabs, they call Hispanic boys at my school Julios or Chicos and I'm sure you know the number of derogatory words they have for us black folk here in America. Words can only hurt you only if you allow them to." Queen replied.

"That's very true Queen, very true."

"Can I ask you a question Ms. Tamara"?

"Ask away."

"You're a very pretty lady and Chong is a good lookin'…well a good lookin' chong. Are you two in a relationship together?" Queen asked.

"How did you pick up on that"?

"Two things give it away. Who'd be goin' out on a case in three hundred dollar Donna Karan pumps and a fly Burberry dress. You two look like you comin' from a date….the second thing that told me you two are an item is the way I saw you looked at him when he left to go into that building. Sista girl, I've seen and given that same look befo'."

"Damn girl! Jeremiah did tell me you were good! If the medical thing doesn't work out for you, you need to be an FBI profiler. List me down as a reference!" Tamara stated as she smiled.

For a moment the two shared a brief laugh. Queen appreciated Tamara's efforts to put her mind at ease. From a distance, I emerged from the Rohde building with a manila file in hand. As I opened the metal gate door of the perimeter fence, a loud voice boomed from a distance…from around Northwest 1st Avenue or so.

"A MAN YOU GOT A DOLLA! A…A…BOSSMAN LE' ME GET A DOLLAR!"

The voice became louder and clearer as he approached the vehicle. I jumped in the passenger seat and signaled to Tamara to drive.

"Hold up…where are we going"? Tamara asked.

"Anywhere but here…we're not safe here. My vehicle is not safe here. Just drive!" I said.

Tamara flushed it leaving the mysterious panhandler and the Rohde Building behind.

"Okay Captain Kirk, where to now"? Tamara inquired

I turned to Queen who was giggling in the backseat and asked, "Hey Queen? Have you eaten yet…are you hungry"?

"I am a little hungry… I didn't get to eat dinner." Queen replied.

I smiled when I saw Poo sleeping peacefully in his sister's lap.

"T, bang a left at the next corner and jump north on I-95 and then head to my uncle's house."

"You sure about this? I'm sure it violates some department regulation." Tamara suggested.

"Fuck the Department and just drive." I stated as I watched the Rohde Building vanish completely from Taurus' side view mirror.

###

I cupped my hands together and let the cold running water fill them until the tiny pool spilled over. Face first; I administered a self-baptism. I filled my hands again and cleansed my face and neck one last time. *It's these moments of solitude that haunt us the most.* I stared into the brightly lit bathroom mirror. I felt the same way for a month after Songbird passed. My short, Halle Berry was a mess, and there was no tellin' when I'd be goin' to the hairdresser anytime soon. No money. No home. No school. Just random memories of Mama flashin' in-and-out of my mind— like the way Mama always sought a front row seat during all of my awards presentations or the times Mama brought home leftover concessions from her jobs with Rainbow Staffing Solutions. My most vivid and recent memories were of the back and foot rubs I gave her after she arrived home from cleaning 2-3 houses that day— right before she landed her dream job. Each fleeting memory weakened me more. I a felt numbness in my legs, which made it difficult to support my tiny, 117lb frame. Even though I was physically fatigued from the day's events the mental fatigue ravaged me even more. The uncertainty of my future— better yet our futures scared the shit outta me. *Where were we goin' to stay? Who would take care of Mama's burial arrangements? What about school? My science project was due in 2 ½ weeks and I didn't conduct one iota of research on my topic! 'Do sound waves affect a plant's growth rate?'*

A knock on the door jarred me back into the moment.

"Hey girl, you awright in there?" Tamara asked.

"Yes Tamara, I'm awright. I'm awright." The crackling of my voice advised otherwise.

I opened the bathroom door which led down a wide hallway that spilled into Chong's Uncle's mammoth great room, I looked up at the vaulted ceilings and I was in awe. I have been in a few nice homes in my life—years of accompanying Mama on her cleanin' jobs—and this home was one of the nicest. One side of the room was a living room area and was decorated with plenty of modern, sleek looking furniture, which didn't look very comfortable. On a sage painted wall hung a 42-

inch plasma television installed over a fireplace. On another side of the room there was a wall dedicated to family pictures. Beside the pictures hung five Philippine-style brooms, Chong called 'em *walis ting ting*, painted goldenrod, white, purple, green and red. The traditional brooms from the Philippines paid homage to their Philippine heritage. The punch of colors drew my eye immediately; I thought they were gorgeous; they also reminded me of the African American custom that Songbird and Mama always harped about, "Jumpin' The Broom." In fact, my parent's broom is still in our closet. From a large espresso-colored dining table, Poo waved at me while Chong's mother, Cynthia served him miniature egg rolls with sweet and sour sauce: my brother never met an egg roll he didn't like.

"Hey Sweetie would you like something to eat? Your brother seems to have taken a liking to our Filipino cooking?" Ms. Cynthia asked.

"No thank you ma'am. I don't have the greatest appetite right now." I responded.

"Understood, my name is Cynthia. I am Jeremiah's mother. If you need anything at all just ask. Tamara and my sister-in-law, Ingrid are trying to find some extra clothes for you. Ingrid is about your size, a 4-6. Unfortunately, my brother, Lonnie, doesn't have any little children in his household, so we have nothing for your brother. Jeremiah told me that he's going to stop by a Walmart to pick up a few things for him."

Ms. Cynthia reached into her back pocket and retrieved a hundred dollar bill and handed it to me.

"I know my son cannot give this too you, so please take it from me."

I balked at the gesture, but was forced to take the money after Ms. Cynthia retreated into the kitchen for more food. I could see where Chong got it from— just like The Collins Family...it all starts at home. The thought saddened me. Now, I have no home. The only thing left I had in this world was Poo, and even he might be taken from me. So many memories...so many emotions from sadness to fury, I must have felt at least each one in these passin' hours. I was even tempted to contact Scrub and tell him to "Handle Dat": I knew he would. He would've laid that nigga flat if I told him what Lil Boy did to my family. But Lil Boy's existence has caused so much pain, no one else need pay for his pathetic existence.

"You gotta try these eggrolls, Queen! They are soooo good! They're even better than Wong's. These eggrolls are all meat—no veggies." Poo stated with a mouthful of *lumpia shanghai*.

My brother's voice jostled me back into reality. I took of a bite out of Poo's eggroll and smiled.

"Yeah Poo...they are good. Where's Chong—Oh I mean Mr. Jeremiah?"

"He out back by the pool." Poo stated.

"Thanks. Remember Poo always use 'Please' and 'Thank you'. I'll be outside talkin' to Mr. Jeremiah."

I walked over to the two pairs of French doors which opened onto the pool deck. Before I exited, I stared at Chong through the glass of one of the French doors. He was sitting at a granite-topped wet bar rubbing his temples with one hand while writing feverishly with the other. He used the lid off a jar of Planters Dry Roasted Peanuts as an ashtray.

Before marking my signature on the last page of the document confirming me as the affiant and author, I glanced over my freshly written shelter petition for errors. I found these types of removals the easiest ones to write for. Removals where the parent/guardian was incapable of caring for a child due to incarceration, hospitalization or death, usually had few issues meriting probable cause from a dependency judge. It took me approximately 30-minutes to draft the Collins petition, but I was so emotionally exhausted after authoring this document. It pained me to envision Queen and Marcus without the love and support of their mother. I wondered if Queen's stellar academic and performance and growth would stymie after this tragedy. I wondered if Poo's heart would be so damaged that he would stop wanting to make people smile. I proofread the document from the back to the front when I reached the narrative description, I read this section aloud:

On or about February 2, 2001 the Department of Children and Families received an abuse report (**01-0009008**) involving the alleged sexual abuse of a child. The allegations provided on this abuse report state that on December 26, 2000, Quintavia Collins DOB: (06/24/85) was in her kitchen cooking her family Christmas breakfast. Mother's paramour, Archie Bedford cornered Quintavia in the kitchen and rubbed his penis on Quintavia, then groped her breast. He may have been under the influence of alcohol at the time. Quintavia's mother, Denise was at work at the time and was unaware of the incident. Furthermore, mother Denise Collins took the appropriate action by protecting her children by driving the A/P out of her home and securing restraining order (#FC-001241-d12r) on A/P Bedford. CPI Jeremiah Abundo, Unit 808 referred the family for a number of services: (1) counseling through Kristi House (2) Flex Funds for the family's utility bills and furniture for the children (3) subsidized aftercare referral; for said child Marcus Collins DOB: (03/24/95). Subsequently on February 3, 2001, Detective Fredrick Nunez of the Miami Dade Police Departments Domestic Crimes Bureau arrested A/P Bedford as a result of the alleged battery. CPI Abundo submitted a diligent search request and attempted to locate the A/P at six different addresses to no avail.

On or about February 18, 2001, the Department received an #02 additional sequence for abuse report (01-0009008). This sequence alleged that A/P Bedford made forcible entry into the Collins Residence and murdered the mother of children, Denise Collins. Ms. Collins expired at the scene; the cause of death is yet to be determined. A/P Bedford is currently incarcerated and being detained at Turner Guilford Knight Correctional facility

This family has no prior history with the Department. At this time, there are no friends or relatives that are capable of caring for the children at this time. Currently, the children, Quintavia and Marcus Collins are currently in shelter. We implore the courts to find probable cause and reasonable efforts in this case.

###

"Very concise Investigator Abundo." I said.

The sound of my voice startled him, but he was slow to turn in my direction. Chong looked a mess.

"Hey Queen. How long have you've been standing there?"

"Long enough to hear your narrative. It's amazing that you can cram two months of my life into three paragraphs. I tend to be a little wordy myself!" I stated as I struggled for levity.

"Listen Queen; please don't think that this brief narrative is a testament to your amazing family because it isn't. Our judges hear a lot of cases and have to make decisions very quickly. Brevity is the rule of thumb in dependency court. Please don't take offense to this."

"Chong, none taken— none taken at all." I stated.

I looked at the enormous amoeba-shaped pool that glistened as the moonlight reflected off its surface. Then I looked up and saw a bevy of stars pepperin' the sky. It seems the further you traveled away from the City, the more you could appreciate our Earth's beauty. I could see why Chong decided to resign himself to this beautiful solitude— to get his mind right and to remain focused. I looked straight ahead and all I saw was darkness. But in the darkness there were still signs of life: like the sound of a bullfrog's call off in the distance and the sound of branches making contact as an owl or falcon left its perch in search for its prey. The uncertainty of darkness can be a scary thing if you choose it to be so or it can be the complete opposite. I choose the complete opposite.

As he lit another cigarette, I blurted:

"Damn Boy! I had no idea you smoked!"

He held out his freshly lit menthol to me.

"No. No thank you Boo. That's all you right there. My father passed away due to smoking." I stated dodging the noxious fumes.

"My father succumbed to pancreatic cancer and emphysema. A double whammy! When he passed away a few years ago he passed me the torch— and I used it to light my first cigarette. I began smoking my senior year in high school and haven't stopped since. Bless the globe with the pestilence, the hard-headed never learn."

His last sentence had me stumped 'cause I heard that line before. A few moments later it came to me.

"Wu-Tang Clan right Chong? Your last sentence was from one of their songs"? I asked.

"Yes ma'am. The song is 'Triumph' and Method Man spits that on one of his verses." Chong said.

"Man you do know your music, but you really need to try to stop smokin'. You're too important to cut your life short. Nowadays, they have gum, patches and a bunch of other things to help people stop." I suggested.

To pacify me, he took one last drag from his cigarette and crushed the butt into the tin lid. The lid was almost full of crushed butts.

"For the record, are there any relatives that might be able to care for you and your brother?—even if the relative lives out of state? I have to document my efforts to locate relatives in the shelter petition."

"My Auntie Belinda lives in Bakersfield, California. I don't have her contact information on hand though." I said

"No worries I can request a diligent search for her information at the office tomorrow."

He added the additional information to his petition then inked his signature onto it. He then tucked the document into a manila file folder along with other documents to be submitted to court tomorrow.

He lifted his left hand up as he remained seated....I paused for a second before I grabbed it with my right. He then spoke:

"Queen, I am so sorry about your mom. Later on this morning, I'm going to refer you and your brother for some grievance counseling. But if you or your brother needs anything... anything at all, I will be here for you. Even if I am not working at the Department, my door will always be open to you."

As I looked down at the back of his head, I couldn't help but feel sorry for him—another casualty of Lil Boy's destruction. When his head sunk into his chest and his grip loosened, I reapplied more pressure.

"A... what are you feelin' sad for Chong? You don't have to offer me no apologies. When I met you three weeks ago, you were there for my family. You took the time to explain the entire process to us and you went outta your way to help with our outstandin' bills, furniture, and even counselin' for me. This evenin' when I was outta my mind ballin' at the precinct...you showed up unexpectedly—and on your day off of all days! Right now, we're at your uncle's palatial home. Chong, I'm not sure what your rules are, but I'm 99% sure your agency frowns on bringin' foster chil'ren back to tha crib."

I lifted his chin with the tip of my index finger and our eyes met.

"Chong, you have nuthin' to feel bad about Baby. You'll forever have my gratitude."

"That means a lot to mean Queen. I've been working here less than a year, but I'm a mess. This job is so taxing— emotionally and physically, not to mention the other shit you have to endure. I don't know how long I can hang on?" He stated exasperatingly.

"Chong, I don't know very much about DCF. I can't imagine your workload and the hundred-or-so other things you're responsible for. But if this job ever changes you into somethin' different then who you are then maybe it is time to go."

The sound of the patio French doors opening interrupted our conversation. Tamara saw us holding hands and paused before she spoke.

"Hey girl, come on inside. Ms. Abundo fixed you a plate! After, you can take a look at some of these clothes we picked out for you."

I leaned over, moistened my lips with the little saliva I could gather and gave Chong a peck on the back of his neck. Then I whispered in his ear:

"Déjà vu, tell you what I'm gonna do, when they reminisce over you…"

As I passed through the French doors, he yelled out:

"Pete Rock and CL Smooth! That's Pete Rock and CL Smooth!"

I looked back, nodded and smiled. The gesture brought him to tears once again.

17 THE HEARD

I raced across the employee's parking lot, traversing it in a matter of seconds almost losing my case file during my sprint.   When I reached the double glass doors, Pepe Olivares of Piedmont Security broke me down before I could pass through the metal detector. I looked at Pepe hoping he'd show some leniency regarding the Department of Juvenile Justice's strict security policy. The sixtyish year old security guard was unrelenting. I emptied my pockets into a red plastic deli serving basket and walked through the metal detector. Two annoying buzzes had me cussing to myself. After a few passes from his metal detecting wand:

(Silence...)

I grabbed my belongings and I bolted down a corridor which led to a set of stairs in DJJ's courtyard. I hopped up the stairs taking three steps at a time. When I reached the top, I entered through the delinquency side of the courthouse and scanned for my case through the lengthy case dockets hanging on the wall, each enclosed in its own glass case. I double checked each docket, but couldn't locate my family on any of the sheets. My heart began palpitating when I realized that I was late for my hearing. I felt a tap on my shoulder and discovered a face I haven't seen in months.

"Oh hi Sara!   I just came from the Rohde. We just finished a mandatory training and I got caught in traffic. Did they call my case yet?" I asked.

"Hi Jeremiah! We were waiting on you...they called your case and the judge was pissed, but I did my best to try to calm her down. Judge Slate still wants to see you in her court room ASAP!" Sara Rothschild exclaimed.

What else could go wrong? It's nice seeing you again Sara. Are you still with the Department?" I asked as I followed Sara to courtroom 2-5.

305

"No Jeremiah, but I managed to transition over to another job with the State. I'm currently working with the Guardian ad Litem program. It doesn't pay as much as a CPI. But I don't have the headaches or heart attacks either. Most importantly, when I'm home from work, I'm home. That means I get to spend more time with Anthony."

"That's wonderful Sara. I'm glad you landed on your feet after you left here." I responded.

Sara held the door open for me and I gingerly entered the courtroom. Immediately, I knew I was fucked. The courtroom was totally desolate. Even Judge Slate's bailiff, Rodney left for the day. A loud crunch echoed in the courtroom. I watched surreally as Judge Slate munched on a large red apple from her bench. I wondered what was for dessert. *My ass more than likely!*

"Hello your honor."

Judge Slate spun around the minute she heard my voice.

"Mr. Abundo I'm glad you could grace us with your presence. I wanted to wait for you personally to see what your excuse was this time…" Judge Slate said as my palpitations increased, and the little bit of saliva in my mouth all but evaporated. She continued. "…Frankly, you CPIs and case managers are a major reason why the system continues to remain broken. That's why I intend on writing Chet Parker, Secretary Kearney and even the Governor Jeb Bush if need be to request your dismissal."

Suddenly, my palpitations morphed into murmurs. I managed to utter a few words before my heart ceased to beat.

"Your honor respectfully… may I know what I did so wrong? I have no idea why you are requesting my dismissal."

Judge Emily Slate peered down at me like a sniper through crosshairs of her scope. The five-foot-two inch judge graduated from UMass Dartmouth with top honors and migrated to South Florida 30-years ago. She immediately fell in love with weather and found a lucrative market defending alleged drug defendants. After a successful stint at the State Attorney Office, she ran for circuit court judge in 1986 and never relinquished her position.

"Well if you ask Mr. Abundo... due to your bumbling ineptitude two children managed to languish in foster care for almost six months, when there was a viable relative in California that could have taken these kids almost immediately. After reviewing your case notes during discovery, you made mention of this relative in your notes, spoke to this relative and even promised the children you'd get them back to this relative. I know personally, CPIs are notoriously bad for initiating the Interstate Compact for Placement of Children, but it is still your responsibility. If you are unfamiliar with this process Mr. Abundo...which appears that you are, an ICPC is a request we make to another state for possible long-term placement of a child. At the very least, you should have made mention of this potential long-term placement at the ISS staffing. Notwithstanding, your carelessness caused undue emotional injury to the children and your tardiness at today's hearing has compromised their futures as well. Due to your, inability to testify at today's trial, I had no choice but to offer the goal of reunification for these children, which frankly burns me up inside. Mr. Abundo the best I can do is recommend and advocate for your dismissal, but in truthfulness... I wish I could levy jail time for your incompetent actions—or should I say inactions!"

Jail time? My head was spinning. I had no counter for the judge's diatribe. Lately my memory has been fleeting. There was no question about my decision to leave the agency now. I looked around for Sara, but suddenly she was gone. Then I looked up at the bench and so was the judge—gone without a trace.

Hold up!...
Reunification?
Reunify with who?

It just didn't' make any sense. I found myself alone.

###

February 19, 2001

They hovered over my body like vultures to carrion: I was slumped over in my cubicle totally drained from this morning's removal episode. Abassi Okafor, Jessica Thompson and Jamie Watkins contemplated waking me up an hour ago, but unilaterally decided I deserved my rest before the big district meeting. At 6am in the morning, placement called me with a tentative home for the Collins children. The placement was in a Family First group home in Homestead. Even though the children would be residing in separate group homes due to their age, Queen and Poo would be only a few buildings down from one another. After I dropped off the kids and Tamara down south, I headed to the office. I balked at Tamara's offer to stay over for the night; I feared any sexual activity would render me physically useless for the rest of the day. Wearing the same clothes for the past 36-hours, I decided to come directly to work. *Who would know and frankly who cares what people think?* I was spent.

"My Lawd, the po' child is a mess. His clothes are all wrinkled and he smells a bit tart." Jessica Thompson said.

"Yes my brother looks like he had a very eventful night. Maybe it's best we wake him up now before someone misconstrues his fatigue for laziness." Bassi stated.

"I agree. Bassi you may have the honor", Supe Watkins replied.

Bassi put his hand on my shoulder and gently prodded me.

"Wake up Jeremiah. Wake up. Our district meeting is going to start in a few minutes my brother." Bassi urged. He had to repeat himself a few times before he saw some movement from me.

I slowly regained consciousness. After the nightmare I just had about Judge Slate dicing my ass up in court; I was never so glad to be back at my desk.

"Good morning everyone." I stated as I stretched my arms and legs.

The members of unit 808 stared at one another amazed that I lost track of the time, *11:50am*, just ten minutes before our meeting. Then I realized all the tasks that remained undone due to my slumber.

"Oh my goodness! I have to staff with legal and get the Collins petition ready for court in an hour! Why didn't you guys wake me up?" I said frantically.

"It's okay Jeremiah. I took the petition down to legal myself. You also probably forgot it's President's Day...so no court today." Supe stated.

"No school today either. Let's pray it's a light day!" Ms. Jessica Thompson added.

A feeling of calm swept over me, but I still remained focused. There was a multitude of tasks that needed to be completed in such a short span of time. I needed to: refer the Collins' children for grievance counseling, complete an incident report within the next 15-hours and submit it to Tallahassee, I needed to check with Detective Salinger to see when I could gain entry into the home to get the kids their belongings, and I needed to initiate a diligent search to find Auntie Belinda from Bakersfield. If I located the children's aunt, I then needed to complete an ICPC to Sacramento if she wanted custody of her niece and nephew. These were just a few items on my punch list for the Collins investigation. But I still had some other obligations on the other cases in my load including: two follow-up homevisits and a case that needed to be closed before 11:45pm that night.

The sound of Rhonda's voice interrupted the pack.

"C'mon boy pick it up, pick it up!" Rhonda stated to her eldest son, Theo as they trudged down the row cubicles.

"Hey y'all!" Rhonda greeted the other members of the 808 as she passed us.

Theo acknowledged everyone with a brief, "Hi" as he headed straight for his mother's cubicle.

Bassi waited for the two to pass before commenting.

"I thought Rhonda was reamed out for bringing her kids to work? Didn't she just get written up for that"?

"She was…we both were. Let me go and speak to her. See you guys at the meeting." Supe stated while walking towards Rhonda's cube.

"Hi Theo. Hi Rhonda." Supe stated as she peered into Rhonda's workspace.

"Hi Supe." Rhonda stated as she unpacked her laptop, while Theo remained quiet as he thumbed through one of his books.

"Rhonda, I need your help with a particular file? Can you please give me a hand"?

Rhonda arose from her seat and followed Supe a few cubicles down to a newly vacated one. Jamie noticed a significant change in her lead worker. Since her birthday, Rhonda became more aloof and withdrawn from the unit. Always a fashionista, Rhonda's ensembles became nothing out of the ordinary. And although her commitment to her work and families never waned, her sharp, trademark personality was all but nonexistent.

"How's everything Dear? Are you doing alright" Supe chose her words carefully.

"What do you mean"? Rhonda replied.

"I mean…Theo. Parker laid into us about bringing children in the office. Actually, we both got written up last time you brought your kids

310

to the office. In a few minutes, the entire investigative area will be in a meeting with this guy. What are we going to do with your little one in the interim? Leave him in your cube by himself for the next two hours? Even Ms. Thompson and support staff with be in the meeting." Supe stated as she scanned for witnesses.

"Jamie, today is President's Day and my children's father gave me his ass to kiss—again. Javon's daycare is open, but as you know school is out for the older kids. I found a sitter for Theo, but she won't be able to get him until 12pm—she's gotta a mornin' class at Miami Dade College. He just needs to be here for an hour-or-so, until I can get him to the sitter."

Jamie was at a loss for words, but remembered the venomous written reprimand she received last time Rhonda brought Theo and Javon to the office. Chet Parker was adamant any further infraction would definitely end up as write-ups and expulsion for them both.

"Rhonda it's not too late to call out sick"? Supe meekly suggested.

"What are you talkin' about Jamie? I'm not sick. I just need a minute or so I can take Theo to the sitter!"

"No I didn't mean anything by that..." Supe stated— her meager attempt to bamboozle Rhonda was unsuccessful.

"Lawd knows this is my third sitter of the year. When they find out that babysittin' for me can be an all-day affair, they quit the next day. I should've just left Theo at the hous.. "

Rhonda tried to catch her words before they left her mouth, but was unsuccessful. Jamie remained quiet as Rhonda continued.

"Jamie I always respected you as a supervisor and a friend, but think back when you were a mother with young children. It ain't easy. Theo will be awright in my cube. Right after the meeting, I'll whisk him away to the sitter, and no one will know he was here. Back in the days, we used to take care of one another in-and-out of this place. But now this place is just starvin' for love. Jamie don't think like these people...you ain't one of them—don't front like you one of them." Rhonda pleaded.

As Rhonda walked back to her cube, her last statement penetrated deep in to Jamie's soul. The CPIS saw her own evolution as of recent and was disappointed with the change. As years passed, her own courageousness and rebelliousness faded. Now Supe was just another mindless cog in the machine. The sound of rustling feet interrupted Jamie's train of thought as the entire 5th floor marched towards the elevators to head upstairs for the big meeting— everyone with the exception of Theo.

In Miami Dade County, the Department of Children and Families Child Investigations Division didn't have a meeting area large enough to accommodate the 200-or so CPIs, supervisors and support staff; I wondered if this was done purposefully or just poor planning. In my time, I've seen investigative sections occupy whole buildings, but the age of smaller government did away with that. In Opa Locka, CPIs were literally sharing cubes thanks to the do-more-with-less attitude. To hell with the Privacy Act of 1974, a client's information was shared openly in this environment on a daily basis— from the casual phone conversations mentioning sensitive case details to clients sitting literally feet away from one another listening to one another's abuse allegations. Child protective investigations was shrinking. Due to the lack of space, the district meeting was held in the Department of Juvenile Justice's meeting area on the sixth floor of the Rohde building. As personnel filed into the 1500-square foot room, which overlooked bustling I-95 and the amazing Downtown Miami skyline, CPIs from the various areas gathered in certain parts of the room. The Central had the front of the room, since this was our home turf. The North occupied the middle of the room. And the South occupied the back. I knew a majority of the CPIs in the district through chance meetings in Dependency court and trainings. But now that I think of it I've either received or transferred an investigation from every CPI in this room one time or another, I found it shameful that CPIs possessing decades of tenure never were formerly introduced to one another, until today.

Todays, assembly marked the first time line staff from all three area (South, Central, and North) were present in one location. All staff was ordered to be at the meeting at 12pm sharp, only a few selected CPIs remained on standby to field Immediate investigations from Tallahassee. In Unit 808, I was the designee, which provided me a perfect alibi should I need to leave the meeting early and tend to Theo. One thing I didn't plan for is the time. When you're on Department time, namely CPI-related, nuthin' starts as scheduled. I eyed my Swatch watch and it was *12:18pm* already.

Like most CPIs, I sat with my unit. Ms. Thompson occupied the end seat; Jamie occupied the other end seat, while the Fellas flanked me –Bassi to the left and Jeremiah's sleepy-ass to my right. As staff awaited the arrival of District Administrator Chet Parker, the room was abuzz with commentary. I leaned over to my right and whispered in Jeremiah's ear.

"Hey Rookie, how you holdin' up? Heard you had a rough one last night"?

"Rho, physically and mentally I'm sapped. I feel like I drank a case of peach Cisco, but without enjoying the euphoria of drunkenness!" He responded.

"I swear if I didn't know you no betta I'd think you was Black Jeremiah." I said jokingly.

"Oh yeah, is that meant as a compliment Rho?"

"Hell yeah Boy!"

We laughed. But my thoughts were elsewhere, namely downstairs in my cube where my eldest son sat patiently waitin' on me. I kept my phone close to me on vibrate, just in case I had to rush down to him.

Jeremiah continued, "…Wonder what Parker has to talk about today? I guess it doesn't really matter. It's nice see to all the investigators in one place."

"Child, probably nuthin'. It's the first time in my tenure, I've see all the CPIs in one place." I said as scanned the room for familiar faces. "What do you say my Nigerian love? Is this the first time you've seen this many CPIs in one place?" I asked Bassi.

"One second my dear, I am just finishing my Dhuhr and giving thanks to the Almighty." Bassi replied with eyes closed…only his lips moved as he continued to recite his prayer silently. A few seconds later he opened his eyes and smiled at me and Jeremiah.

"Thank you both for your patience my brother and sister. I've never seen this many CPIs in one place before and I've been here forever. The Department dispels any type of unity, that's how they control us. They keep us separated, often pitting us against one another through statistics and petty rivalries." Bassi stated as he kept smiling and waving whenever he came across a familiar face.

"Hey Jeremiah, is that your Boo Boo over there?" I pointed at Tamara Norvil who was sittin' with her unit members in 413 in the back of the room. Tamara made brief eye contact with me. I lifted up my hands, as if to say I was no threat. *Yeah, right Bitch! Yo' man ova here on my hip! Best believe…*

"Yeah I guess you can call us an item. She met my mom and my family and actually helped me out with my removal yesterday." Jeremiah replied.

"She comes off as a bit jealous— but she's a beautiful girl though. You guys will have some real pretty chil'ren with good hair." I stated.

I checked my watch again and it was *12:32pm.* The longer the people waited, the more they grew restless and began airing out their dissatisfaction with the agency aloud from the brutal case assignments, which were now up to 3-a-day to the Department's flagrant disregard to adequately compensate its employees. Apparently, the 808 wasn't the only faction dissatisfied with the Department at the moment. Suddenly, a wild thought danced in my head.

What if we all got together and told administration or even better— Tallahassee about our dissatisfaction with this district's working conditions?

If they ignored us, we'd have an answer for them…

A petition?...A one day sick out?...A strike perhaps?

Could this be the day?…

We took action rather than wait as the system picked us off one by one?

…now the crowd's murmurs broke out into uncensored denunciations.

"Administration needs to do better and hire more bodies." **An unknown voice chimed.**

"Judge Slate is bi-polar maniac. When is someone gonna' put that bitch in her place!"

Half asleep, Jeremiah bust out laughin'.

"When is this meeting goin' to start? I still have to close two cases!"

Jeremiah stopped laughin' when he realized his butt had a case to close before 11:45pm tonight himself.

"…I hope administration doesn't act funny, when I hit 'em ova the head with overtime 'cause I have to work late tonight!

I found reassurance that others felt like me. Maybe change was on the horizon. Maybe there was a reason to stay.

All the commentary and noise ceased when District Administrator Chet Parker entered the room followed by two administrative assistants who worked in the program office. One pushed a huge cart crammed Willie Wong's Chinese Food and the other cart was stocked with beverages.

The garrulous Chet Parker spoke:

"Don't worry folks dessert is on the way. We just didn't have enough room on these carts to hold all those sweet potato pies and vanilla bean ice cream!"

The crowd rancor's metamorphosed into jubilant praise.

"With this type of spread Mr. Parker, we should get together every week!"

I looked spitefully at the commentator Evelyn Bonner, a CPI from the south. *Fuckin' sellout.*

"Honey garlic chicken from Wong's and sweet potato pie, you definitely have my undivided attention!"

I wanted to vomit. *Slaves…every single one of 'em— slaves. Their souls so easily procured for some trays of cheap-ass fried rice and a few store-bought pies from Publix.*

Jeremiah leaned over and whispered in my ear.

"Hey Mama are you alright"? He asked as he put his left hand on my shoulder.

"I'm good Jeremiah. Just wakin' up that's all."

"Me too— literally" Jeremiah added.

The voices ceased as Mr. Parker made his way to the podium in front of the room.

"First of all, Happy Presidents Day and thank you all for coming, I didn't want to keep you guys here long because I know there is plenty of work to be done…" Chet Parker stated.

I felt my Nokia 5110 vibrate in my Coach hip holster at *12:41pm.* I looked at the display and it was a picture of Theo and I quickly rejected the call. I eyed the time and responded back to Theo in a text.

Almst Done. Back 10-min.

"I know things are rough right now, but we are all family here and have to work together. You have my word that if we can get a handle on this overtime, we will be able to offer some of you guys bonuses next fiscal year and hire for more positions. I know things are tough but we will get through this!" Parker continued.

I felt my phone vibrate again. This time it was a text from Theo.

Hury up. Im scared.

I nudged Bassi, who in turn nudged Jamie. With a quick nod, I signaled that I was off to take Theo to the sitter. *I couldn't believe my po' baby has been downstairs by himself fo' almost an hour. What kind of mother am I?* As I gathered my belongings to make my exit, I couldn't help but draw the attention of my district administrator.

"Ms. Jackson, please do not deny us of your presence. I'd love to have your input in the Q&A session after. To have one of the most respected CPIs in the district chime in on this would truly be an honor. You don't know how many more families you'd be helping if you didn't leave. Please stay."

I took a second before responding. I could have excused myself and said I was going out on an Immediate, but I opted to say on it...besides there was nuthin' left for me here anymore. I looked around at my peers and glanced at the picture of Theo on my Nokia. There was no turning back.

"First of all Mr. Chet Parker, we are not family— and if we are...we are more dysfunctional than some of the clients we service. A couple of weeks ago, I got my first write up in almost 10-years of workin' here not because I lied about facts on a case or stole from the State, or placed a child in danger...but because I brought my chil'ren to work with me on a Friday at 4pm! You have no issues with me workin' countless of unpaid hours helpin' everyone else's family, why do my chil'ren deserve second best? I've sacrificed football games with my boys, family reunions, birthdays all for this..." I extended my arms as I looked around at my peers, "….my DCF family. Now durin' one of the biggest forums to voice our dissatisfaction of this unfair system you stuff your faces, while panderin' to those who've never went on an investigation in their lives. They could never understand how it feels to work this dangerous job with such little respect. We all…an' I mean all should be ashamed that we let it get this far. This job is way too important to remain silent, but my family and my physical and emotional state outweigh even this job. Right now my eight year old son has been waitin' downstairs for me in my cube for over an hour and I'm ashamed I would even put him in that position— I was scared of the consequences for violating our precious "district policy". Now I must go 'cause he needs his mama. He's been patient with me long enough."

I stormed out of the meeting room, bludgeoning the crowd into silence. As I passed Jamie, I whispered in her ear,

"See Supe, I was listenin'… listenin' all the while."

I didn't see his face, but I was told Chet Parker was livid.

I sat in my cube thinking about Rhonda's condemnation of the Department and all its pieces— from the higher ups to the grunt-level line staff. She definitely laid it out and now I had something else to respect her for. If anything, my brief tenure with the Department of Children and Families allowed me to meet some extraordinary people and the experience I gained was invaluable. I thought about all the "A" list women in my life: Quintavia, Rhonda, and Tamara. All will always occupy a special place in my heart. Quintavia was the kid sister I always wanted—strong, smart and too responsible for her age. Yesterday at Bayani's, she provided me solace on the eve of the worst night of her life. Words cannot describe how much strength that tiny little girl possesses. Rhonda was the mature, flirtatious woman who taught me the ins-and-outs of investigation. I wondered how our working relationship would be if I took it to another level with her—smashed her and *broke her back*. I smiled and was content keeping her a good friend. Although she possessed a natural radiance and beauty, when vexed Rhonda was the type of chick to flatten all four tires on your vehicle and leave it on stomach if you caught her on right day. Her outburst at today's meeting was just an example. But you cannot deny she has heart. As for Tamara, she was just too damn beautiful. I got a kick when I saw guys approach her to possibly get her name and her number, and get turned away flatly when she'd point to me and say three words, "I'm with him". At first, she lacked a bit of confidence about her abilities, but she found herself eventually. I wondered if we'd have future if she left the Department, but if it was our time to part ways, I will always be happy with the little time we spent. How lucky was I to meet these three women in less than a year's span. *Too lucky if you ask me.*

As I finished my incident report on the Collins case, I was startled by the sound of my supervisor's voice.

"Jeremiah, Parker wants you upstairs"

From the look on Supe's face, my pending meeting with the District Administrator wasn't to pat me on the back for a job well-done. Then it hit me. *Shit! They must of have found out about my pre-placement pit stop at Bayani's.*

"What's this about Supe"?

"It's about the Collins Case. Please bring your case file and all your documentation."

"No problem Jamie." I replied. From Jamie's laconic response, I didn't know if my supervisor was pissed off at me or still mortified at Rhonda's outburst.

###

Jamie and I sat side-by-side at a honey, maple laminate conference table in Chet Parker's office. It was my first time being summoned to the 10th floor. We waited patiently until Parker arrived, we both remained quiet. I looked at my watch, *4:15pm.* Then I looked at the various fishing paraphernalia and pictures that adorned the administrator's office walls. He had pictures of him holding his fallen catch: grouper, swordfish, tarpon, and even a spinner shark. *"Bayani would love this friggin' guy."* I said to myself. On Parker's desk, he had a photo cube of himself partaking in various activities involving water: spear fishing, surfing a log on Reef Road in Palm Beach and one side of the cube was a picture of him holding a Florida spiny lobster, while giving a thumbs up. I didn't see any pictures indicating any semblance of family. Chet Parker a veteran of the agency for 30-years began working with the Florida Department of Health and Rehabilitative Services (HRS) when he was 25. He worked at the juvenile court house as a clerk and moved up the ranks eventually becoming a court liaison. In his capacity, he acted as the middle man for children who had open dependency and delinquency cases. In 1994, when Florida Legislature created a separate division to address Florida's juvenile delinquents, Parker began working with the newly titled, Department of Juvenile Justice. In 1996, Governor Lawton Chiles signed legislations splitting HRS into two components: the Department of Health and the Department of Children and Family Services. That same year, Parker transitioned to DCF and took a supervisory role in a daycare licensing unit. His wealth of connections and his uncanny ability to communicate, internally and externally, afforded him much success at the Department. His favorable hue placed him in his current position as the head administrator of one of the biggest child protection outfits in the country without ever having to step foot in a client's home.

I promised that if asked about my decision to bring the Collins children back to my home, I'd tell the truth. I had a good run while I was here and I learned a lot. My recent doubts of this agency and my physical and mental fatigue have consumed my whole being. A Florida employee is considered vested after his sixth year of work; I didn't know if he'd make my first year. If I left now I wouldn't regret putting so much into this agency. If I left now I could start fresh with a laudable, untainted record.

Parker walked into the room followed by an unknown Hispanic man, who wore wrinkled a white button down and ill-fitting blue Dockers. When the man squinted, the slits of his eyes were more narrower than mine. The man spoke before Parker could introduce him.

"Dean Dominguez, reporter for the Miami Star."

So much for the laudable, untainted record. I thought as I edged from my seat. I nodded to the reporter and stared straight ahead with my arms crossed.

"Mr. Dominguez is doing an exclusive on the Collins case. He needed to ask you a couple of question since you're the investigator on this case. Plus, we're bound by the Sunshine Law to provide any information if the public requests it from us that includes media inquiries." Chet Parker stated.

"Chet, I beg your pardon, this investigation is open, do we volunteer information openly just like that? Aren't there privacy concerns that need to be addressed? Maybe we can get legal in on this before continuing any further." Supe stated vehemently. Thoughts of her own experience with the media prompted her to come to my aid. Her own incident, **Jealous Boyfriend Kills Mother and 2-children**, occurred almost thirteen years ago, but the experience stays fresh in her memory. Chet Parker's face turned redder than the lobster he was holding in his picture cube.

"Ms. Watkins, there is no need for any of your recommendations. Tax payers fund this agency and they have the right to know what their money is being spent on. It's called Transparency; I will explain it to you after this meeting. CPI Abundo will answer this reporter's questions. The law is clear and the public has the right to know what goes on here!" Parker deftly countered to the reporter's liking: Dominguez enjoyed the tension.

I turned and looked at Jamie after our administrator's uttered his last statement: "...the public has the right to know what goes on here!" *Transparency my ass! More like invisibility! Where was Dean Dominguez four hours ago when Rhonda laid it all out in our district meeting? I'm sure you don't want that type of press coverage?*

"Mr. Abundo, according to the record you had an open case, **Abuse Report 01-0009008** with the Collins family prior to the mother being murdered at the hands of Archie Bedford. Did you ever meet up with Mr. Bedford at anytime during the course of your investigation?" Dominguez asked.

I was relieved that the inquisition wasn't about my choice to feed and clothe Queen and Poo at my home earlier today, but the thought of having my name in the paper for negligence was just as unappetizing.

"No sir, I did not make contact with the Mr. Bedford at any time during my investigation, but I did make multiple attempts to locate him at various addresses throughout Dade…and I even ventured into Broward." I responded.

"Did you know that Mr. Bedford had an aggravated battery charge in 1990? And did you ever discus a safety plan with the mother should Bedford come back to the house?" Dominguez asked.

"I did know of the battery charge and mother took a proactive approach to file an injunction against Mr. Bedford." I retorted.

"Was any grievance counseling offered to the children and are there any relatives at this time that can take custody of the children?

I looked at my watch *4:45pm* and grew restless with the questioning. I felt tempted to pull a Rhonda— speak my peace and storm out of the meeting, but I didn't.

"Not yet. Awaiting data." I replied curtly.

"I'm sorry…what does that mean Mr. Abundo?" Dominguez inquired.

"Simple. I have not yet submitted the request for grievance counseling because I am here discussing case matters with you. And I am awaiting data from our diligent search unit to see if we can locate a possible relative in California." I stated exhaustedly.

"Please forgive him. Jeremiah has been up since yesterday night working on this case— he wasn't on duty at the time. He has plenty of more work to do on this case before day's end." Supe interjected.

The sound of Jamie's phone blared before a response was offered. Jamie excused herself and answered the call.

"Yes Ms. Thompson..........Jeremiah has a 24?..........Please pull the case for me and I'll take a look at it in 10-to-15 minutes...............Thank you."

The room went silent for a moment. I rubbed my neck and shut my eyes. Thoughts of Queen and Poo entered my mind, specifically this morning when I dropped them off at their placement in Homestead. Before I said goodbye, we shared in our customary group hug; I wish I didn't have to leave them— ever. The brief memory brought a smile to face once again.

"Mr. Dominguez, how much longer do you need? As you see we're a busy bunch over here." Parker asked.

Dean Dominguez glanced over his notes and jotted a few extra ones down then spoke, "I just have a few more questions ...I'll just be another 10-minutes or so."

I clutched Jamie's hand and sat there quietly.

18 CARREFOUR

March 9, 2001
(Homestead)

As the children waited for transportation to arrive, they decided to play a pick-up game of tag to pass the time away. Poo couldn't care less. Mama was gone. His friends from school were gone. And earlier today, he found out I was being transferred to another foster home, which was closer to my high school in the City. When the judge found out that I was enrolled at Northwestern High's Medical and Allied Health Science Program, Judge Slate gave the Department 24-hours to withdraw me from Homestead High School and reenroll me back at Northwestern or suffer the penalty of $1000 per day I remained at Homestead. Unfortunately, my new foster home only had room for one, so Poo would have to wait here until something else opened up. I almost dropped out of my program, so I wouldn't be apart from my brother. But my worker told me that she's actively trying to find a placement to accommodate, Poo and myself. I offered to care for Poo myself, *I mean— I've already been carin' for my little brother way befo' this shit.* But my worker told me that this was impossible because no judge would cosign on a deal as risky as this.

"Awright Poo you it!" A young girl yelled as she slapped him on the left shoulder blade.

Poo attempted to chase after the other six kids—all were about his same age, but his lackluster effort showed. When the other children recognized Poo's sluggishness, they taunted him all the more, as he reached and grabbed, they juked and laughed. The more dexterous ones came just inches from Poo's touch then to add to the sting, they'd hurl a verbal mud pie in his face.

"Poo you slow as shit bwoy!" A voice yelled out.

"Yeah, they need to change your name to Poo Poo!" Another voice quickly followed.

After minutes of flailing and chasing, Poo was winded and tired. He ceased his pursuit. I watched the scene unfold. My normal instinct would be to intervene—straighten anyone messin' with my lil brother, but things were different now. A few taunts might be the least of his concerns during our separation. *Time for Poo to grow up. Mama would feel the same way!* Poo slowly walked over to me.

"Hey little brother, givin' up so easy?" I asked.

"I ain't feelin' right Queen. Feels as if I'm walkin' around with a broke heart. It seems every little thing I try to do reminds me of her. I miss Mama." Poo said before beginning to sob.

"It's awright to cry, lord knows I did my fair share these past few weeks, but rest assured Poo— Mama is always wit' you smilin' at whatever you do."

"You mean dat"? Poo stated.

"I do Poo. I do. You definitely got Ms. Denise's beautiful spirit in you. Like the way you make me smile even if I'm havin' the worst day ever that's yo' Mama in you and no one can take that away. In a few minutes the bus will be here and you'll be headed out to the fair. Mama would want you to have so much fun so much fun that you'd fall deep asleep on the ride back home. Promise us you'll enjoy yo'self?"

He nodded.

I kneeled down and gave my brother a big hug. I marveled at Poo's stature. In a year or so, he'd be taller than me. *Even if he grew taller and bigger than Alonzo Mourning himself, he'll still be my lil Poo.*

"Poo, I'm headed to another foster home, but they told me they'd be moving you too once they find space. I need you to be a big boy when I'm gone. At night, I want you to call me so I can make sure you're awright. Remember to do your homework and ask Ms. Donna for help if you get stuck." I said holding his dense wrist.

I reached into my breast pocket and pulled out a ten dollar bill. I always hustled on the side; I made this little bit from braidin' another foster girl's hair. As I stuffed the money in Poo's pants pocket, I felt a hard, metallic object scrape my hand as I made the deposit. A second later, I fished out Mama's thin, 14kt gold Figaro chain and her wedding ring. The set never left Mama's neck.

"I'm sorry Queen. I forgot that was in there? You ain't mad at me?" Poo said as he looked at me apologetically.

Tears welled in my eyes as I held the jewelry in the palm of my hand. The sound of a '95 Blue Bird School Bus roared as it entered the facility grounds. The kids stopped playing tag almost immediately, and flocked to the bus. Poo began slowly hovering to the Blue Bird. As I watched my little brother fade into the distance I yelled over the Bird's loud engine.

"I love you Poo!"

He glanced back at me and screamed at the very top of his lungs…

"I love you my Queen!!!"

I watched as my brother climbed into the Blue Bird and I stood there motionless as it drove away. I walked back to my room where I still had to pack. Within the hour, my family service worker (foster care worker) was going to take me to my new placement.

###

My luggage consisted of three State-issued Hefty garbage bags that contained all of my worldly possessions. I checked to see if I had my red plastic Hello Kitty wallet which contained some money I saved up from doing hair and sculpting eyebrows. I even kept the $100 bill Ms. Cynthia gave me— I doubt I'll ever spend it. Ms. Donna, my foster parent told me the State would soon give me a stipend while I remained in care, part of the Subsidized Independent Living Program. I took an inventory of my belongings. My most treasured possessions were the few family pictures I salvaged. There was a picture of me holding my 3rd grade spelling bee championship certificate minus my two front teeth and a baby picture of Poo splashing in his infant tub and I had a tattered picture of Ms. Denise and Songbird kissing while under some mistletoe one Christmas. I let out a long sigh. *First Songbird, then Mama and now Poo, if God wanted to test one of his children, he certainly knew how to do so!*

As I waited for transportation, I sat on foot of my bed clutching the 14kt Figaro chain and Mama's wedding ring. I eyed my Hello Kitty wristwatch, *5:03PM. Transportation was running a little slow.* I scurried to one of the Hefty bags and rummaged through it until I found my travel sewing kit. Using a tiny safety pin and some thread, I manufactured a modified clasp. I walked to the dresser mirror and admired my handiwork. *Songbird and Ms. Denise would be proud. Even during the most trying times always strive for normalcy.*

Two knocks on the door interrupted my reminiscence.

"C'mon in." I ordered.

"Transportation…." Chong stated, "…at your service."

I quickly moved toward him and gave him a big hug. In similar fashion, I quickly pulled away from him.

"Boy, I'm mad at you…I've tried to call you for the past two weeks? Why you iggin me?" I asked.

"Sorry Queen, I had to take a couple of weeks off to recharge my batteries. It's been quite a ride working for the Department these past few months. Between the pressure to meet deadlines and the volume of cases, I needed a break. I also need time to explore a few options. My good friend just resigned the other day." Chong responded.

"So you came back to take me to my new placement, so you could make up for your actions? I forgive you!" I hugged him once more.

"I'm not going to lie. I came back to check on you and your brother, plus my investigation is past 30-days old so I'm required to make face-to-face contact with the all the children listed on my case again. Don't take it personal, just business… but I am very happy to be here."

"The consummate professional…I respect your work ethic." I stated.

"Not too professional. According to my co-workers…they think I'm insane. They say I shouldn't be transporting a 15-year old female by myself. I say fuck it."

Chong grabbed two of the heavier Hefty bags while I grabbed the lightest of the three. As we walked outta the door, I caught a glimpse of our images in the dresser mirror. Chong had a low, fresh fade, a blue plaid Nautica button down and a pair of khaki-colored shorts and a pair of suede Clark Wallabies. He seemed less pensive than normal while I looked a hot mess. My hair was wrapped in Mama's red bandana and I wore: an oversized white t-shirt, a Champion sports bra, some gray sweatpants and a pair of Poo's foam slides. I felt and I looked old. After signing me out of my current foster placement, we walked slowly to Chong's Ford Taurus. He told me in less than a year of employment, he racked up an extra 30,000 miles on her and he plans to ride her until the wheels fall off.

"I heard your brother went to the fair. How's he holding up?" Chong asked.

"He'll be okay. He's a little withdrawn from the other kids but that's to be expected. I hate leavin' him here by himself, but I need to get back into my program. I need to make somethin' out of myself; it will benefit us in the future." I replied as we placed my luggage in the trunk of his car.

"You are something, and you will always be. You're one hell of a sister and a wonderful daughter. Your family is one of the reasons I'm still working with the Department." Chong replied.

To refrain from crying, I changed to topic.

"Any word on Lil Boy? What's the State gonna' do wit' him"?

"The State is going after him for murder, but even though Florida promises the right to a speedy trial that might not take place for years to come. You gotta love the State, if it was up to me, a quick double tap would save the taxpayer's time and headache…forgive me if I have a love hate relationship with my employer right now." Chong stated while holding my car door open for me.

Gauging my facial response, he realized his reference was too caustic for the moment. Immediately, he tried to apologize.

"No need for any apologies Chong. I just can't preoccupy myself by hatin' him. Carryin' on and being vengeful isn't gonna change my life. I need to stay focused for Poo and me. Besides they say the best form of revenge is success." I stated as I clicked the buckle of my seat belt.

I chose to sit in the back seat to spare Chong from any additional problems if questioned. Once he was seated, Chong scoured for the address of my new placement, which he jotted down on the right-hand corner of one his investigation folders. As he turned to look at me through the smudged glass of his rearview mirror, he caught the twinkle of Mama's wedding ring that hung from around my neck, all I could see was his beautiful eyes...I couldn't see his mouth, but I could tell he was smilin'."

"Nice ring." Chong blurted.

"Could've been lost forever but it was salvaged in a 5-year old's pocket. Fate can be a beautiful thing some times."

A molten red and orange sky emerged as the sun descended. I eyed the display on his car radio and saw the time, *5:51pm.*

"Have you ever had conch Chong"? I asked while looking at the sky.

"No, isn't that some sea snail, slug or something"?

"No crazy boy...I know of a place that serves the best conch in Miami. Do you mind if we stop for a bite before you drop me off at my placement— my treat?"

"I definitely don't mind my queen." He said as he slipped the Taurus in DRIVE and zoomed off.

—KLR

ABOUT THE AUTHOR

When he was 11, Kevin L. Ramos began his journey helping people, when he worked washing dishes at his parent's ACLF (Adult Congregate Living Facility) in Miami, Florida. His commitment to bettering the lives of others steered him to a career working with the Florida Department of Children and Families.

During more than a decade of service to the Florida Department of Children and Families as both a Child Protective Investigator and Supervisor, he dedicated his life to the care and service of the children and families he served. As a tireless Investigator and Supervisor, Kevin never missed an opportunity to come to the aid of his co-workers and staff during moments of triumph and profound difficulty. Anyone who has ever dealt with the abused, abandoned, and neglected, knows it takes a caring and sensitive person to help make sure that children are protected and families receive the help needed to heal and become whole. THE DEPARTMENT is Kevin's chance to tell the stories of the amazing and challenging experiences that face child welfare professionals and the families entwined in this difficult system.

Kevin is a husband and father who lives in Miami, Florida. He graduated from Florida International University with a Bachelor's of Arts Degree in Communications and interned at Hallmark Cards in Kansas City, Missouri.

Kevin can be contacted at: kevin@thedepartmentbook.com

THE DEPARTMENT